10 GREAT IDEAS *from* CHURCH HISTORY

A DECISION-MAKER'S GUIDE TO SHAPING YOUR CHURCH

Mark Shaw

InterVarsity Press
Downers Grove, Illinois

InterVarsity Press® is the book-publishing division of InterVarsity Christian Fellowship®, a student movement active on campus at hundreds of universities, colleges and schools of nursing in the United States of America, and a member movement of the International Fellowship of Evangelical Students. For information about local and regional activities, write Public Relations Dept., InterVarsity Christian Fellowship, 6400 Schroeder Rd., P.O. Box 7895, Madison, WI 53707-7895.

ISBN 0-8308-1681-X

Printed in the United States of America ♾

Library of Congress Cataloging-in-Publication Data

Shaw, Mark, 1949-
    Ten great ideas from church history: a decision-maker's guide to
shaping your church / Mark Shaw.
        p.   cm.
    Includes bibliographical references.
    ISBN 0-8308-1681-X
    1. Pastoral theology.   2. Church history.   I. Title.
BV4011.S47   1997
253—dc21   96-46370
                                                                          CIP

| 22 | 21 | 20 | 19 | 15 | 14 | 13 | 12 | 11 | 10 | 9 | 8 | 7 | 6 | 5 | 4 | 3 | 2 | 1 |
| 13 | 12 | 11 | 10 | 09 | 08 | 07 | 06 | 05 | 04 | 03 | 02 | 01 | 00 | 99 | 98 | 97 |

To the ministers in our family:

the late Rev. Donald Douglas, the Rev. Paul Shaw,
the Rev. Ronald Sylvester and the Rev. Robert Clement—
men of God, men of vision, classic decision-makers

Introduction _____ 9

1/ A VISION FOR TRUTH: Luther's Theology of the Cross _____ 16

2/ A VISION FOR SPIRITUALITY: Calvin on the Christian Life__ 42

3/ A VISION FOR UNITY: Jeremiah Burroughs & the
Denominational Theory of the Church _____ 63

4/ A VISION FOR ASSURANCE: William Perkins's Model of
Conversion & Assurance_____ 76

5/ A VISION FOR WORSHIP: Richard Baxter's Directions for
Delighting in God_____ 93

6/ A VISION FOR RENEWAL: Jonathan Edwards's
Theology of Revival _____ 111

7/ A VISION FOR GROWTH: John Wesley's Concept
of Discipleship_____ 135

8/ A VISION FOR THE LOST: William Carey's Model
of Mission _____ 151

9/ A VISION FOR JUSTICE: William Wilberforce's Model
of Christian Social Action_____ 172

10/ A VISION FOR FELLOWSHIP: Dietrich Bonhoeffer's
Principles of Christian Community _____ 191

EPILOGUE: From Vision to Decision_____ 215

Notes_____ 226

Introduction

Just south of Boston, Massachusetts, lies the city of Quincy. Tucked between the sea and the urban sprawl of Boston, Quincy is best known for two American presidents, John Adams and John Quincy Adams, who were born and buried there. Like many New England towns, Quincy is full of historic churches. One of these, First Presbyterian, was founded late in the nineteenth century—just yesterday by New England standards. The church was organized in 1884 by Scottish immigrants.

For the first fifty years "First Pres" enjoyed steady and stable growth. By the 1950s the spiritual descendants of the original sixty-two charter members had come to number seven hundred. Watching over this flock in the decade of *Ozzie and Harriet* and "I like Ike" was the Reverend Roy Schoaf. Under his ministry the church was nominally Christian, "not distinguished by either extreme fundamental, or evangelistic zeal; or by any of the various brands of liberalism which swept the mainline churches."[1]

All of this changed in 1961, with the retirement of Schoaf and the hiring of the Reverend David Muir. Muir was sensitive to the changes going on in America. Civil rights and the cultural revolution were shoving aside the world of Ike and Ozzie. But Muir's confrontational sermons and his passion for social justice failed to mobilize the church to action. Much to his surprise, his ministry had the opposite effect. People began leaving in large numbers, complaining that traditional values were being violated. Dwindling numbers soon produced a financial crisis that hastened Muir's departure in 1964.

In 1967 Steve Brown became First Presbyterian's new pastor. He found a congregation that was deeply divided and financially unstable. Brown chose a style of ministry very different from those of his two predecessors. His sermons were filled with promise and hope rather than confrontation and criticism. He downplayed politics and stressed the evangelical truths of the Bible. A new atmosphere of community was created, and the numbers began to increase.

In his 1967 annual report Brown laid out his plan for the church: "Every church, at one time or another, stands at the crossroads of its church life. One road leads to mediocrity, frustration and failure. The other leads to greatness, fulfillment, and the advance of the Kingdom of God. I believe that now is our time of decision."[2] Brown laid out a blueprint of that path of greatness, stressing classic Christian values such as believing the gospel *(kērygma)*, serving others *(diakonia)* and building community *(koinōnia)*.

After Brown's departure the church faced another critical juncture. Not everyone had been happy with Brown's conservative theology. Yet rather than reverse direction, church leaders made the decision to continue pursuing the course Brown had charted. Roger Kvam became pastor in 1974. During his long pastorate Kvam initiated an aggressive evangelism program and moved the church toward mainstream evangelicalism, all without causing a major split between the "old lights" (pre-Brown members) and the "new lights" (post-Brown members). Throughout the 1980s and into the 1990s First Presbyterian Church of Quincy followed the old paths of *kērygma, diakonia* and *koinōnia,* and it paid off. The decision-makers who chose to follow this "path of greatness" helped the church grow in both size and quality.

The Old Paths

This is a book about following old paths—some of the great ideas in church history—to find the path of greatness for your church today. The aim is to help you make better decisions and become a better decision-maker. One of this book's assumptions is that church history can clear your vision and help you see where you are going.

Have you heard that old Russian proverb, "He who dwells on the past loses an eye, but he who forgets the past loses both eyes"? Personally I'd like to hold on to both of my eyes. Probably you would too. It's hard to see where you are going if something is wrong with your vision.

Every Christian decision-maker needs to keep both eyes in good working order. I believe that two-eyed decisions are better than any other kind. In the pages that follow I argue that we can make better decisions if we avoid the blind decision-making of those who dismiss history as irrelevant *and* the one-eyed decision-making of the tradition-bound, who are prisoners of the past and blind to contemporary needs and opportunities.

What kind of decision-maker might benefit from a book like this? I have in mind primarily leaders of local churches (pastors, elders, deacons) as well as leaders of Christian organizations. For this reason the decision-making examples given at the end of each chapter are heavily oriented toward the local church.

But someone in the back row has a question. "How can looking at a few cases and classic ideas from the past help me make better decisions?" That's a fair question. I've asked it myself over the years as I've struggled to become a better decision-maker. In the course of my quest to find the answer, I have made some discoveries. In the chapters that follow I'd like to share these discoveries—great ideas from key decision-makers in the past. You will learn how . . .

☐ Martin Luther's theology of the cross can deepen the faith of your congregation.

☐ John Calvin's model of holiness can combat "me-centered" Christianity.

☐ Jeremiah Burroughs's denominational theory of the church can be a tremendous force for unity within your congregation.

☐ William Perkins's idea of assurance through true conversion can overcome the extremes of apathy and anxiety within the church.

☐ Richard Baxter's directions for delighting in God can revitalize worship.

☐ Jonathan Edwards's vision of revival can defend the church against the attacks of secularism.

☐ John Wesley's strategy of small groups can turn slumbering churchgoers into zealous disciples.

☐ William Carey's model of missions can inspire boomers and busters to fulfill the Great Commission.

☐ William Wilberforce's paradigm of evangelical social action can guide Christians in opposing the evils of our time.

☐ Dietrich Bonhoeffer's vision of Christian community can bring your people together and counter the tribalization and radical individualism of postmodern life.

I see another hand raised. You want to know whether digging up the past is really worth the effort. After all, doesn't one have to get through numerous shovelfuls of academic dirt before finding a few spoonfuls of wisdom? Let me answer that question this way. The fact is that major groups outside the church—groups like the United States federal government, major universities and select Fortune 500 companies—are spending significant amounts of money each year to raid the treasuries of the past. Let me give you a few examples.

Several years ago Richard Neustadt and Ernest May of the Kennedy School of Government at Harvard University pioneered a course on the use of history in political decision-making. Soon their lecture hall was spilling over with "legislators, bureau chiefs, colonels, generals, ambassadors and the like."[3] Similarly, the University of Chicago started a public policy program that showed leaders how to use history to improve decision-making effectiveness. Leaders came. Riding this same wave of interest in the decision-making value of historical study is Carnegie-Mellon's

School of Urban and Public Affairs, which offers a course on "Historical Perspectives on Urban Problems." The Harriman School of Urban and Public Affairs (part of the State University of New York) offers a similar course. History is speaking, and government leaders are listening.

The world of business is also waking up to the value of history for a decision-maker. The Rand Corporation's Graduate Institute in California offers a "uses of history" course to Ph.D. candidates who are working part time on Rand projects. Business schools are getting the message. The M.B.A. program in the Graduate School of Business Administration at the University of North Carolina at Chapel Hill includes a course on using history in decisions.

Unfortunately, many Christian leaders have yet to discover the value of history for their decision-making. For many years at both college and seminary levels I have taught a course on the uses of church history in decision-making. My students, many of them church leaders, are enthusiastic about the value of church history and wonder why Christian churches and organizations (including their own) generally fail to consider history when making decisions. These students are used to church decision-making that is essentially pragmatic—knee-jerk reactions to the crisis of the moment or the pressures of the bottom line. Principled or vision-based decision-making is relatively rare.

Principled Decisions

Management gurus like George Barna *(The Power of Vision)* and Stephen Covey *(The Seven Habits of Highly Effective People)* stress the long-term (as well as short-term) benefits that come from basing our decisions on principles and ideas. Barna calls for decision-makers to use vision and not unprincipled pragmatism as the basis for choices:

> Pastors who actively seek to fulfill God's vision for their ministry are a treasure for the church. They are leaders driven not by a need for self-aggrandizement or ego gratification but by a burning desire to see God's will done to its fullest. . . . Their churches

will accomplish something unique, meaningful and special because the Holy Spirit has enabled them to capture an image of the future and to chart a course of action to reach that goal.[4] The kind of visionary leadership Barna is describing, however, seems to be oriented toward the future, not the past. Is church history relevant for visionary decision-making? Barna answers this question directly:

Tradition is generally a reflection of the past. Vision is always a reflection of the future. Is there any room for a marriage between the two? Absolutely! Because He is the God who created and reigned over the past, He can use history to His advantage in your life and ministry. . . . He will use your past to enhance your future.[5]

God can use history to enhance your future. In fact, God's power to use the past to shape a significant future through good decision-making in the present is the premise of this book.

In the chapters that follow we'll look at some great ideas from the last five hundred years of church history. Though I could have chosen great ideas from earlier centuries, I believe the ten I've selected are the most helpful ones for contemporary Christian leaders. I will not only examine how each of the ten ideas builds vision but also suggest some decisions that might flow from the vision. The ten ideas are culled from the lives and writings of Reformers (Luther and Calvin), revivalists (Wesley and Edwards), social activists (Wilberforce and Bonhoeffer), pastors and pioneers (Baxter, Perkins, Burroughs and Carey). Two tests were used to select ideas that can enhance your decision-making: (1) Is this idea or model deeply rooted in biblical truth? (2) Does this model or idea have a track record in building more effective Christians and churches?

Each chapter will describe the leader and the situation he faced. Then it explores the central idea this individual discovered or articulated. I will offer some suggestions as to how the idea might apply to the church today and the kinds of decisions that might flow from it. A few questions for reflection and discussion are given at the end of each chapter to help you process the idea and take a few steps toward implementing it.

Acknowledgments

Before we launch our study, let me express thanks to those who have helped this project at key points. Once again I am indebted to students who were willing to be guinea pigs for both the ideas and the approach of this book. My thanks then to students at Gordon-Conwell Theological Seminary, Conservative Baptist Seminary of the East, Nairobi Evangelical Graduate School of Theology and Scott Theological College. Thanks also to dear friends Karl and Debbie Dortzbach, who got this book rolling by inviting Lois and me on a "writing retreat" at their house. Cindy Bunch-Hotaling of IVP has now been my editor for two book projects, and I have come to depend greatly on her common sense and wise counsel. Two Wheaton College professors, Timothy Beougher and Mark Noll, gave encouragement by their willingness to read selected chapters. Three great friends who are also great pastors read and critiqued this work in its manuscript form. My thanks to the Reverends Irfon Hughes, Tom Kenney and Ron Sylvester, who gave honest feedback that helped me greatly.

A special embrace is due to Lois, my wife of twenty-six years, who believed in this project from the very beginning, sometimes more than I did. And I cannot proceed without reminding two of the best kids in church history, Anne Bradstreet Shaw and Jonathan Edwards Shaw, that their gift of producing laughter in our home has kept their sometimes stodgy father from taking himself too seriously. Finally, four men to whom I owe special debts are mentioned in this book's dedication.

But enough of the preliminaries. The best way to show you how this kind of decision-making works is simply to jump right into one of these great ideas and squeeze out its decision-making potential. We turn to Martin Luther, the great Reformer, who had a few ideas of his own about what the "path of greatness" looked like.

1

A VISION FOR TRUTH
Luther's Theology of the Cross

Lois and I were new in town and new at the church, a conservative evangelical church that was well established in the community. The first two Sundays we felt a warmth and excitement in the worship service that drew us back. The worship was so electric that we had high hopes for the adult Sunday-school class as well.

The class got off to a good start. The teacher was very friendly. We sat next to George and Jane, church members who were actively involved in outreach ministry. They too were quite friendly. Our teacher got the discussion rolling with a few case studies. The stories he told succeeded so well at triggering discussion that we didn't get to the Bible passage that morning. People were sharing and interacting and seemed to need the chance to talk about their problems.

When we returned to the class the next Sunday, though, the same thing happened. Lots of time for sharing and personal opinions. No time for the Bible. With about ten minutes left before the end of class, the teacher read a chapter from 1 Corinthians, and we were asked for our reactions.

Jane spoke up. "I don't believe this passage. I think Paul was messed up when he wrote this. I wouldn't even let my kids read this." There was a short silence as Jane's words sank in. The teacher said nothing.

Though I was new, I decided somebody needed to respond. I made a few comments, as gently as I could, about the inspiration, authority and trustworthiness of Scripture. Eyes rolled. My comments seemed to fall flat.

The class ended, and we made some small talk with George and Jane as we filed out. To be honest, I was a bit shocked by Jane's words, given the reputation of the church. I had to wonder if I was in the right place. People in this congregation carried their Bibles to church, but at least some of them left their theology at home. I wasn't sure about next Sunday.

Wanted: Theological Literacy

It's clear to me now that Jane is not alone. In evangelical churches all across the land theological literacy and doctrinal clarity are falling faster than a bungee jumper. A 1994 Barna report documented a decline in evangelical beliefs. Barna found that those willing to affirm the inerrancy of the Bible, the sovereignty of God and the necessity of a new birth through faith in Christ declined from an estimated 12 percent of Americans in 1992 to only 7 percent in 1994. "The movement of the data," concludes Barna, "suggests that we may see a continued shrinkage of the ranks of evangelicals in the immediate future, short of a miraculous outpouring of God's Spirit upon the people of our land."[1]

For those who point to the evangelical debate about the Bible in the 1970s and 1980s as evidence that we are still concerned about biblical truth, David Wells counters by noting the appalling irony that "while the nature of the Bible was being debated, the Bible itself was quietly falling into disuse in the church."[2] The consumer mindset has invaded not only the church but also our theology. A therapeutic Christianity that helps me raise my kids, renew my sex life and become all that I can be has replaced an older theological and doctrinal Christianity that concerned itself with questions of God, sin, salvation and the cross. As a 1990s book title suggests, the church increasingly has no place for truth.

Where do we begin in our quest for theological renewal in the church? "Ultimately," writes historian Mark Noll, "the greatest hope for evangelical thought lies with the heart of the evangelical message concerning the cross of Christ."[3] Decision-makers who want to see the church move forward need to rediscover the cross. As useful as contemporary Christian thinking is about church growth, evangelical social action, global missions and worship renewal, the narrow channel of long-term progress for the church lies in a new engagement with the message of the cross.

This is an apparent folly. To say that insight into the cross has more renewing power than evangelistic action or savvy marketing is the kind of scandal Paul described in 1 Corinthians 1:27: "God chose the foolish things of the world to shame the wise; God chose the weak things of the world to shame the strong." As G. K. Chesterton once suggested, a proper diagram of the Christian mind should be shaped not like a circle that encloses everything into a system but like a cross that, beginning with a central paradox, moves out in every direction to shed light on all aspects of reality. Indeed, the cross is the foundation of all the classic decision-making we will look at in this book.

Unleashing the power and significance of the cross for all of life is the key to the long-term health and wholeness of the Christian church. To uncover the full significance of the cross is the greatest decision a church leader can make.

No figure in history has grasped this insight into the power of the cross more deeply than the sixteenth-century Reformer Martin Luther. Luther's theological breakthrough is sometimes summarized by the phrase "justification by faith in Christ alone." What is not always appreciated is that Luther's understanding of the cross went beyond its power to save and included its power to help us *see.* Oxford theologian Alister McGrath has called Luther's theology of the cross "one of the most powerful and radical understandings of the nature of Christian theology which the Church has ever known."[4]

If life and ministry seem a riddle to you, the cross has an answer. The older riddle of the cross can solve the newer riddles of our fragmented existence in the modern world. Luther's theology of the cross points like a compass needle to a passageway of progress that we might otherwise miss and dismiss.

But how does Christ's death provide solutions for muddled leaders and muddled Christians? What did Luther mean by "the theology of the cross"? How can decision-makers apply this insight today? To these questions we now turn.

Luther's Life

Martin Luther (1483-1546) was born into a world in which passion for the truth was fading and boredom with the gospel was growing. European Christianity was in trouble. Three of its most serious problems were nervous Christians, worldly churches and moralistic reformers.

Timothy George has written of the sixteenth century as an age of anxiety. That anxiety had three faces. The fear of sickness and death produced a sobering *physical* anxiety. Fear of guilt and condemnation, and the church's inadequate answers to these terrors, produced a crippling *moral* anxiety. Fear that life had no meaning and purpose produced a profound *existential* anxiety. In the sixteenth century and the late Middle Ages there was a morbid obsession with death. The prospect of punishment in the fires of purgatory and hell increased a sense of guilt and condemnation. Fear of anarchy and chaos along with the dread of an imminent apocalypse raised numerous questions about life's meaning and purpose.

Popular theology's answer to these terrors was simple: Work as hard as you can and then hope for the best. Deliverance from the anxieties of the age was not primarily through Christ but through one's own efforts. But how much was enough? How perfect did one have to be to receive divine grace that would lift the anxious soul out of the abyss of fear? The typical late medieval Christian found little help for dealing with these anxieties. Christians were nervous, and their anxieties were growing.

The church to which anxiety-ridden Christians turned was ill-equipped to ease troubled souls. On the upper levels a growing spirit of secularization ate away at church and parachurch structures (schools, monastic orders, hierarchy and so on). Leo X (1475-1521) symbolizes this attitude. He had been elected pope in 1513. Son of Lorenzo de Medici ("the Magnificent"), Leo was generally sincere in his faith, but his areas of weakness were money and politics. Because Leo spent huge sums for patronage of the arts, music and the theater, the papacy's money was in short supply. In order to finance his most extravagant project, St. Peter's Basilica in Rome (including the Sistine Chapel), Leo renewed the practice of indulgences (paying money to reduce one's stay in purgatory), which precipitated the Protestant Reformation. He excommunicated Luther in 1520 but never fully appreciated the depth of Luther's protest or the extent of his impact. For Leo the only real problem in the church was lack of money. Leo also played politics in order to enhance the secular power of the papacy. And the story was pretty much the same wherever one looked. From top to bottom, church leaders yielded to those three familiar temptations: money, sex and power.

Many sought to reform the church to overcome the abuses of money, sex and power and to meet the needs of anxiety-ridden believers. Numerous cures for the ills of the church were offered. Desiderius Erasmus (1466 or 1469-1536), the most famous scholar of his day, represented those who called for moral and spiritual reform. Influenced by the Brethren of the Common Life, a pietistic movement that emphasized the imitation of Christ, Erasmus wrote a number of popular and scholarly works to address the declining morals of church and society. Notable among these works were *The Enchiridion* (1501), *The Praise of Folly* (1509) and a pioneering critical edition of the Greek New Testament (1516). Erasmus and the humanists called for fresh study of the Scriptures and the fathers of the early church. They spoke out against abuses like indulgences. But Erasmus and his fellow reformers failed to see that the problems of the church and of the age pointed to a truth issue that was theological at root. A different kind of reformer was needed who would not just hack at branches but would work at the root.

During his student years Martin Luther showed little concern for these problems or their solutions. He entered the University of Erfurt in order to become a lawyer and help his father, Hans, with his small mining business. When Luther received his M.A. from the university in 1505, he threw a party for his friends at a local pub to celebrate. To the shock of his drinking buddies, however, Luther announced that he was not going into law; instead he would join a monastery.

His friends laughed at first, thinking this was just another joke by their jovial former classmate. But Luther was dead serious. A brush with death in a thunderstorm had brought him face to face with his own mortality. He had promised St. Anne that he would become a monk if she spared his life. His prayers had been answered, and Luther intended to keep his promise. He entered the Augustinian monastery in Erfurt and sought rest for his troubled soul.

But the rest that Luther sought eluded him. He wanted to be sure of his salvation, but no amount of religious exercise or discipline seemed enough to quiet his troubled conscience. Luther quickly exhausted the Catholic means of grace and found them wanting. No full assurance could be given. The moral, physical and existential anxieties of the age were simply too much for the late medieval version of the gospel.

Luther's superior in the monastery, Johannes Staupitz, became concerned about his anxiety-ridden colleague and suggested that Luther should get his mind off himself and put it on the Bible. From 1510 onward Luther became a serious student of Scripture, and eventually he was appointed professor of Bible at the University of Wittenberg—a tiny school of sixty students with little reputation or promise.

Sometime between 1514 and 1516, through his studies of Psalms and Romans, Luther discovered that we are justified by faith alone. That is, God declares us to be perfectly righteous in his eyes, not on account of our actual righteousness (which is insufficient) but only on the basis of the perfect righteousness of Christ, which is transferred to our account and superimposed on our standing before God. In other words, we are right with God through what Christ does and not what we do.

For a spiritually exhausted monk in an age already weakened by the fever of unresolved anxiety, the truth of justification by faith seemed a miraculous cure. Luther wrote that when the truth of this imputed (or transferred) righteousness of Christ became clear to him, it seemed as though "the gates of paradise" opened before his eyes.

Luther acted swiftly to share his discovery with the rest of Europe's nervous Christians. The hammering of his Ninety-five Theses (protesting not only the traffic in indulgences but also the church's loss of truth) on the door of Castle Church in 1517 inaugurated the Protestant Reformation. Luther had noisy debates with John Eck in 1519 in the German city of Leipzig. In 1520, defying papal excommunication, Luther wrote his magnificent Reformation booklets *The Babylonian Captivity of the Church, Address to the Christian Nobility* and, thundering above the others, *The Freedom of the Christian Man.* "Here I stand!" he thundered in 1521, as he faced the scowl of Holy Roman Emperor Charles V and refused to recant his new discovery. The explosions that followed right up to Luther's death in 1546—spiritual explosions that revolutionized Europe and had a lasting impact far beyond—still ring in our ears today.

Paradox and the Theology of the Cross

In contrast to the "roaring" years of Luther's life, 1518 appears to have been a quiet and neglected whisper. It's easy to miss this hushed year when we tell the story of Luther, but that would be a mistake. In 1518, at a convention of Augustinian monks in Heidelberg, Luther quietly spoke words that have shaken the church periodically ever since. His thoughts were an extended meditation on 1 Corinthians 1:25: "For the foolishness of God is wiser than man's wisdom, and the weakness of God is stronger than man's strength." Luther knew that what Paul was saying about the cross opens up an entirely new view of God.

Luther further discovered that the key to understanding biblical truth in light of the death of Jesus Christ is that God now speaks through *paradox*. A paradox is a statement that seems to contradict apparent truth but actually contains a deeper truth. For example, Christ said that those who would save their lives must lose them (Mt 10:39). That sound backwards to most of us. But what Jesus meant was clear. To find real life we must give up our independence and give our lives over to him.

Don't miss the point. *If I want to understand the Bible today I need to learn to think in terms of paradox.* Christian theology fails when it uses straight-line logic alone. The road to ultimate truth is like a twisting, winding mountain road. Luther's thinking on the cross illustrates the way we must think if we are to grasp scriptural truth. The paradox that runs through the points we'll examine below is that God makes things out of their opposite. He makes something out of nothing. He wins by losing. He lifts us up by bringing us low. He turns Good Fridays into Easter Sundays. He works opposite to the way humanity logically expects an omnipotent God to work.

Luther hoped to restore a love for biblical truth by putting the cross of Christ in the central position of Christian theology. Centuries of medieval theology had attempted to combine Greek philosophy with Christian theology. The sick state of the church convinced Luther that this experiment was a failure. As he studied Romans and the Corinthian epistles, he made a stunning discovery: God works through opposites. The only salvation that works is one that renounces works. The might of Christ was revealed in the death of Christ. When we are weak, then we are strong. Luther saw that the gospel is chock full of paradoxes.

If we don't grasp this central idea of divine paradox, Luther will make no sense to us and, more important, the deepest truths of the Bible will be beyond our reach. So hold on for the twisting ride around the paradoxes of the cross, and don't give up. The twists and turns may be severe, but they will get us to the top of the mountain, where we'll gain a new vision of truth.

The God Paradox

Back to Heidelberg. Sifting the text of 1 Corinthians 1:25 like a miner panning for gold, Luther's words fell like nuggets into that solemn assembly of monks. He described a theology of the cross that opened up a new way of seeing salvation, God, reality, suffering, the church and theology itself. What was this all about?

"For the foolishness of God is wiser than man's wisdom, and the weakness of God is stronger than man's strength" (1 Cor 1:25). From this verse and its context Luther pulled out a number of propositions that he felt went to the heart of both the mystery of God and the predicament of humanity.

What does the cross say about God? That is the question with which Luther began and we too should begin. But Luther didn't get to the heart of his answer to the "God question" until he arrived at his nineteenth thesis. If any Augustinian monks were dozing as thesis eighteen was read, Luther woke them up with number nineteen.

Luther began by attacking the way we talk about God. "He is not worth calling a theologian" who tries to describe God's nature and attributes "on the basis of things that have been created." What's wrong with God-talk that's based on our observations about life and nature? "Knowledge of all these things," insisted Luther, "does not make a man worthy or wise."[5] That is to say, speculation about God based on sunny days or solar systems doesn't change our hearts. Lofty ideas, however beautiful or breathtaking, cannot save our souls.

Luther called any theology based on human speculation and natural theology "a theology of glory." Theologians of glory come in all shapes and sizes. A sixty-year-old Sunday-school teacher or a six-year-old angel in a Christmas pageant can be an agent of this soul-damaging theology of glory. "Natural theology," writes Luther scholar Paul Althaus, "and speculative metaphysics which seek to know God from the works of creation are in the same category as the works righteousness of the moralist."[6] In other words, talking about God primarily based on what we think about his works produces pride in us. This theology of glory "leads Man to stand before God and strike a bargain on the basis of his ethical achievement in fulfilling the Law."[7] Theology or worship done wrongly can produce a plague of spiritual pride—something God hates.

What's the alternative? We have to talk about God and think about his glory if we're going to worship and serve him. What does Luther suggest we do? The kind of thinking and speaking about God that leads to vital spiritual life and avoids deadly spiritual pride is rather strange. Luther tells us bluntly in thesis twenty: "But he is worth calling a theologian who understands the visible and hinder parts of God to mean the passion and the cross." What is God's visible "backside"? "These visible parts mean the humanity of God, his weakness, his foolishness."

Why would our glorious and almighty God want to be understood in terms of weakness and foolishness? How can we worship a God of folly? Luther's answer hurts: "For because men put to wrong use their knowledge of God which they had gained from his works, God determined to be known from sufferings."[8] Why sufferings? Because we do not benefit from our natural knowledge of God ("I think God is like this or that") unless he is known "in the humility and shame of the cross."

Focusing on the cross, not meditating on the Milky Way, is the proper approach to God because it confronts us with two truths that we would not otherwise face squarely: first, we are God's enemies, and second, God has loved his enemies in Christ. Knowing God through the weakness and foolishness of the cross humbles us because it is our weakness, our foolishness, our shame that God wears when he climbs onto the cross. God on the cross becomes an accurate picture of humanity as it truly is—weak, helpless in the face of death, yet under the judgment of death. Our lofty thoughts about God turn into an ugly game of taking the place of God. So God's appearance as a defeated fool is a life-giving game of taking the place of fallen humanity. The cross is a telescope that locates God in the cross-hairs of our weak and foolish sinfulness and his vulnerable, unmerited love for such enemies. To know God through the cross is to know our sin and his redeeming love.

But doesn't such talk about God border on blasphemy? How can we hold up clownish pictures of God as weak and foolish and still worship? Luther proclaimed that God's glory is magnified, not minimized, when we think and speak of him in terms of the crucifixion. How? "God shows that he is God," explains Althaus, "precisely in the fact that he is mighty in weakness, glorious in lowliness, living and life-giving in death."[9] Only God is great enough to win by losing. Only God is loving enough to love the unlovable. Only God is eternal enough to be swallowed by time and death and live to tell the tale. The cross magnifies the divine King who played the fool in order to end the folly of sin and death.

What does all this talk of the foolishness and weakness of God mean for us? It means that all our God-talk in worship and in preaching should be shaped by the vocabulary of the cross. As sinners we have no right to worship God's attributes of holiness, infinity and sovereignty until we come in brokenness and repentance before his costly love proclaimed on the cross. Worship or sermonizing that gets people feeling good about themselves or self-satisfied in their lofty words and thoughts about God is a worship of glory that damns our souls and divides us from God. But worship or preaching that first puzzles over the paradox of the apparent defeat of the King of kings on Good Friday will then be raised to the newness of Easter life.

God is thus never to be known through circumstances. Circumstances are frequently confusing and sometimes negative. We will not understand him unless we look at him where he is hidden most—in the dark shadows of apparent weakness and defeat that surround the death of Christ on the cross.

The Salvation Paradox

The world is full of religions that build ladders on which humanity may ascend to God. Christianity, envious of the achievements and strengths of rival religions, can be seduced to follow suit and turn itself into a religion of good works and performance reviews.

The medieval salvation system that Luther inherited as a young priest had attempted just such a facelift. Gabriel Biel, a fifteenth-century theologian whose teaching on salvation shaped Luther's generation, spoke of the "spark of God" within every person. If we do our very best, the teaching went, God will fan that spark of divinity within us, and we will become fuller each day with holiness and love.

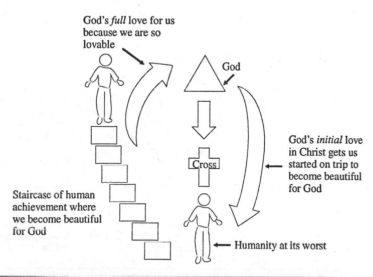

Figure 1. The medieval understanding of the cross as accomplishing only partial salvation and union with God

In this scheme, through grace and good works we can climb the staircase of religious and moral achievement to the point where

God will be so impressed with our performance that he will declare us righteous and reward us with the gift of eternal life in heaven (so we avoid the remedial torments of purgatory—see figure 1). If we slip on the way up the staircase, the sacrament of penance is there to catch us. Confession to a priest coupled with fear of punishment is enough to win a penitent another crack at the climb.

This system of staircase climbing failed for Luther. Try as he might, he always found himself bruised and battered at the bottom of the stairs, angry at God and in despair about his salvation. But a new understanding of the cross changed all that (see figure 2). God's love is shown to us in that Christ climbed the staircase of religious and moral achievement for us, then met us at our point of sin, anger, defeat and judgment and took our place. God's saving love is given at the bottom of the climb to crippled pilgrims, not at the top of the stairs to spiritual overachievers. The cross is thus a paradox: God rejects the proud but gives grace to the humble; he rejects beautiful heroes and sheds his justifying love on ugly

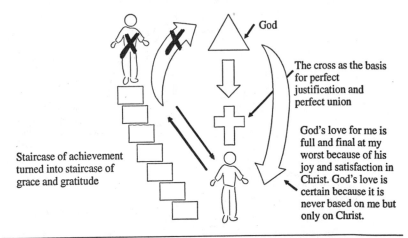

Figure 2. Luther's evangelical breakthrough: the cross as a new way to see salvation

failures. The sinner at the bottom of the staircase needs only to believe in order to be delivered.

Luther was so excited about this aspect of the theology of the cross that it became the area of his greatest emphasis. "It is Christ who is grasped by faith," he told his audience of Augustinian monks, "who is the Christian righteousness, on account of which God beckons us to be righteous and grants us eternal life." Christians are righteous before God, then, only when they give up on their own righteousness.

The theology of the cross, applied to the issue of salvation, transforms my understanding. Christ's death is the achievement that saves me, not my fancy footwork on the staircase. Unless I live by faith in the achievement won by the events of Good Friday and verified by the surprises of Easter Sunday, I will never grasp how God can justify and accept as his own a sinner who deserves his curse and not his blessing. But when I learn to see God and his salvation through the cross, I see things differently.

The principle of the cross is that God does things in surprising and contradictory ways. To inspire our praise he wears the clownish costume of weakness and folly. To make everything he begins with nothing. To deliver sinners he becomes defeated by them.

When I become accustomed to this "cross-eyed" way of seeing, salvation becomes clear and wonderful. I can be assured that I'm righteous in God's eyes because God is cross-eyed too—he sees me through the substitutionary death of his beloved Son. Thus I can have confidence in God's love even when I lose all confidence in my own love. I can be full of joy in God even when I despair of myself.

What does this mean for us? The theology of the cross should change the way we view salvation. If we want our churches to foster competitive rat races for moral and spiritual superiority, we can silence the theology of the cross and scramble up the staircase of self-righteousness. But if we want to fill our churches with people who glow with grace, gratitude and unshakable assurance of God's love and acceptance, we must unleash this theology of the cross and God's strange way of making successful saints out of broken sinners.

The Reality Paradox

Luther's twenty-first thesis pushed the cross in new directions. "The theologian of glory," he declared, "says that bad is good and good is bad." In contrast, "the theologian of the cross" calls things "by their proper name."[10] What is Luther talking about?

Luther's reasoning goes something like this. Not only do theologians of glory misunderstand God and salvation because they fail to see these things through the cross, but they also distort the rest of reality, evaluating everything in wrong-headed ways. Paul Althaus explains Luther's meaning:

> True reality is not what the world and reason think it is. The true reality of God and of his salvation is "paradoxical" and hidden under its opposite. Reason is able neither to understand nor to experience it. Judged by the standards of reason and experience, that is, by the standards of the world, true reality is unreal and its exact opposite is real. Only faith can comprehend that true and paradoxical reality.[11]

"Only faith can comprehend that true and paradoxical reality." When Christ was dying on the cross, the reasonable explanation was that he was a liar and a failure. The reality was that his magnificent defeat vindicated all his words and marked the greatest victory in all of history—the conquest of sin and death. When Pilate and Christ stood face to face on Good Friday eve, the reasonable explanation would have been that Pilate was in charge and the shackled Jewish rabbi was at the mercy of Rome. The cross tells me, however, that things are not what they appear to be. Reality from the perspective of the cross is that Christ was in charge of the events of Good Friday, that Pilate was swept along by the force of a kingdom and a king that he did not recognize.

"To believe," concludes Althaus about Luther's paradoxes, "means to live in constant contradiction of empirical reality and to trust one's self to that which is hidden."[12] When God brings me low, the reality of the cross leads me to conclude that he will lift me high. Why? Because the cross's principle of paradox reflects the way God has structured all reality. Death will lead to life. The grave becomes the place of hope. The status quo will be transformed into a God ordained opposite. The first shall be last, and the last shall be first. "Faith must endure being contradicted by reason and experience," but if it endures it can "break through the reality of this world by fixing its sights on the word of promise."[13]

The Pain Paradox

One reason, says Luther, that people want a theology of glory rather than a theology of the cross is that "they hate the cross and suffering."[14] But in light of the cross, suffering serves an important purpose—the cultivation of self-denial. "It is impossible for a man not to be inflated by his own good works unless the experience of suffering and evil, having previously taken all the spirit out of him and broken him, has taught him that he is nothing and his works are not his own but God's."[15]

The way to Easter Sunday is through Good Friday. Suffering heals us by breaking us. It brings us high by bringing us low. It empties us of our self-confidence so that we might have confidence in God. It destroys our boastful tongues so that we might boast even more of Christ. Alister McGrath explains:

It is through experiencing the wrath of God that man is humbled, and forced to concede that he cannot, by himself, stand in the presence of God—and thus he turns to God in his helplessness and hopelessness, and by so doing is justified. Paradoxically, it is thus through God's wrath that his mercy is made to operate, in that man would not seek that mercy unless he knew how much he needed it.[16]

But what about suffering as an ongoing part of the Christian life? Why does God bring us through painful and humiliating circumstances after we have been justified? The answer is that the pattern of the cross becomes the pattern of my entire Christian journey. The experience of apparent abandonment by God and the despair that accompanies it will be followed by the surprise of grace and renewal. McGrath comments:

> As Good Friday gave way to Easter Day, the experience of the absence of God began to assume new significance. Where was God? And as those bystanders watching Christ gazed proud, looking up to the heavens for deliverance, they saw no sign of God and assumed he was absent. . . . The presence of God was missed, was overlooked, was ignored, because God chose to be present where none expected him—in the suffering, shame, humility, powerlessness and folly of the cross of Jesus Christ.[17]

God chooses to continue to be present with his children in unexpected ways. Just as he was present in the suffering Christ, so God's presence in our trial is not apparent unless we see him as present inside our weakness and pain.

Why does he do this? Why doesn't he make our lives smooth and trouble-free? Luther's answer would be to look at the cross. God's way of working in the lives of those he loves as his children—whether it is Christ, his only begotten Son, or us, his adopted children—is to bring them low in order to raise them high. The pattern of Christ's life, spelled out in the Gospels and summarized in Philippians 2:1-11, is the pattern of humiliation and exaltation. This is God's pattern for us as well.

When our stories begin to conform to the story of Christ, we need to respond by exercising faith. "Reason is scandalized by the cross; faith embraces it with joy."[18] To trust that the God who brings us into a Good Friday of pain, rejection and defeat will also bring us into an Easter Sunday of victory and gladness is to guarantee blessing and deliverance. Unbelief that misses the meaning of pain will also miss the experience of exaltation. The mystery of Romans 8:17 is thus unraveled by the theology of the cross: "Now if we are children, then we are heirs—heirs of God and coheirs with Christ, if indeed we share in his sufferings in order that we may also share in his glory."

The Truth Paradox

So extensively did the theology of the cross transform Luther's thinking about God, salvation, reality and suffering that he declared, "The cross alone is our theology."[19] This dramatic statement seems to be a clear exaggeration. After all, there are so many more doctrines in theology (God, creation, humanity, sin, church, last things) than the doctrine of the cross. What did Luther mean?

Luther is proposing that the cross should change the way we look at every doctrine. How does the cross do this? The cross tells us that God's revelation of himself as Creator, Sustainer and Judge must be understood in a new way because of the work of the cross. In all God's other works, such as creation and providence, God shows himself as infinitely powerful. But in the cross he shows himself as apparently weak, thereupon contradicting our entire theology.

Further reflection on the cross contradicts every doctrine we hold in one particular sense: the assumption that God's power is directly revealed by his actions. The doctrine of creation reveals God's power to make things. The doctrine of eschatology reveals God's power to judge and transform. But the cross shows us something deeper about the way God reveals truth about himself. The work of the cross shows God's indirect way of working. God, at his heart, shows his power best through apparent weakness. He displays his wisdom best through apparent folly. The fullness of his deity was displayed paradoxically, according to Colossians 1:19, in the frailty of Christ's incarnation. God is revealed best where he is hidden most.

The cross is a hermeneutical key that unlocks new dimensions and correct understanding in every area of theology. Explaining Luther's point, Althaus writes:

All true theology is "wisdom of the cross"; this means that the cross of Christ is the standard by which all genuine theological knowledge is measured, whether of the reality of God, of his grace, of his salvation, of the Christian life, or of the Church of Christ. The cross means that all these realities are hidden. The cross hides God himself. For it reveals not the might but the helplessness of God. God's power appears not directly but para-

doxically under helplessness and loneliness.[20]
Thus when critics attack the narrow-mindedness of evangelicals who insist on the uniqueness of Christ in a pluralistic world or the supreme authority of the Bible in a world of many competing authorities, the cross helps us to understand our position. The apparent weakness of our position (going against the mainstream, which insists that God must reveal himself universally to all, not in unique ways to particular peoples) is actually a hidden strength. The theology of the cross recognizes that God does not work as we might expect. God did not give saving truth in nature, from which we might expect a universal Word to come. He whispered to the world in a totally surprising and scandalous way, through the cross of Christ. Our whole theology needs to be reinterpreted in light of the cross because true theology is but a theology of the cross.

The Ministry Paradox

In church ministry nothing is more powerful than weakness. Luther's theological crisis was first experienced as a crisis of ministry. He could neither give to others nor find peace and assurance of salvation for himself within the traditions of the church. The Protestant Reformation was the result of Luther's attempt to fix the ministry of the church from bottom to top. But what is remarkable about the young Luther (though he grew more negative in his later years) is that he never gave up on the church. His theology of the cross helps explain why.

"The Church," Luther admitted, "would perish before our very eyes, and we along with it, . . . were it not for that other Man who so obviously upholds the Church and us." The crucified and risen Christ is at work in the weakness of the church, preparing to show his strength. Likewise, the crucified and risen Christ "passes judgment upon the Church where she has become proud and triumphant, or secure and smug, and recalls her to the foot of the cross, there to remind her of the mysterious and hidden way in which God is at work in the world."[21] McGrath explains this final paradox:

The scene of total dereliction, of apparent weakness and folly, at Calvary is the theologian's paradigm for understanding the hidden presence and activity of God in his world and in his Church. Where the Church recognizes her hopelessness and helplessness, she finds the key to her continued existence as the Church of God in the world. In her weakness lies her greatest strength. The "crucified and hidden God" is the God whose strength lies hidden behind apparent weakness, and whose wisdom lies hidden behind apparent folly. The theology of the cross is thus a theology of hope for those who despair, then as now, of the seeming weakness and foolishness of the Christian Church.[22]

When the church has lost almost everything and radically chooses to believe that the gospel of the cross of Christ is still its greatest treasure and hope for future success, God will lift it up. But when the church loses the cross, exchanging it for the applause of the age or the world's measure of success, it actually faces a dismal future. The triumphant liberal churches of the 1950s and 1960s became the declining churches of the 1990s. The culturally peripheral but "cross-eyed" evangelical and charismatic churches of the 1950s and 1960s became the megachurches of the 1990s. God works in his church through opposites. The cross of Christ helps us see that.

The Theology of the Cross in Our Decision-Making
Luther's quiet year, 1518, was actually a year of momentous importance. Like a north star, Luther's theology of the cross now points to the way ahead for the bewildered church and disoriented Christian in a postmodern world. But how can decision-makers translate Luther's great idea into good decisions? Let's look at some possible decisions that might unleash the power of the cross in our churches, families and organizations.

Use #1: The cross and preaching. By "preaching the cross" I don't mean we should preach only evangelistic sermons. Instead we need to bring the perspective of the cross into everything we preach.

William Willimon, chaplain at Duke University, writes about preaching to consumer-oriented audiences who appear to want entertainment more than enlightenment. It's easy for preachers to make one of two mistakes in responding to such congregations. One mistake is to give in "to their consumer mind-set" with "feel-good" sermons that avoid biblical truths. The second mistake is to give up. We can develop the attitude that "my people don't care about the gospel. They just want to be entertained."[23] What Willimon has discovered about beating the consumer mindset is striking:

> My first priority, then, is to preach a sermon that speaks about the gospel, not a speech that explores people's experience. In the admirable attempts to be relevant, too many sermons I hear whitewash therapeutic solutions with biblical "principles" where the Bible ends up sounding like the latest rage of popular psychology.[24]

What we need in our churches is talk "about Jesus Christ and what he has done for us and what he calls us to do for him and for one another."[25] When we lift up the cross of Christ each week as both a way of salvation and a way of seeing, we will turn an audience into a church and consumers into the committed. As David Wells has written: "The Church is called to declare the message of the cross, not to uncover God's hidden purposes in the world or the secrets of his inner therapy."[26] We must bring people under the cross to get them over the world.

Use #2: The cross and theological literacy. If theology in general is despised in our churches and organizations, then the theology of the cross will be marginalized as well. When we cultivate our people's appetite for doctrine, however, the theology of the cross can be unleashed.

George Barna has described the "theology of the typical American" as "nothing less than frightening." What's the problem? "The lack of accurate knowledge about God's Word, about his principles for life, and the apparent absence of influence the Church is having upon the thinking and behavior of this nation is a rude awakening for those who assume we are in the midst of a spiritual revival."[27]

This theological slippage also appears among evangelicals. Denominations that were once known for their defense of the faith now talk only of marketing their churches or ordering their private worlds. Yet "to value theology," argues David Wells, "is to value the means by which the Church can become more faithful and more effective in this world."[28]

Providentially, the structures for theological renewal are already in place. Adult Sunday-school classes and weekday small groups dot the landscape. Useful resources that could be studied by those in such networks abound. Alister McGrath's *The Mystery of the Cross* would be one place to begin. New theological methods such as narrative theology, which employs story forms to communicate theological truth, have made theological study more accessible to a wider audience.[29]

When theology matters, the theology of the cross will matter more. Keeping in mind Luther's warning that a theology of glory will do more harm than good, wise decision-makers will take practical action to raise the theological literacy of their congregations.

Use #3: The cross and public worship. What do people need when they file into church at 11:00 a.m. on Sunday? Some are bored to tears, but most are looking for some kind of contact with God, although many have stopped expecting that. What we can offer them is not just a feel-good pick-me-up but a reliving of history's most famous weekend, which changed forever the future prospects of lonely sinners.

When the cross is raised up through prayers of confession, hymns and choruses of praise, sermons saturated with Christ and other elements that look at life with a cross-eyed magnificence, something happens to people. Good Friday realities that everybody faces turn into Easter-morning possibilities that few have dared to hope for. "There are no hopeless situations," writes Winifred Newman, "only people who think hopelessly." Cross-centered worship changes hopeless people into heartened worshipers. Deciding to worship this way is a decision we can't afford to miss.

Use #4: The cross and working with people. I sometimes get frustrated with people. They don't always do what I want. I have friends who disappoint me, kids who have their own ideas, students who aren't always on my wavelength. I am sometimes tempted to give up on certain people, write them off as incorrigible, hopeless cases. But God won't let me. The cross reminds me that the frustrations of Good Friday were winning a secret victory that only Easter morning revealed.

God may do his best work through an incorrigible student, a strong-willed child or a callous friend. He may make something marvelous out of its opposite and use those who in my eyes are "weak and foolish" to confound the wise. The cross reminds me that *I* was "weak and foolish" in God's eyes, yet he chose me to do a job for him. The cross keeps me proactive and works against my reactive tendencies to give up on people. Decide to look at problem people in your church or organization with new eyes because of the cross.

Use #5: The cross and the bottom line. Leaders of Christian organizations may wonder how the cross relates to money raising and the practical realities of running a Christian organization. It is true that marketing, promotion, businesslike management and shrewd stewardship are all necessary if we are to be effective in competitive times. But each of these things must be looked at through the perspective of the cross.

In 1995 many Christian organizations were affected by the collapse of a charitable organization known as New Era Philanthropy. Millions of dollars were lost. Scores of Christian organizations and churches were shaken.

Leaders of some organizations responded by focusing on the loss of funds. Heads rolled. Programs were cut. Ministries were weakened. Others focused on the pattern of the cross and found in the experience of financial loss the opportunity to exercise faith. They believed that Good Friday experiences can be times of hidden victories, even though to the world they appear to be defeats. The faith that was exercised was rewarded, and some organizations rebounded from the New Era crash with new energy, vision and strength. Deciding to filter bottom-line realities through the perspective of the cross was a significant factor in their renewal.

Times of financial crisis or constraint are opportunities to win hidden victories. But leaders must decide to exercise faith in the midst of discouraging events and expect God to conform our present realities to the master realities of the cross.

Use #6: The cross and social justice. Many churches, families and Christian organizations are concerned about matters of social justice in their communities and nations. How can the perspective of the cross help us make good decisions in this area? In an interview Archbishop Desmond Tutu revealed how the pattern of the cross empowered the Christian struggle against apartheid in South Africa. Tutu, who was awarded the Nobel Peace Prize for his efforts to promote racial equality, was asked how his small, understaffed and poorly financed Christian organization, the South African Council of Churches, was able to sustain its nonviolent struggle against injustice over the decades. Was it Marxism? capitalism? humanism? His answer was the cross. "The Bible enabled one to reply" that God "is always on the side of the weak, of the small, the 'unimportant.' " Because of this, "whatever may be the case now, however powerful the government may be militarily and in all other kinds of ways, be assured that victory is going to be ours." Because Tutu believed the cross revealed God to be on the side of the weak of the world, he was able to say to the government: "You have lost. You may be powerful now but that doesn't say anything about the eventual outcome."[00]

A decision to base the campaign against apartheid on the theology of the cross and what it taught about God produced an indomitable spirit that sustained the South African civil rights movement through several discouraging decades until its eventual triumph in the early 1990s.

Of Boulders and Gateways

I remember a grueling canoe trip with my brother-in-law John many years ago. We took a week to canoe from northern Ontario to the Hudson Bay. We experienced uncomfortable campsites, swamped canoes, wild rapids and long portages. But the most bizarre episode of the trip occurred when we lost the river. How do you lose a river when you're paddling down it? Easy. At one point the river had been flooded by a dam and became a wide, island-studded lake. We lost the current. We lost our way.

After two days of paddling around the lake, studying our maps and consulting our compass, we concluded that the river must resume on the far end of a certain bay. As we scanned the shoreline, however, we could find no outlet. All we saw was a huge boulder rising near the shore like a fortress. The outlet to the river was nowhere to be found.

We decided to persist. We moved closer to the boulder, and as we sailed around it, much to our surprise we discovered a small, narrow channel that curled around the rock and led to the continuation of the river on the other side. The boulder that looked like a barrier to our journey actually was a gateway that made it possible to continue our journey.

I believe the cross is like that boulder. The cross does not appear at first to hold the secrets of our journey through life. It seems irrelevant to many of our plans and needs. Yet if we explore it closely, a powerful paradox is revealed. This unpromising barrier actually becomes the gateway to growth and progress in every area of life.

When John and I finished our canoe trip, we arrived at river's end in the Cree town of Moosenee. We caught the Polar Bear Express, a train that brought us back along parts of the river we had traveled. It looked easier now, this canoe trip we had taken. The rapids, the long portages, the bumpy campsites were behind us.

Though they were history, out there amid the dark spruce was a thin crack of water that made our train ride back to civilization one of triumph rather than defeat. To explore that unlikely passageway was the best decision we had made on the trip. Like Robert Frost's diverging roads, it was a decision that made all the difference.

For Discussion
1. A key text for Luther's theology of the cross is 1 Corinthians 1:18-31. How many paradoxes can you spot in this passage? How does the cross produce these paradoxes?

2. Which of Luther's six paradoxes is the most relevant to you and your church right now? Why?

3. Which of the six applications might be the most useful for your church right now? Why?

For Further Reading
On the life of Luther I recommend James M. Kittelson, *Luther the Reformer* (Minneapolis: Augsburg, 1986), though Roland Bainton's classic *Here I Stand* (Nashville: Abingdon, 1950) is still excellent reading. On the theology of the cross, two books by Alister McGrath are recommended: *Luther's Theology of the Cross* (Oxford: Blackwell, 1985) and *The Mystery of the Cross* (Grand Rapids, Mich.: Zondervan, 1988). A useful collection of primary source readings including the Heidelberg Disputation can be found in Timothy Lull, ed., *Martin Luther's Basic Theological Writings* (Minneapolis: Fortress, 1989).

2

A VISION FOR SPIRITUALITY

Calvin on the Christian Life

Afunny thing happened to secular society as it was rushing toward postmodernity. It discovered a thing called spirituality. Men and women who had spent decades as religious agnostics and "ignostics" (ignorant of God) now talked about their newly discovered spirituality as though it were the latest vacation hot spot.

Take the case of novelist Douglas Coupland. Coupland is the reluctant guru of Generation X, the gloomy generation of baby busters facing a future of downward mobility in a world where "McJobs" seem to be the only reliable employment. Coupland's novel *Generation X: Tales for an Accelerated Culture* not only coined a term but also defined a generation of post-baby boomer twentysomethings made cynical by a lifetime of *Brady Bunch* reruns and baby boomer self-absorption. He chronicled a religion-less generation that numbed itself to this loss with "drugs, stupid jobs, empty sex."[1]

Coupland's later novel *Life After God* traced a new trend within Generation X. One of the characters confesses that he is searching for salvation from cynicism. "I'm trying to escape from ironic hell: Cynicism into faith; randomness into clarity; worry into devotion." In another place the central character, Scout, wonders out loud whether cynicism "is the price we paid for the loss of God." The novel ends with a cry for a rediscovery of God.[2] On behalf of this first generation raised without religion and the hope of an afterlife, Coupland longs for a way out of the wasteland. He hints that if there is a way out, it probably has to do with finding God.

God or Self?

Among baby boomers, secularists, Depression-generation skeptics and baby buster "ignostics," a new search for God is on. Psychiatrists Thomas Moore and M. Scott Peck produce bestsellers that purport to guide the search for spiritual fulfillment. In the early 1990s *Newsweek* devoted a cover article to the phenomenon entitled "The Search for the Sacred: America's Quest for Spiritual Meaning."[3]

What kind of spirituality are the returning prodigals discovering? As the *Newsweek* article indicated, the new pilgrims seem to have post-Christian appetites. New Age spirituality, selfist spirituality, pantheistic mysticism and other forms of self-absorbed pseudopiety seem to appeal to many of the new seekers. The real object of their worship seems to be themselves.

Over a decade ago, psychologist Paul Vitz saw that this rising spirituality of self-worship was really "a popular secular substitute for religion."[4] He argued that selfism could masquerade as spirituality. Self-actualization and self-fulfillment rather than truth or God's glory are the real goals of selfist piety. Vitz also noted that selfism is destructive whether it appears in secular or spiritual guise. The joys of serving and loving others slowly wither under selfism's narcissistic gaze.

Generation X spiritual consumers and their parents and grandparents need more than selfist spirituality whitewashed with the language of revivalism. This kind of me-centered piety, though initially attractive, is ultimately unsatisfying. Vitz predicted that by the 1990s "millions of people will be bored with the cult of the self and looking for new life." The signs of just such a boredom with selfism are everywhere to be seen.

The reason for this boredom is not hard to find. Self-absorption does not make people happy. Psychologist Abraham Maslow, famous for his "hierarchy of needs," revised his theories significantly at the end of his life. He had believed that the highest level of human fulfillment was self-actualization, a point of total development achieved by meeting basic physical, social, mental and spiritual needs. In his last years Maslow realized that *self-transcendence,* not self-actualization, is the highest human experience. Living for others is a more satisfying spiritual state than merely "feeling good about myself."

How can the church help confused and wayward pilgrims find true spirituality? Vitz is convinced that the great need of the hour is to return to the spiritual resources of historic Christianity, which teaches, "very simply, [that] the only way out is to lose the self, to let it go and once more willingly become an . . . object in the love and the service of God."[5]

Historically evangelicalism taught that knowing God is the key to self-transcendence. It also taught that this knowledge of God was the climax of human happiness. "In your presence there is fullness of joy," sings the psalmist; "in your right hand are pleasures forevermore" (Ps 16:11 NRSV). Thus a truly God-centered approach to piety was our hallmark in the past.

But on the way to the late twentieth century our spiritual legacy of self-transcendence through God-centeredness became muddied by a variety of American ideas such as pragmatism, self-reliance and more overt forms of humanism. For many evangelicals the search for a new spirituality has meant wandering around in the theological wine cellars of Christian traditions, so depleted has our own current stock become.

Vitz, aware of the spiritual poverty of the modern church, insists that the key question is not whether spiritual prodigals will return to the church but "whether their Father's house, the true faith, will still be there to welcome and celebrate their return." And, we may add, will the Father's house have the true spirituality that the returning prodigals seek and need?

John Calvin, a younger contemporary of Luther, spent a lifetime mapping out a spirituality that put the true and living God of Scripture at the center of the spiritual quest. Because his model of Christian living avoided many of the ancient and modern pitfalls on the road to spirituality, it deserves a place as one of the great ideas in church history. Calvin believed that spirituality is produced by following daily disciplines rather than by a few bursts of inspiration or enthusiasm. His great idea was that we can best overcome the me-centered spirituality of our age by learning the habits of a biblical holiness.

What are these habits of holiness? Calvin stressed six. Like most effective Christian leaders, he learned these habits the hard way.

Calvin's Life

John Milton once said of Oliver Cromwell that "he first acquired the government of himself and over himself won the most singular victories so that he was a veteran in arms before he ever faced an external foe." Winning victories over the self was a lifelong battle for John Calvin. He wrestled with the issue of meaning and direction in his life just as Luther had wrestled with the question of death and condemnation. The search for direction consumed much of Calvin's life.

John Calvin was born in 1509 in the village of Noyon, France. His father, Gerard, worked for the local bishop and determined that his son should pursue a career in the church. Calvin was sent off to the University of Paris to study for the priesthood.

After Calvin had begun his studies, however, his father was excommunicated from the church. So Gerard, perhaps disillusioned with Catholicism, ordered his son to change his direction and study law. But no sooner had the young Calvin begun to study law than he received news of his father's death. He was devastated. What direction now? Free to follow his own inclinations, Calvin pursued humanist studies, which involved the study of ancient pagan and Christian literature.

By 1533, when Calvin was completing his studies, another change of direction had occurred. Luther's ideas were circulating in Paris, and a bright, inquisitive student like Calvin could scarcely avoid their influence. Sometime before 1533 Calvin underwent a change in heart that he later described in the preface to his commentary on the Psalms:

> God at last turned my course in another direction by the secret rein of providence. What happened first was that by an unexpected conversion he tamed to teachableness a mind too stubborn for its years, for I was so strongly devoted to the superstitions of the papacy that nothing less could draw me from the depths of that mire.[6]

What was nearly as remarkable as his "unexpected conversion" was the rapid growth in his understanding of the new faith. Calvin wrote that conversion "set me on fire with such a desire to progress that I pursued the rest of my studies more coolly, although I did not give them up altogether. Before a year had slipped by anybody who longed for a purer doctrine kept on coming to me, still a beginner, a raw recruit."

Calvin's reputation as an evangelical soon got him into trouble: an uproar against evangelicalism at the University of Paris forced him to run for his life. From 1533 to 1536 he was on the run, living under assumed names and donning different disguises. He settled in Basel, Switzerland, long enough to write a small book intended to explain the evangelical faith in simple terms. His book, *Institutes of the Christian Religion,* became a bestseller and went through many editions and revisions during the course of his life. The publication of the *Institutes* brought Calvin immediate fame as an articulate spokesperson for the evangelical cause.

Calvin's new celebrity made him a target for zealous reformers eager to enlist his aid. While visiting Geneva, Switzerland, Calvin heard a knock on his door one night. The visitor was William Farel, an evangelical reformer who was eager to renew the church in

Geneva but needed help. Farel insisted that Calvin join him as copastor of the Geneva church. Calvin politely refused, explaining that he intended to live the life of a quiet scholar. Farel was not impressed. He called down the curse of God on Calvin's studies if he refused to help in the reform of Geneva. Calvin was shaken by this threat and decided that God was changing the direction of his life once again.

Calvin ministered in Geneva for two years until he was fired by the city council, which had become disenchanted with church reform. Thereupon he moved to the peaceful city of Strasbourg, then part of Germany, and from 1538 to 1541 spent three idyllic years as a pastor of the refugee church in the city. He also wrote a commentary on Romans, the first of many biblical commentaries which would add to his enduring fame as an exegete. During the Strasbourg years Calvin also married a young widow, Idellette de Bure. He was content at last.

All was going smoothly until the day that Farel appeared to call him back to Geneva, where the city fathers had undergone a change of heart. Calvin refused, but when Farel threatened him once again with the curse of God, he packed up and returned to Geneva.

From 1541 to his death in 1564 Calvin labored to reform the church and the city that had become his personal Nineveh. This time God granted success. As the decades passed Geneva was transformed into what one visitor, John Knox, called "the most perfect school of Christ since the time of the Apostles." Calvin's influence spread throughout Europe. By the time of his death he had become the international leader of the Reformation and one of the most significant figures in the shaping of the modern world.[7]

At the heart of Calvin's public victories as the champion of reform were private victories gained through a relentless pursuit of the secrets of holiness. Piety was uppermost in Calvin's mind as he wrote the *Institutes,* which he subtitled *A Sum of Piety.* He particularly treasured the chapters in the *Institutes* that dealt with Christian living; at one point he reprinted them as a separate booklet. These chapters on the Christian life gave the church the secrets of a true spirituality that would transcend the self and connect with God. Calvin saw the spiritual life not as a series of spine-tingling experiences but more as daily "habits of the heart" (to borrow a phrase from de Tocqueville). Stephen Covey claims there are "seven habits of highly effective people"; Calvin upheld six habits for highly effective Christians.

Habit #1: Depend on the Holy Spirit

For Calvin, the greatest secret of holiness is the inner working of the Holy Spirit. And the greatest work of the Spirit is the work of putting us in union with Christ. What did Calvin understand by this phrase "union with Christ"? It is a relational union similar to marriage, and the Spirit plays a prominent role in it. "The Holy Spirit is the bond by which Christ effectually unites us to himself."[8] How does the Holy Spirit unite us to Christ? This union is experienced by faith, which for Calvin is the "principal work of the Holy Spirit" (3.1.4).

The content of this Spirit-produced faith that leads to union with Christ is *Christ as redeemer.* True faith is "a firm and certain knowledge of God's benevolence toward us, founded upon the truth of the freely given promise in Christ, both revealed to our minds and sealed upon our hearts through the Holy Spirit" (3.2.7). A faith union with Christ produced by the work of the Holy Spirit is thus vital for true spirituality.

If we harbor any uncertainty regarding this dynamic, holiness in our theology becomes the nervous manipulation of an unpredictable God. Gratitude is the only truly evangelical motive for holiness, but it cannot flow swiftly in us if justification by faith is perceived only dimly. Servile fear or haughty self-righteousness becomes the destructive motive for spirituality if the evangelical impulse is weak or absent.

Union with Christ is not static but produces two internal actions called *mortification* (killing off the old life) and *vivification* (creating a new life). The Spirit is central to both actions. Calvin saw these two actions as the real content of repentance, which is "the true turning of our life to God, a turning that arises from a pure and earnest fear of him; and it consists in the mortification of our flesh and of the old man and in the vivification of the Spirit" (3.3.5).

Consider the action of mortification. Union with Christ is first of all union with his death. The task of the Spirit is to do to sin in us what Christ did to sin on the cross—remove its curse from our lives. Daily killing of the power of sin is necessary because indwelling sin remains in the believer's life. Indwelling sin is an orientation to self-centeredness and must be destroyed (3.3.8). True spirituality for Calvin is therefore a lifelong repenting and fighting against sin. For Calvin it is only "through continual and sometimes even slow advances [that] God wipes out in his elect the corruptions of the flesh, cleanses them of guilt, consecrates them to himself as temples renewing all their minds to true purity that they may practice repentance throughout their lives and know that this warfare will end only at death" (3.3.9).

This mortification of sin is followed by a second action of the Spirit—vivification. Just as mortification was based on the believer's union with the death of Christ, so also vivification is based on the union of the believer with the resurrection of Christ. The Spirit brings to the Christian the same power that Christ experienced when he rose from the dead. United with him in his resurrection power, we can live a new life on earth. This wonderful process of vivification "comes to pass when the Spirit of God so imbues our souls, steeped in his holiness, with both new thoughts and feelings, that they can be rightly considered new" (3.3.8).

The basic attitudes that Calvin later extols as expressions of true piety are given to us through this experience of union. Because I am in union with Christ, I am no longer an autonomous person (who has "got" religion); I am now only a person-in-Christ.

Wilhelm Niesel summarizes Calvin's first habit of holiness thus: Christ is the crucified and Risen One not in and for Himself. He does not remain aloof from us but He who once-for-all has experienced death and resurrection meets us today and really communicates to us those benefits which for our sakes He has obtained. Our old man is seized upon and crucified by the power of the death of Jesus Christ. We are awakened into a new life by the power of His resurrection. This happens through the Spirit of Christ which binds us to Him and evokes in us faith and obedience.[9]

For Calvin the bottom line of true spirituality is union with Christ through the Spirit. From this deepest root flows faith, justification, sanctification and every other benefit of salvation. When Calvin discusses the life of the Christian as journeying with Christ through self-denial, cross-bearing and meditation on the future life, we must not think of the lonely pilgrim, winding his solitary way. We must think of the connected Christian unable to be separated from his loving Savior who fights with him and for him each step of the way.

Habit #2: Practice Self-Denial

From Matthew 16:24 Calvin drew three central elements of the Christian life—self-denial, bearing the cross and following Christ. What did he understand by *self-denial?* Self-denial for Calvin was not just punishing the body or giving up sweets for Lent. True self-denial is much deeper than such superficial things. At heart, self-denial is about the question of ownership: Who is really in charge of my life—God or me? For Calvin the selfist answer was unacceptable. The true owner of each self is the God who creates, sustains and redeems the self.

Calvinist spirituality is built around Romans 12:1-2 and the double denial of self that it teaches: (1) we are not our own, and (2) we belong to God. It is not any particular sin that must first be mortified, but the root of sin, which is personal autonomy from God.

What did Calvin mean when he said that we are not our own? "We are not our own: let not our reason and will, therefore, sway our plans and deeds. We are not our own: let us not see it as our goal to seek what is expedient for us according to the flesh. We are not our own: in so far as we can, let us therefore forget ourselves and all that is ours" (3.7.1). If we are not autonomous selves, then who are we? Calvin's answer is that we are creatures who belong to God. The essence of Calvinism is captured not in the doctrine of election or predestination but in Calvin's declaration of God's ownership of our lives:

> Conversely, we are God's: let us therefore live for him and die for him. We are God's: let all the parts of our life accordingly strive toward him as our only lawful goal. O, how much has that man profited who, having been taught that he is not his own, has taken away dominion and rule from his own reason that he may yield it to God. (3.7.1)

This basic denial of self leads to specific denial of our self-concern and self-will. We need to be concerned with God's name and will and agenda and not our own: "For when Scripture bids us leave off self-concern, it not only erases from our minds the yearning to possess, the desire for power, and the favor of men, but it also uproots ambition and all craving for human glory and other more secret plagues" (3.7.2).

A life of self-denial changes the way we relate to others. Calvin noted that pride, jealousy and envy (and the rivalry they produce) are endemic in human relationships: "But there is no one who does not cherish within himself some opinion of his own pre-eminence. Thus, each individual, by flattering himself, bears a kind of kingdom in his breast. For claiming as his own what pleases him, he censures the character and morals of others" (3.7.4). This being the case, gentleness, humility and lowliness before others are the primary marks of self-denial in relationships.

When we deny self, we seek to use our resources for the good of others and not just ourselves. Calvin insists that "Scripture, to lead us by the hand to this, warns that whatever benefits we obtain from the Lord have been entrusted to us on this condition: that they be applied to the common good of the church. And therefore the lawful use of all benefits consists in a liberal and kindly sharing of them with others" (3.7.5). Self-denial will seek to serve even the most undesirable, for it arises not from a selfish love but from love of others for God's sake. Even "if [someone] has not only deserved no good at your hand, but has also provoked you by unjust acts and curses, not even this is just reason why you should cease to embrace him in love and to perform the duties of love on his behalf."

Contentedness is the primary expression of self-denial before God: "It remains for us not greedily to strive after riches and honors—whether relying on our own dexterity of wit or our own diligence, or depending upon the favor of men, or having confidence in vainly imagined fortune—but for us always to look to the Lord so that by his guidance we may be led to whatever lot he has provided for us" (3.7.9).

In summary, the practice of self-denial will lead to attitudes of detachment and contentment. Calvin concludes that the person who has learned self-denial will be content with "whatever happens, because he will know it ordained of God; he will undergo it with a peaceful and grateful mind so as not obstinately to resist the command of him into whose power he once for all surrendered himself and his every possession" (3.7.10). Such is the spiritual secret of self-denial.

Habit #3: Bear the Cross

The third habit of effective spirituality is to harness the power of suffering. This power comes into play in the ongoing spiritual warfare in which believers are engaged. For Calvin true spiritual warfare is not primarily wrestling territorial spirits or confronting the demonic. The true war is within. "The believer," observed Calvin, "is in perpetual conflict with his own unbelief." The primary attack of Satan is against our faith in Christ. Life is a daily war to keep faith alive and growing.

How do we win this daily war? What is the believer's secret weapon? Calvin's answer is surprising: our secret weapon is suffering. In ways reminiscent of Luther's theology of the cross, Calvin speaks of the importance of suffering and the power it unleashes. We must bear our life's crosses in imitation of Christ. Christ himself "learned obedience from what he suffered" (Heb 5:8). If our battle is to become like Christ, suffering helps us win because it conforms us to Christ.

What are some of the specific benefits of suffering in the life of the Christian? It conforms us to Christ. It breaks our pride in self and enables us to transfer trust to God. It purifies us from sin (3.8.6). It increases our spiritual rewards, for if we suffer for righteousness' sake "we but have a fuller place in the kingdom of God" (3.8.7).

Is Calvin's praise of suffering extreme? Is this a "grin-and-bear-it" brand of Christianity? Calvin denies that it is and speaks against Christian stoics who say it is sinful to sorrow (see Mt 5:4; *Institutes* 3.8.9). Stoicism taught that we should be patient in affliction simply out of the intellectual realization that God cannot be resisted: if you can't beat him, endure him. Calvin rejects this line of thinking as fatalism. Instead he offers an evangelical understanding of why we should be patient in affliction: "Now, because that only is pleasing to us which we recognize to be for our salvation and good, our most merciful Father consoles us also in this respect when he asserts that in the very act of afflicting us with the cross he is providing for our salvation" (3.8.11). For this reason there is a secret joy hidden beneath every external cross.

Habit #4: Focus on the Eternal
Alongside the habits of self-denial and cross-bearing is an even more mysterious habit of the Christian life: following Christ by fixing our gaze on heavenly realities. Calvin called this "meditating on the future life." Since Christ rose from the dead and ascended into heaven, to follow Christ means to meditate on the eternal and future dimension where Christ reigns in power and from which he will return in power. Christ is still on the move, ruling from heaven and preparing to come again to this earth. Following him means keeping in step with his new activities. Calvin believed that we see 20/20 only when we focus on the vanity of this life with one eye and the glories of eternal life with the other.

For Calvin, earthly life lived in ignorance of the reality of the future and eternal worlds is empty. Why? He gives two reasons. First, this life is a seething sea of unpredictable fortune, and therefore to trust in it is to build our house on sand (3.9.1). Second, we really have to choose which world will have first place in our hearts: the passing world around us or the world that is coming (3.9.2).

Calvin does not mean that we should hold this life in utter contempt (more on this shortly). He readily affirms that this earthly life merits a proper appreciation. In fact, God's benevolence shines forth through this life, but not so brightly that we lose our longing for the greater good of eternal life (3.8.3). The proper love of this world in all its created goodness is to love it in a secondary way. First place in our hearts must go to the risen and ascended Christ. Following him means loving his exalted position now and drawing from him all that we need to sustain us in our earthly pilgrimage. Eschatology is thus the proper framework for present joy and hope: "Let us, however, consider this settled: that no one has made progress in the school of Christ who does not joyfully await the day of death and final resurrection."

But the believer needs to know that the power of the resurrection to come can break into our present life. "To conclude in a word: if believers' eyes are turned to the power of the resurrection, in their hearts the cross of Christ will at last triumph over the devil, flesh, sin, and wicked men." How? Faith feeds on this future glory and justice and contentedly waits with joy. These attitudes of faith, contentment and joy give us happiness in our present existence. Following Christ by meditating on the future life can thereby transform us in the present.

Habit #4: Use All of Life for God's Glory

In light of Calvin's strong emphasis on eternal things, how are we to regard God's material creation and human cultures? Calvin would not have us misunderstand his emphasis. Thus his fifth habit of true spirituality is that we should use this good life for the glory of God. All the good things of this life are spiritual food if used for their intended purposes.

What are the intended purposes of created things? Calvin mentions two—beauty and utility (3.10.2). We can even grow in holiness when we use material things for pleasure and recreation:

> The use of the gifts of God is not unruly when it is limited to the purpose for which God created and designed them, seeing that he created them for our good. . . . If we consider to what end God created foods, we shall find that he wished not only to provide for our necessities but also for our pleasure and recreation. . . . With herbs, trees and fruits, besides the various uses he gives us of them, it was his will to rejoice our sight by their beauty, and to give us yet another pleasure in their odors.[10]

But how can we specifically use creation and culture in a way that keeps God central in our affections? Calvin offers four rules for the holy use of creation. (1) *Detachment* means developing a "take it or leave it" attitude to the passing things of this earth. (2) *Contentment* with little enables us to have fairly constant joy in times of plenty *and* times of want. (3) *Accountability* means we realize that God will judge us for the ways we use the gifts of creation and culture. Because of this, it is not enough to do a job well when the boss is looking. We work for the Lord, who is always looking at our work. Ethical integrity and social justice must be concerns of the Christian worker, because his God is concerned about these things as well (3.10.5). (4) *Diligence* leads us to persevere in our calling and work hard. Why is this so important? Think of it as a prime indicator of self-denial, cross-bearing and focus on eternal life. The career gadfly is developing none of these three disciplines of the godly person. Diligence in our humble callings is not a dreary duty, for "no task will be so sordid and base, provided you obey your calling in it, that it will not shine and be reckoned very precious in God's sight" (3.10.6).

Calvin's piety avoids the errors of both an uncritical world-affirming piety and an overly critical world-denying piety. According to sociologist Max Weber, the Puritan ethic was an inner-worldly piety as opposed to the otherworldly piety of monasticism. The inner-worldly piety of the Puritans was derived from Calvin's model of the Christian life. As Alister McGrath has written, Calvin believed in what "could be termed the critical affirmation of the secular order. You live in the world; you address yourself to it; you value it, in that it is the creation of God; but you also recognize that it is a fallen creation, in principle being capable of redemption."[11] In light of the escapist pieties of our day, this fifth habit of holiness is a useful corrective.

Habit #6: Persist in Prayer

The final habit of effective spirituality is prayer. If we need the ministry of the Spirit to mortify sin and give us new life in Christ, and if we follow Christ by fixing our gaze on him in his heavenly glory, then we must engage in prayer. Calvin calls prayer "the chief exercise of faith . . . by which we daily receive God's benefits." Through prayer we "we dig up . . . the treasures that . . . our faith has gazed upon" (3.20.3).

Calvin offers four rules for effectiveness in prayer. The first rule is *reverence for God.* "Let us therefore realize," proclaims Calvin, "that the only persons who duly and properly gird themselves to pray are those who are so moved by God's majesty that freed from earthly cares and affections they come to it" (3.20.4). The rule of reverence should lead us to depend on the Spirit, who helps us to pray. "God gives us the Spirit as our teacher in prayer, to tell us what is right and temper our emotions" (3.20.5).

The second rule of prayer is *sincere need.* Calvin opposes repetitious prayers, which he believes are insincere. In contrast "the godly must particularly beware of presenting themselves before God to request anything unless they yearn for it with sincere affection of heart, and at the same time desire to obtain it from him" (3.20.6).

The third rule of prayer is *a humble and contrite spirit.* Union with Christ by faith is thus a necessary precondition of prayer: "Nor should anyone, however holy he may be, hope that he will obtain anything from God until he is freely reconciled to him" (3.20.9).

The fourth and final rule of prayer is *confident faith*. We must pray with bold hope. Calvin mocks those who pray as though God had not sent a redeemer to cover their sins: "O Lord, I am in doubt whether thou willest to hear me, but because I am pressed by anxiety, I flee to thee, that, if I am worthy, thou mayest help me." Such a prayer is not acceptable to God. "For only that prayer is acceptable to God which is . . . grounded in unshaken assurance of hope" (3.20.12). How can we pray with such confidence, knowing our own sin and ignorance? Christ is the foundation of our hope (3.20.17). Christ has given us the Lord's Prayer to guide us.[12]

The discussion of prayer and the importance of faith in prayer brings Calvin to his first habit—depending on the Holy Spirit, who produces the faith that we need. Calvin's piety thus begins with God and ends with God, and the six habits form a cycle of spiritual growth (see figure 3).

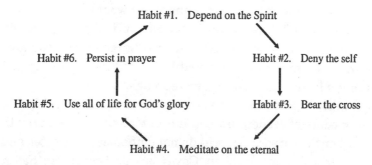

Habit #1. Depend on the Spirit

Habit #6. Persist in prayer

Habit #2. Deny the self

Habit #5. Use all of life for God's glory

Habit #3. Bear the cross

Habit #4. Meditate on the eternal

Figure 3

How good can one expect to get at this kind of spirituality? Though these six habits are powerful agents of change, Calvin is realistic about progress along the path toward spirituality. "No one in this earthly prison of the body has sufficient strength to press on with due eagerness, and weakness so weighs down the greater number that, with wavering and limping and even creeping along the ground, they move at a feeble rate." Does this mean that real spiritual progress is futile? Not at all, says Calvin. "Let us not despair at the slightness of our success; for even though attainment may not correspond to desire, when today outstrips yesterday the effort is not lost." In summary, as we move through each of these habits of effective spirituality we can expect growth but should never expect perfection.

As the six habits of this cycle become part of the rhythm of our lives, we grow in a spirituality that transcends the self and ushers us into conscious intimacy with God. How to cultivate that intimacy with God in our church or organization remains to be discussed.

Applying Calvin's Habits of Effective Spirituality

How can we apply Calvin's model in our ministry? Let me mention some possibilities.

Use #1: True spirituality and the character of the leader. According to James Means, "too many pastors err in thinking that change in other people or a change in circumstance would foster success in their ministries." What many fail to realize is that "God rarely blesses the ministry of those with dubious character, questionable behavior, and unremarkable spirituality."[13] First Timothy 3:2 states that a leader "must be above reproach."

Spirituality is necessary for authentic Christian leadership. Yet popular models of leadership coming out of the church-growth movement or the corporate world do not emphasize character and godliness. In contrast, Stephen Covey, in his bestselling *Seven Habits of Highly Effective People,* speaks of the importance of winning private victories before seeking to win public ones. The habits of personal leadership (a vision for one's life) should be coupled with personal management, where one puts that integrated vision into practice.[14] If we are going to help those we lead experience true spirituality and avoid the pitfalls of selfism, we must be able to say with integrity, "Follow me as I follow Christ." To plan for personal spiritual retreats as well as for spiritual life retreats for the entire leadership team could be key decisions calculated to lead our organization down the path of greatness.

Use #2: True spirituality and accountability. One of the most helpful aids to spirituality is an accountability group. Patrick Morley believes that "the missing link in most of our lives is accountability." He advocates what he calls the "Weekly One-Hour Accountability Check-up." This involves gathering with a small group of trusted fellow believers and asking key questions about one another's spiritual life, home life, work life and critical concerns. I have experienced the benefits of such an accountability group, and I have seen how powerful these groups can be in changing lives.

A few years ago I had the privilege of working at the Billy Graham Center at Wheaton College. The director of the center at that time, Jim Kraakevik, immediately struck me as a man of unusual godliness and grace. I watched him work under enormous pressure, deal with serious medical emergencies at home and handle knotty personnel problems in the organization. What was his secret for keeping his spiritual life in shape, given the pressure of being a high-level decision-maker? In addition to practicing a number of other spiritual disciplines, Jim belonged to an accountability group where tough questions were asked and honest answers were given. Of all the excellent decisions he made as a leader of an important organization, the decision to pursue true spirituality through an accountability group was perhaps the most critical one.[15] We need to make the same kinds of decisions.

Use #3: True spirituality and the leader's family life. The culture of narcissism has seeped into the Christian home. Instead of being nurseries of piety, many Christian families have become service centers for the "me generation." In the hostile sea of modernity some of our homes have become private islands of indulgence. Os Guinness argues that the private sphere "has become the sphere of spending rather than earning, and of personal fulfillment rather than public obligation. . . . Privatized man is not only an anxious atlas but a spoilt narcissus."[16] True spirituality needs to be modeled by fathers and mothers, taught to children and practiced in the day-to-day routines of life.

The truth is that the family setting is the ideal place to work on true spirituality. Every day in the typical home, opportunities abound to practice dependence on the Spirit, denial of the self, bearing the cross, godly use of culture and sincere prayer. Two valuable aids to cultivating this kind of piety are regular family worship and formulating a family life mission statement.

Some years back my wife and I, together with our two children, formulated a mission statement for our family. It contained an element of service to others along with emphasis on learning to love God as Christ did. Reviewing that statement as we face decisions has helped to get us thinking about others and their needs rather than ourselves.

Use #4: True spirituality in the workplace. Guinness warns against an empty piety that fails to penetrate the sphere of work:

Look for a place where the Christian's faith makes a difference at work beyond the realm of purely personal things (such as witnessing to colleagues and praying for them, or not swearing, or not fiddling income tax returns). Look for a place where the Christian is thinking "Christianly" and critically about the substance of work (about, say, the use of profits and not just personnel; about the ethics of a multinational corporation and not just those of a small, family business; about a just economic order and not just the doctrine of justification). You will look for a very long time.[17]

Such a faith is "privately engaging but socially irrelevant." It produces the Christian businessman who regularly attends church and Sunday school even while he pulls off shady deals at work. This kind of spiritual schizophrenia damages the testimony of faith. Where is the detachment from earthly treasure, good though it is, that prevents us from putting money ahead of God? True spirituality learns to use the things of this life without dualism or deceit.

Men's breakfasts and men's retreats are great times to discuss issues of true spirituality in the workplace. Career women could benefit from luncheon Bible studies, seminars or even courses on

Christian business ethics. Identify the lay leaders in your church who have been given great grace in this area, and let them minister this grace to Christian men and women struggling in the marketplace.

Use #5: True spirituality and a broken life. If you as a decision-maker have been knocked out of the race of the Christian life by sin or failure, Calvin's habits of effective spirituality still apply to you. His model of spirituality is not just for unblemished heroes. It is also for wounded soldiers.

Gordon MacDonald, an outstanding New England pastor, saw his ministry destroyed by a serious moral failure. In the months and years that followed—months and years that were sometimes filled with despair, bitterness and brokenness—God did a work of restorative grace. Spirituality was restored. Character was rebuilt. Leadership was regained. A number of Calvin's six habits are mentioned in MacDonald's poignant book *Rebuilding Your Broken World.*[18]

Although *Newsweek* neglected the resources of Christian orthodoxy in its search for spirituality, the church of Christ must not make the same error. In Calvin's model of true spirituality the church can recover the vision for holiness that is greatly needed in today's culture of narcissism.

For Discussion

1. A key text on holiness is Romans 6:1-14. How well do Calvin's six habits of holiness match up with the model of holiness presented in Romans 6?

2. Review the five uses of Calvin's model of spirituality. Which ones are the most relevant for you right now? Why?

For Further Reading

Reading through the *Institutes* can be a spiritually rewarding experience, as I discovered as a young Arminian not at all sure whether Calvin had anything worth saying. I was forced to change my mind. Use the Battles translation found in the two-volume

Westminster Press edition. An important recent biography of Calvin is Alister McGrath, *A Life of John Calvin* (Oxford: Blackwell, 1990). On Calvin's theology in general see François Wendel, *Calvin: Origins and Development of His Religious Thought* (1950; reprint Durham, N.C.: Labyrinth, 1987). On Calvin's spirituality the older work of Ronald Wallace is still useful: *Calvin's Doctrine of the Christian Life* (Grand Rapids, Mich.: Eerdmans, 1952).

3

A VISION FOR UNITY
Jeremiah Burroughs & the Denominational Theory of the Church

When I came to Africa as a missionary I was struck by two outstanding features of African Christianity. The first was the growth of the church during the course of the twentieth century. The figures that were commonly circulated were simply astounding. In 1900 there were an estimated 8 million professing Christians in Africa, or about 10 percent of the continent. By the 1980s the figure was 250 million, or half the population of the whole of Africa. Never before in the history of the church has such dramatic growth taken place in a single century.

My excitement at discovering this feature of African Christianity was soon dampened by my discovery of a second feature. I learned about the enormous disunity of African Christianity. Statistician David Barrett estimated that there were over five thousand different independent churches in Africa by the late 1960s.[1] These groups claimed over seven million members, drawn from 290 tribes all over the continent. More recently church historian John Baur estimates that there are nearly ten thousand such groups.

The broken body of Christ is fracturing still.

It would be one thing if this were only an African problem, but it is not. At the beginning of the twentieth century there were approximately nineteen hundred denominations in the West. By the late 1980s the estimate was twenty-two thousand.[2]

Alongside traditional denominational church structures are new church structures that add to the growing diversity in the body of Christ. Leith Anderson's *A Church for the Twenty-first Century* describes new shapes and forms of church that are multiplying like McDonald's franchises. "Megachurches," with two thousand or more people, "are like shopping malls offering a broad array of services to enormous numbers of people." "Metachurches" are "based on a network of small groups that function as centers for assimilation, training, pastoral care, and evangelism." "Wal-mart churches" "serve regional rural markets"; they "transcend the deep traditions of small communities and give permission to worship without alienating family histories and relationships." The list grows on. Many of these new models of the church are appearing outside traditional denominations. They are seeds for the next generation of denominations and harbingers of growing diversity in the body of Christ in the future.

Peril and Promise

Some see the diversity of the worldwide church described above as a dangerous thing. Like a runaway cancer, destructive cells are multiplying in the body of Christ. Denominationalism has been the bogey man behind the brokenness of the body of Christ. H. Richard Niebuhr called denominationalism "the moral failure of Christianity." Bishop Lesslie Newbigin has declared that denominationalism is "the religious aspect of secularization."[3] What makes Newbigin see it that way? Denominationalism is a concession to individualism, permitting the self to decide what to believe; it therefore relegates the gospel to the private sphere and allows secular ideologies to reign in the public arena. Such a privatized faith, says Newbigin, "cannot confront our culture with the witness of the truth since even for themselves they do not claim to be more than associations of individuals who share the same private opinions." Newbigin believes that the visible unity of the church must be manifested in ways that move beyond denominationalism before the church can mount a credible witness to a lost world.

I would like to differ with Newbigin's diagnosis. While I believe that denominationalism has indeed been secularized, I do not believe that denominationalism is beyond redemption. Nor do I believe that it is the real cause of the church's disunity. On the contrary, I want to propose that the denominational theory of the church, as originally conceived, is our greatest hope for promoting the kind of visible agreement of the body of Christ on earth that Newbigin calls for.

I find myself drawn to the statements of Hans Küng. "The co-existence of different Churches does not . . . in itself jeopardize the unity of the Church," writes Küng. "Unity is only endangered by co-existence which is neither co-operation nor support, but basically a hostile confrontation."[4] Even where there are serious and sometimes hostile confrontations, he asks, "Are such divisions in the Church always the result of narrow-mindedness, lack of charity and selfishness?" He answers thus: "They can also arise from the honest conviction that anything else would be a betrayal of the Gospel of Jesus Christ."[5]

In these statements Küng draws our attention to the two underlying causes of Christian disunity—*sectarianism* and *syncretism*. Sectarianism is an attitude of exclusiveness: "Only my church has the truth." Its relationship to other churches involves "hostile confrontation." Spiritual pride is the real cause of sectarian divisions, not denominationalism. Winthrop Hudson elaborates:

> Denominationalism is the opposite of sectarianism. A "sect" claims the authority of Christ for itself alone. By definition a sect is exclusive—separate. The word "denomination," on the other hand, is an inclusive term—an ecumenical term. It implies that the group referred to is but one member, called or *denomi-*

nated by a particular name, of a larger group—the Church—to which all denominations belong.[6]

A sectarian attitude can infect a denomination and turn it into a force for disunity. This does not change the fact, however, that in its uncorrupted form a denomination is an ecumenical structure, not a separatist structure.

Küng fingers more than sectarianism in his diagnosis of church disunity. The second problem he alludes to is syncretism, or the corrupting of the gospel by mixing it with the ideologies of the day. When a church or group corrupts the gospel, there must be a separation in order to preserve the only kind of unity the Bible knows—unity in the gospel. When the confessing church of Germany in the 1930s separated from the mainline churches which had compromised the gospel with Nazism, they were not sinning against Christian unity. They were in fact preserving the very foundations of Christian unity—the confession that Christ, not Caesar, is Lord. Syncretism, like sectarianism, can invade denominational structures and make it appear that denominationalism is the problem. Küng is correct, however, that the problem lies deeper.

So in contrast to the critics of denominationalism, I propose that denominationalism, as it was originally conceived, can be a great force for unity precisely because it resists sectarianism and syncretism, the two real enemies of unity. I would even go so far as to say that classic denominationalism is one of the most powerful allies we have in overcoming sectarianism and syncretism and restoring the visible unity of the body of Christ. To persuade you of the truth of this statement I need to introduce you to one of the architects of classic denominational theory, Jeremiah Burroughs.

Burroughs's Life

Jeremiah Burroughs was born in 1599, in the last years of the reign of Elizabeth I. Little is known of his life as a youth until he entered Emmanuel College, Cambridge University. Emmanuel, founded in 1584 by the godly Laurence Chaderton, was "the greatest seminary of Puritan Preachers" in England. The Puritans were not the pharisaic killjoys they are so often made out to be. Actually they were some of the most devoted evangelicals of their generation, passionate about the purity of the church and of the gospel. Burroughs himself "combined harmoniously in his own person what might be considered incompatible qualities: a fervent zeal for purity of doctrine and worship, and a peaceable spirit, which longed and laboured for Christian unity."[7]

Burroughs agonized over the nature of church unity. He learned his first lesson about what church unity was *not* in 1624, the year he received his master's degree. In that year he was chased from the university by church officials, who objected to his ideas that congregationalism rather than episcopalianism might be the better form of church government. Burroughs refused to believe that church unity meant a forced conformity. The church, he believed, might be so structured as to maintain the gospel and yet allow for diversity of opinion in such areas as church government, worship and the sacraments.

Burroughs eventually found places of ministry, serving two congregations in East England. In 1636, however, a renewed persecution of nonconformist ministers, organized by the new and unpopular Archbishop William Laud, deprived Burroughs of his pulpit. Forced into exile, he became pastor of the English congregation in Rotterdam, Netherlands. The Netherlands, though officially Reformed in its ecclesiology, tolerated a wider diversity of Protestant worship and theology than did England. There Burroughs began to formulate an answer to the question of how to have unity in diversity.

Meanwhile, the situation in England was changing rapidly. In the early 1640s Charles I was opposed by an angry Parliament that demanded reform of both church and state. This "Long Parliament" invited exiled ministers to return to England. Burroughs was among those who accepted the invitation. But no sooner had he settled in a new ministry in London, preaching regularly at two of the city's leading churches, Stepney and Cripplegate, than war broke out between king and Parliament.

This civil war gave the Puritan party the opportunity to reform the Church of England. Ministers from all over the country were summoned to the Westminster Assembly (1643-1646) in order to reform the church's theology and government. Among those chosen was Burroughs. Presbyterians and Congregationalist sympathizers made up the majority of the delegates, and Burroughs became the main spokesperson for the group of independents.

Along with others, Burroughs was saddened by the harshness of the debate over church government that threatened to divide the Puritan movement. He decried this contentious spirit:

We are wrangling, devising, plotting, working against one another, minding nothing but to get the day of one another. . . . Love and unity are Christ's badge, the arms of a Christian, whereby he shows of what house he is. . . . We cry out exceedingly against [divisions], . . . yet scarce a man does anything . . . towards any help against divisions or furtherance of our union.[8]

Burroughs opposed the rigidity of the Presbyterians at Westminster, many of whom taught that theirs was the only form of church government authorized by Scripture. So he decided that it was time to express his views on a new kind of unity in diversity. In 1644, along with four other "dissenting brethren," he offered his denominational theory of the church in the *Apologetical Narration*, which laid out the framework of a strikingly original theory of church unity.

The ideas of Burroughs and his fellow dissenters were rejected by the assembly as it concluded its work in 1646. Burroughs, discouraged by the decisions of the gathering, returned to his churches. Later that year he had a fall from his horse. Within a matter of weeks he died from complications of that fall. He was mourned even by those who had opposed him at Westminster. Richard Baxter, an ardent supporter of Presbyterian polity, paid him a high tribute when he declared that if all Episcopalians had been like Archbishop Ussher, all Presbyterians like Stephen Marshall and all independents like Jeremiah Burroughs, "then the breaches of the Church would have soon been healed."[9]

Something of Burroughs's passion for unity was captured in a book published shortly after his death entitled *Irenicum: To the Lovers of Truth and Peace Concerning the Causes and Evils of Heart Divisions* (1646). In this work Burroughs "pleaded for the unity of all who loved the truth, and argued that what made comparatively minor differences into causes of rigid divisions were a wrong spirit and wrong motives."[10]

Though Burroughs lost his battle at the Westminster Assembly, he did not lose the war. England experimented with the denominational theory of the church with some success during the protectorate of Oliver Cromwell (1653-1658), when Baptists, Congregationalists and other groups were part of the "voluntary national establishment." When the Stuarts regained the throne of England in 1660, Cromwell's experiment with denominationalism was scrapped. In 1689, however, the Act of Toleration paved the way for a permanent acceptance of denominationalism in England and the beginning of its worldwide practice.

The Denominational Theory of the Church

What were the central ideas in Burroughs's vision that have proved so influential over the long haul? Burroughs and his associates at Westminster argued for a denominational theory of the church based on six principles.

Principle #1: Doctrinal differences are inevitable. "Considering the wants and weaknesses that do ordinarily attend men's apprehensions," argued Burroughs, differences of theological opinion are unavoidable. While the Bible's teaching on salvation is sufficiently clear for all true Christians to agree on, other issues are not as clearly spelled out. "Christians in all ages," notes Winthrop Hudson, "have differed in judgment about the patterns of organization and worship that best serve to express and safeguard the Christian faith."[11] If for two thousand years Christians have disputed these secondary issues, it is unrealistic to expect that disagreements will somehow disappear.

Principle #2: Doctrinal differences in secondary matters are still important. Though these other matters are secondary to the primary truths of salvation, they cannot be ignored, because they are addressed in the Word of God. "Every Christian is under obligation to practice as he believes and to pursue to the end the implications of the convictions he honestly holds."[12] Because the Bible alone, and not human authority, has the right to dictate to the conscience, its statements even on secondary matters of doctrine (not fundamentals of the faith) are still binding. These different opinions (on worship, government, Christian freedom, eschatology and so on) must be preserved because the Bible has binding authority on our conscience. To be forced to violate one's conscience even in secondary matters is wrong. Organizing churches and denominations to preserve these distinctives is therefore in order.

Principle #3: Differences can be useful. God can use our differences, argued Burroughs, to bring out the truths of the Bible just as "sparks are beaten out by the flints striking together." Rather than being threatened by differences of opinion in secondary matters, Christians can be strengthened by the give-and-take of "discussing, praying, reading, meditating" on issues over which they disagree. To be threatened by differences is already to move toward a sectarian spirit.

Principle #4: No single structure can fully represent the church of Christ. The heart of sectarianism is the tendency to identify the true church with a single organizational expression. Denominationalism strikes against this spirit by preserving the "Protestant principle": no single ecclesiastical structure can ever fully represent the true church of Christ. "God is not the exclusive possession of any church, and the existence of different churches—each striving to the best of its understanding to be a faithful and worthy representation of Christ's church in the life of the world—serves as a constant corrective to the pretensions of all churches."[13]

Principle #5: True unity is based on the common gospel and should be expressed through cooperation between denominations. The diversity of churches does not justify the neglect of visible unity. Our agreement in the gospel is more important than our disagreement in secondary areas. Burroughs points out that though our differences are sad enough, yet they come not up to this to make us men of different religions. We agree in the same end, though not in the same means. They are but different ways of opposing the common enemy. The agreeing in the same means, in the same way of opposing the common enemy, would be very comfortable. It would be our strength. But that cannot be expected in this world.[14]

How do we then express this unity? Through cooperation in common causes. Continuing the military metaphor, Burroughs insists that "soldiers who march against a common enemy all under the same captain, who follow the same colors in their ensign and wear them upon their hats or arms, may get the day though they be not all clothed alike." The common "colors" and common "captain" would be an evangelical understanding of the gospel as outlined by Luther and Calvin.

Works of cooperation by Christians of different denominations are not only possible but keenly necessary for displaying the visible unity of the body of Christ. Unity is therefore to be expressed through cooperation between denominations in matters of mission and service, not necessarily through mergers of churches. Hudson says, "When it is remembered that, although Christians may be divided at many points, they are nonetheless united in Christ, it then becomes possible, Burroughs insisted, for them to work together for the common ends of 'godliness.'"[15]

Principle #6: Denominational separation is not schism. Some members of the Westminster Assembly accused Burroughs of advocating schism—that is, splitting the church into rival factions. Burroughs's calm reply was that "the true nature of schism is . . . an uncharitable, unjust, rash, violent breaking from union with the church or members of it." What Burroughs was advocating was different. If "loving and peaceable" separation into distinct church structures while still working across denominational lines for the advancement of the gospel "be called schism, it is more than yet I have learned." Though individual Christians "may be divided from a particular society, yet they are not divided from the Church."[16]

Burroughs and the dissenters were convinced that if these principles were followed by evangelical Christians in a spirit of humility and peace, we could be confident that "Christ will not charge us at the Great Day for retarding his cause."[17]

Applying Burroughs's Great Idea

Can the denominational theory of the church work for us today? Consider the following uses of Burroughs's idea.

Use #1: Teach the denominational theory to your church or organization. A few years ago a pastor friend of mine asked me to address a board of elders on the subject of denominational distinctives. He knew that I supported Burroughs's denominational theory of the church. My friend was encountering some resistance to change based on the objection that "we don't do it that way in our denomination." I was able to show to the elders the difference between being a closed denomination (sectarian and resistant to the free flow of ideas and partnerships with other groups) and an open one (holding to true distinctives while remaining open to new ideas and partnerships with other groups). God blessed that teaching time, and some new opportunities for growth opened up in the church.

Even if you belong to an independent church without denominational affiliation, Burroughs's teaching is still relevant, for it should encourage you to seek active partnership with other churches for the cause of the gospel. Take Burroughs's principles seriously, and teach and discuss them at the leadership level in your church or organization.

Use #2: Seek new partnerships with parachurch agencies. For the last couple of decades evangelicals have debated the nature of parachurch organizations. Do they really have any biblical basis? Don't they end up draining people and money from our local churches? Some are willing to accept parachurch organizations on pragmatic grounds. After all, they seem to get the job done where the local church often fails.

Still, theological foundations for the existence of parachurch agencies have been hard to find. Ralph Winter's suggestion in the 1970s about biblical modalities (local church structures) and sodalities (single-purpose parachurch structures) as both being crucial in the book of Acts was a major step forward. But it is the denominational theory of the church that provides the needed theological foundation. .

Unity between churches has been aided by parachurch organizations, which act as brokers of "pluriformity" (unity in the midst of denominational diversity) and agents of cooperation between denominations. Where would we be as evangelicals without the Lausanne movement, the Billy Graham Evangelistic Association, the World Evangelical Fellowship, Navigators, mission agencies, InterVarsity, Campus Crusade, Young Life, Focus on the Family, interdenominational evangelical publishing houses, colleges, seminaries, radio and regional fellowships (like the Evangelistic Association of New England)? What parachurch agencies bring to the equation of unity is an emphasis on "mere Christianity" that strengthens our grip on evangelical essentials and does not necessarily compromise denominational distinctives.

One of the challenges that parachurch agencies face is learning how to be more accountable to and involved with local churches. On that count too, rediscovering the denominational theory of the church can help.[18]

Use #3: Rebuild the theological foundations of cooperative unity. The denominational theory of the church brings us back to this book's first great idea—the theology of the cross. If denominationalism is to be a force of unity and not of disunity, we need theological renewal along the lines suggested by Luther. When we so treasure the cross and the new way of seeing and saving that it opens up, we will be able to put our differences in perspective and envision ways to cooperate in furthering the cause of the cross.

Remember that along with sectarianism the other great agent of disunity is syncretism—compromising the gospel by mixing it with human ideologies. Only a theology of the cross which extends the implications of the saving death of Christ in every direction can act as an adequate safeguard against theological compromise.

Use #4: Do a "unity check." What has your church done in the last year or so to increase its meaningful participation with other local churches on behalf of the kingdom? What parachurch agencies have been effective vehicles for your church's missions program, evangelistic outreach or education and training? What local or regional fellowships is your church or organization involved in? Do your people know the difference between their denominational distinctives and old-fashioned narrow-mindedness? Spend some time discussing such questions, and evaluate where your church is in terms of a vision for unity.

I began this chapter bemoaning the brokenness of the body of Christ. But rather than blaming denominationalism for this sad state of affairs, I suggested that sectarianism and syncretism are the two real causes of contemporary disunity. I went on to try to persuade you that denominationalism, as it was originally conceived, can be a powerful force for unity precisely because it resists sectarianism and syncretism. Whether I have succeeded in my purpose only you can tell. But I would encourage you to look again at Burroughs's vision for unity and consider its relevance. I'm convinced that if we follow this great idea and explore its implications, "Christ will not charge us at the Great Day for retarding his cause."

For Discussion

1. Do you agree or disagree with the statement that "sectarianism and syncretism are the two real enemies of the unity of the church"?

2. Review the points of Burroughs's denominational theory of the church. How might this model help a church overcome sectarianism and syncretism? What are some other benefits of following Burroughs's model?

3. Select one application and suggest practical steps that might be taken to implement it in your church. What kind of time frame

is needed? What teaching would need to precede the application?

For Further Reading
The best discussion of the denominational theory of the church and the role Burroughs played in forming it is found in Winthrop Hudson, *American Protestantism* (Chicago: University of Chicago Press, 1961). For a taste of Burroughs's piety one could do no better than read *The Rare Jewel of Christian Contentment* (1648; reprint Edinburgh: Banner of Truth Trust, 1964).

4

A VISION FOR ASSURANCE
William Perkins's Model of Conversion & Assurance

If I were ever asked to nominate a title for our times, my choice would probably be "the Age of Self-Esteem." For today's North American culture in particular, to regard oneself as a valuable person and to be so valued by others is not just a "nice extra" but rather an absolute essential to a healthy life. The concept of self-esteem or self-acceptance has reshaped much of contemporary parenting, politics, education, counseling and even religion. Though I sometimes tire of an exaggerated stress on self-esteem (as in "Don't criticize Junior for scribbling in your books, or you'll ruin his self-esteem"), in my more objective moments I realize what damage a lack of healthy self-esteem can inflict on our homes, our organizations and our churches.

Nominals and Neurotics
Intriguingly, the search for self-esteem—when it goes bad—may produce two types of problem people. The first type is the *nominal Christian* who suffers from inflated self-esteem. The nominal

Christian is often full of self-satisfaction and self-justification. The nominal Christian is sure that he or she is "just as good as the next person" and therefore is resistant both to change and to true Christianity. This is spiritual presumption, a false confidence in one's spiritual health and security.

The second type is the *neurotic* or *nervous Christian,* who suffers from deflated self-esteem. Despite the promises of the gospel, neurotic Christians are miserable and full of self-loathing. They lack the assurance of salvation. They question the depth of God's love for them. They are critical of themselves and others.

Churches, families and organizations that are full of nominal Christians and neurotic Christians must suffer an unpleasant mixture of cold indifference on the part of some and feverish insecurity on the part of others. Trying to lead a congregation of such extreme types can be a harrowing experience. How can we light a fire under the false self-esteem of the nominal Christian and simultaneously cool the fever of the nervous Christian? The problem requires a little more analysis.

The true foundation of healthy self-esteem is, as Calvin wrote, "a firm and certain persuasion of God's benevolence towards us." Such a God-centered and grace-based self-esteem can boldly ask the rhetorical question of Romans 8:31, "If God is for us, who can be against us?" To accept ourselves, we must internalize God's gracious acceptance of us in Christ. A failure to experience this internal assurance contributes to the phenomenon of the nominal Christian (who bases her self-esteem on her exaggerated opinion of herself) and the nervous and discontented Christian (who bases his self-esteem on his negative and despairing opinion of himself).

But simply being able to parrot the doctrine of justification by faith is not the answer. A cavalier acceptance of the truth of justification by faith can produce a nominal evangelicalism. In the generation after Luther's death, Luther's profound insight into the gospel, summarized by the formula "justification by faith," had been reduced in the mind of the masses who attended the state church to a bare creed with no life-changing power. "Dead orthodoxy" is the name for this phenomenon. Dietrich Bonhoeffer labeled such a barren profession of the gospel "cheap grace." The theology and pastoral strategies in many European Protestant countries between Luther's time and Bonhoeffer's were unable to overcome this spiritual blight.

The English Puritans confronted these twin problems of nominalism and nervousness in the pew and suggested some creative pastoral remedies. Puritan pastors believed the way to unleash the power of the gospel of justification by faith was to fuse it with an evangelical concept of conversion. Puritan covenant theology—a theology that explains both what God does and what we must do in salvation—sought to bring about this fusion.

The magic cure for the apathetic, nominal Christian is "true conversion." The magic cure for the anxious, neurotic Christian is "full assurance." It was the particular insight of the Puritan William Perkins to put these two pastoral strategies together. Perkins pioneered the concept of *full assurance through true conversion.* From his time onward the idea that being "born again" meant experiencing a profound but visible conversion became a central part of evangelical identity.

Perkins's idea of assurance through true conversion is one of the best ways to produce truly Christian self-esteem and overcome the extremes of apathy and anxiety within the church. I'd like to take you on a tour of Perkins's idea and show you why I believe it is one of the best ideas in church history.

Perkins's Life

William Perkins was born in 1558 to Thomas and Hannah Perkins in the village of Marston Jabbet, Bulkington Parish, Warwickshire, England.[1] We know little of his early life until he left home and began his studies at Christ's College, Cambridge, in June 1577.

Perkins matriculated at Christ's as a "pensioner," suggesting that he came from a solidly middle-class background.[2] Life at the university challenged Perkins's religious upbringing. He seems to have lost whatever Christian faith he had. Into the spiritual vacuum came a new, more exciting substitute—the occult. Years later Perkins described this addiction to magic and the occult: "I have long studied this art, and was never quiet until I had seen all the secrets of the same: but at length it pleased God to lay before me, the profaneness of it, nay, I dare say boldly, idolatry, although it be covered with fair golden shows."[3]

By 1584 Perkins had become soundly converted to Reformation Christianity.[4] At some point between his B.A. of 1581 and his M.A. of 1584 William Perkins experienced the new birth. In that same year, the twenty-six-year-old Perkins became a teaching fellow at Christ's. It was a calling to which he brought a special talent. As a teacher he grew in stature and repute until "few students of theology quitted Cambridge without having sought to profit in some measure from his instruction."[5] A part of his appeal to students was his love of logical symmetry and precision. According to Robert Hill, his friend and the translator of his most important theological work, *A Golden Chain,* "An excellent gift he had to define properly, divide exactly, dispute subtly, answer directly, speak pithily and write judicially."[6]

Besides his regular duties as a fellow, Perkins was for the remainder of his life lecturer at Great St. Andrews, located directly opposite Christ's College. His pulpit ministry pulsed with the same force that animated his teaching. "From the pulpit he would pronounce the word 'damn' with such emphasis," Thomas Fuller tells us, "as left a doleful echo in his auditors' ears a good while after."[7]

In 1596 Perkins married a widow named Timothye and immediately found himself the father of seven children. It must have been a shock for this long-time bachelor. Perkins wrote a book on Christian family living, *Christian Economy,* which no doubt helped him work through this sudden change in his quiet life. As a married man Perkins was required to resign his fellowship at the college. He remained active, however, as a preacher at Great St. Andrews. His last years were spent writing and preaching.

Perkins died in 1602 at forty-four years of age, at the height of his powers and the peak of his fame. At his grave his good friend John Montague, the future bishop of Winchester, exhorted those who stood with Perkins's widow and her seven children from Joshua 1:2, "Moses my servant is dead." Yet Perkins's death did not bring an end to his influence.

Perkins had belonged to a part of the Puritan movement within the Church of England that advocated passive resistance. A little background may be helpful. *Puritanism* was originally a term of abuse applied to those within the Church of England who opposed the Elizabethan Settlement of 1559—an agreement on religious issues—as too "catholic." Puritans sought to complete the Reformation in England by purifying the church of elements they believed were contrary to biblical standards of worship, theology, piety, polity, pastoral care and ethics.

Historian Leonard Trinterud has distinguished four main groups within Elizabethan Puritanism. The original Anti-vestment party surfaced in the 1560s in reaction to clerical dress too similar to that worn by the Roman Catholic priesthood. The main concern of this original branch of Puritanism was purity of worship. Elizabeth's first archbishop of Canterbury, Matthew Parker, opposed the Anti-vestment party and enforced uniformity. Many clergy were expelled. In 1563 the term *Puritan* was first used of this dissident group.

In the 1570s and 1580s a second kind of Puritanism appeared: Presbyterianism added a concern for polity to the list of Puritan issues. The lectures of Thomas Cartwright (1535?-1603) on Acts at Cambridge University in 1570 are sometimes seen as the beginning of English Presbyterianism. His outspoken support of the priesthood of all believers, the abolition of episcopacy and its replacement by presbyterianism forced him into exile. John Field and Thomas Wilcox continued the attack on bishops in a 1572 document, *Admonition to Parliament*. An underground "classis" (group of ruling elders) movement developed. The tracts of "Martin Marprelate" (pseudonym for Job Throckmorton) popularized the antiepiscopalian campaign. Lay Puritans and members of

Parliament like Peter Wentworth sought to establish presbyterianism by legislation. Puritan presbyterianism also sought the patronage of powerful members of Elizabeth's court such as Robert Dudley, Earl of Leicester. John Whitgift (1530-1604) became archbishop of Canterbury in 1583 (succeeding Grindal, who tolerated Puritanism) and by 1593 had crushed the movement.

A third Puritan group emerged in the 1580s under Robert Browne. Browne was the champion of the Separatist Puritan position. His *Treatise of Reformation Without Tarrying for Any* clearly spelled out his position. Browne's ideas were not always warmly received by the authorities. Henry Barrow and John Greenwood were hanged for following Brownist principles. Separatists found safer havens for their views in Holland. Many of the *Mayflower* Pilgrims who landed in Plymouth, Massachusetts, traced their spiritual ancestry to this group.

The fourth Puritan group was the Passive-Resistance party. The great names of this branch of the movement include Laurence Chaderton, Richard Greenham and William Perkins. Avoiding much of the debate about polity and vestments, Perkins and his disciples forged a new strategy for Puritanism in the late 1580s and 1590s. They sought to win the masses to the evangelical faith and lifestyle by returning to the New Testament strategy of preaching, training leaders and persuading. Perkins and his colleagues were convinced that such a strategy would bring about a deeper transformation of England than could be achieved by applying government pressure or playing games of ecclesiastical politics. Popular books on holy living and salvation poured from the presses, and this fourth branch of the movement grew in influence.[8]

In retrospect, Perkins must be given credit for much of the success of this program for reform through teaching and persuasion. Perkins wrote a number of bestselling books to promote popular reform. These writings fall into three categories, each representing a key area where Perkins saw the need for reform. First and foremost, Perkins worked for *theological renewal* by teaching simplified Calvinism in such books as *A Golden Chain* and *The Reformed Catholic.* The second area of reform was the clergy. Perkins labored to bring about *ministerial renewal* by training a new generation in the arts of expository preaching (he wrote *The Art of Prophesying,* the first book on preaching in the English language) and pastoral counseling. Finally, Perkins called for *moral renewal* through manuals for practical Christian living. One of the most famous of his numerous works in this area was *Whole Treatise of Cases of Conscience.*

Here we shall focus on this third area of reform, moral renewal. Perkins wrote much on practical Christian living, and in his practical works he returned repeatedly to the question of assurance and true conversion. What did he discover about these crucial topics?

Perkins's findings about conversion and assurance can be summarized under six points. While it is wonderful to know that Christ died for sinners, the burning need in my heart is how I can know for sure that he died for *me.* This becomes particularly tricky when we say we are saved by grace. How do I know that my conversion is a genuine one (was it truly of God's grace, or did it come from my own effort?) or that I am part of the elect? Perkins's answers to these important questions can be summarized in six statements. Taken together, these statements are a description of Puritan covenant theology. More important, they are a prescription for a confident faith and a peaceful conscience.

1. Assurance Is Possible Only Through a True Conversion

When· a seeker came to Perkins's study for counsel about the salvation of his or her soul, Perkins had a ready response. He realized that Luther and Calvin had laid the foundation for a true understanding of salvation, but they had left something out. Luther and Calvin had stressed what God does in salvation. Justification by faith in Christ was the great answer. But they didn't really answer the question of what the seeker should do to receive this grace and experience this faith.

For the transforming power of the gospel to be unleashed, the evangelical truth of justification by faith needed to be fused with the evangelical process of conversion. Puritan covenant theology, as shaped by Perkins and others, sought to bring about this fusion. Perkins wanted to avoid the Pelagianism (belief in salvation by human effort) of pre-Reformation covenant theology (remember Gabriel Biel, mentioned in chapter one?); thus he stressed the divine side of the covenant of grace. Perkins also sought to avoid the "cheap grace" of dead orthodoxy; thus he simultaneously stressed the human side of the covenant with its demands.

Both sides are real, argued Perkins. The divine side is the ultimate cause of salvation, but the human side is also real. What we do is merely a response to what God is doing mightily within. Yet it is a necessary response. God is the primary cause, but he works through secondary causes as well.

This combination of the human factor and the divine factor in salvation can be called "coaction." Salvation is grace-initiated coaction. Like an iceberg, salvation has an immense base of grace below the surface which produces the glistening and visible shapes of conversion above the surface. Figure 4 illustrates this principle of coaction.

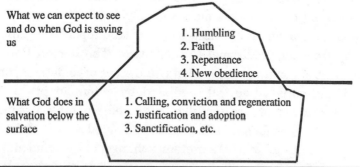

What we can expect to see and do when God is saving us

1. Humbling
2. Faith
3. Repentance
4. New obedience

What God does in salvation below the surface

1. Calling, conviction and regeneration
2. Justification and adoption
3. Sanctification, etc.

Figure 4. The "iceberg" of salvation: divine and human coaction

Perkins's *Golden Chain* sought to present both sides of the covenant of grace to the common person. The divine side of the covenant is God's decree to save and involves several expressions of God's love, such as election, calling, regeneration, justification, adoption, sanctification, preservation and glorification. The human side of the covenant involves a four-stage conversion followed by a life of ongoing spiritual warfare against the world, the flesh and the devil. The four stages of conversion, according to Perkins, are humbling, faith, repentance and new obedience.[9]

Stage 1: Humbling. The Holy Spirit usually prepares the elect for salvation by humbling them. They experience a sorrow for sin that softens the heart, making it teachable and receptive to the gospel. Humbling takes place normally through a "law work": the holy demands of God and the depths of human sin are proclaimed to the sinner in order to destroy all vestiges of pride and self-right-eousness. The visible result of humbling is primarily negative. The seeker despairs of salvation through any kind of self-effort. He or she is convinced that sin renders one morally and spiritually incapable of saving oneself.

Stage 2: Faith. Perkins defines faith as a "supernatural gift of God in the mind, apprehending the saving promise with all the promises that depend on it." This faith has various degrees, but one can be saved by even the weakest degree of faith—a simple desire for Christ to be one's Savior. Even the weakest faith has the seeds of assurance within it—a certain conviction that the saving promises of Christ apply to me personally.

Stage 3: Repentance. Perkins's view of true repentance differed greatly from the traditional Catholic view. The Roman Catholic sacrament of penance consisted of ritual steps of confession, absolution and satisfaction, all mediated by a human priest. For Perkins, true repentance is a full turning from sin. It has two parts: (1) a godly sorrow for sin, that "we have offended so merciful a God and loving Father," and (2) a profound change "of the mind and the whole man in affection, life and conversation." At its deepest level, true repentance was evidenced by the regenerate heart's resolution not to sin against God in anything but to please him in everything.

Note that Perkins is not asking the new convert to exhibit the *behavior* of total repentance. What he insists on is the *pledge* of total repentance. In initial repentance we promise to leave off sin and obey God in all things. The ongoing life of repentance that follows seeks to put that promise into action. Repentance is therefore both an initial experience (the promise) and a lifelong process (the actual transformation of behavior).

Stage 4: New obedience. The final step of conversion is conformity to the law of God (loving God and others radically). New obedience involves cooperating with the Spirit in mortifying the old habits and attitudes of sin and cultivating (vivifying) new Christlike habits and attitudes of holiness. The convert embarks on this life of new obedience armed with the commands of Christ in Luke 9:23: (1) self-denial (exalting God's grace rather than natural abilities, and desiring the growth of the kingdom of Christ [his rule over people's lives through law and gospel] more than worldly wealth or personal advancement); (2) taking up the cross—patiently and cheerfully bearing burdens and afflictions; and (3) following Christ by practicing the virtues of meekness, patience, love and obedience through mortification and vivification. Perkins thus connects Calvin's model of true spirituality with the final stage of conversion.

The true convert must be a cross-carrying disciple. Teaching, counseling and preaching such a model of conversion can go a long way toward reducing the problem of nominal Christianity in our churches.

2. Assurance Is an Action of the Holy Spirit

What about the nervous Christian? Perhaps she has gone through just such a fourfold conversion experience. How can she be sure that her faith is genuine and her sins are truly forgiven?

Perkins spent a great deal of time and energy wrestling with such a question. His basic conclusion was that *a true conversion persuades the conscience, and a persuaded conscience issues the verdict of assurance.*

Let me elaborate. For Perkins the human conscience is that inner faculty that accuses us or excuses on the basis of God's law. The conscience is always at work, passing hundreds of verdicts about us daily. It condemns us when we break God's law (or even the laws of the culture). It comforts and assures us when we are right before God and his law.

The basic method the conscience uses to accuse or acquit us is the practical syllogism. The practical syllogism is a method of moral reasoning that follows three logical steps. First is the identification of the rule or law that applies to my case. The second step is the description of my behavior in comparison to the law. The third step is the rendering of the verdict. For example, if I have lied, the conscience, in the blink of an eye, makes the following declarations:

All who lie are sinners worthy of condemnation.

You have lied.

Therefore you are a sinner worthy of condemnation.

Such moral reasoning may seem cold and detached, but Perkins makes a crucial point about the conscience and its practical syllogism: *Most of our emotions flow from the verdicts of conscience.* Guilt and condemnation produce shame, sadness, fear, desperation and restlessness.[10] The sense of acceptance and approval by God registered by the regenerated conscience cleansed by the gospel produces joy (which Perkins calls "alacrity"), peace, patience in affliction and other fruits of the Spirit.

So far so good. The key question for nervous Christians, however, is this: How do we get this sense of certainty of God's forgiveness and love so that our conscience issues a positive and assuring verdict? The answer is that the conscience now is controlled first by the facts of the gospel and second by the facts of one's conversion. Perkins explains:

Infallible certainty of pardon of sin and life everlasting is the property of every renewed conscience. . . . The principal agent and beginner thereof is the holy Ghost, enlightening the mind and conscience with spiritual and divine light: and the instrument in this action, is the ministry of the Gospel, whereby the word of life is applied in the name of God to the person of every hearer. And this certainty is by little and little conceived in a form of reasoning or practical syllogism framed in the mind of the holy Ghost on this manner: *Everyone that believes is the child*

of God: But I do believe: Therefore I am a child of God.[11]
Once my conscience has the word of the gospel for its major premise
and my true conversion as the minor premise, the only conclusion
it can reach is one that will give me joy and gladness.

3. Assurance Must Be Rooted in God's Sovereignty
If the conscience is still acting up, all is not lost. The nervous
Christian needs to feed the conscience with more gospel truths;
Perkins recommends injecting a heavy dose of sovereign grace.
Perkins was a strong Calvinist who believed that salvation begins
with God's choice of us, not with our choice of God.

One might argue that such a view breeds spiritual uncertainty
in the heart of a Christian, because the inscrutable counsels of God
cannot be known. But Perkins argues in just the opposite way.
Unless salvation is by the decree of God, it can never be certain in
the human conscience. For support Perkins quotes Romans 8:30
with its "chain of many links, whereof everyone is so coupled to the
other, that he which taketh hold of the highest, must needs carry
all the rest with him." To have justification necessarily requires
that I am elect and will be glorified because this chain of salvation
cannot be broken. If I hold on to a genuine conversion experience,
I can be assured that this link is connected to all the other links
and I will be preserved and glorified. Such a confidence that
"nothing can separate me from the love of God" produces a strong
sense of assurance that can quiet the most stubborn conscience.

4. Assurance Focuses on Christ by Faith
The nervous Christian objects. Doesn't all of this depend on my
faith? What if I have a bad day? If my faith is weak, my focus on
these truths will be weak. Consequently, my assurance will suffer,
and the anxieties of a troubled conscience will return. What then?

Perkins has an answer for this problem. We can know for certain
that we belong to God even if our faith is weak because true faith,
though it be weak, is like "the hand of the child or of the palsy man,
though it be feeble, it is able to reach out itself and receive an alms

of a prince, so the faith that is but weak, is able to apprehend and receive Christ with all his benefits."[12] To enjoy the comforts of a fully assured conscience one must be careful "not to behold faith, but the object of faith which is Christ."[13] Naked reliance on Christ is the focus of the faith that brings assurance. And even a weak faith can cling to Jesus.

5. Assurance Is Strengthened by Sanctification

Just as sin can trouble our conscience and interrupt the flow of assurance, so holiness strengthens and stabilizes the testimony of the conscience that we are children of God. Basing his argument largely on 1 John, Perkins insists that loving God and others is a secondary but important support to our sense of assurance.

Perkins warns, however, that the saint should not be troubled by the question of how much holiness is needed to provide evidence of true faith. For Perkins "one apple is sufficient to manifest the life of the tree."[14]

6. Assurance Does Not Eliminate Spiritual Depression

From all that has been said above one might conclude that once assurance is gained the believer is on easy street. Not quite. Perkins issues a warning to the Christian that qualifies the previous statements. Though assurance can be certain and full, it is assailed by doubts and depression. After all, we are in a state of war with the kingdom of darkness. In the midst of these attacks the enemy of our souls will tempt us to doubt God and question the power of the cross. Such doubt can lead us to despair of our salvation and of God's grace.

Perkins has a powerful word for those whose consciences are under such an attack: *The attack of doubt is itself a testimony of your salvation.* The enemy lulls the hypocrite to sleep with a "carnal presumption" (a false sense of assurance), but he attacks the saint with the arrows of doubt and depression. "There is no child of God," says Perkins, "but more or less, one time or another, he feels the sting of sin and the buffeting of Satan . . . but this grief is a notable grace of God," for it keeps us from ever trusting in ourselves and forces us to flee to Christ for safety and help.[15]

The attacks of doubt are a sign of genuine faith. The strategy of the enemy thus backfires, and his darts become fuel for a deepening assurance of God's redeeming love.

Applying Perkins's Great Idea

Perkins's idea of assurance through true conversion is one of the best ways to produce a truly Christian self-esteem and overcome the extremes of apathy and anxiety within the church. A remedy for such serious problems surely must constitute one of the best ideas in church history. But how can decision-makers use Perkins's idea?

Use #1: As an answer for the charge of cheap grace. The evangelical understanding of the gospel remains hard for many people to accept. The idea that we are saved by faith and not by works can be a real stumbling block. Dietrich Bonhoeffer's oft-repeated phrase about "cheap grace" comes to mind—and in too many cases the charge of cheap grace is deserved. James Means writes about the "theological flaccidity" that has cheapened the evangelical concept of conversion:

> The new theological wrinkle offers quick and permanent assurance of salvation in response to an easy professed belief, while at the same time allowing the convert to live indefinitely with contempt for Christ's teaching. Today's theological flaccidity separates historically unified concepts: justification from sanctification, faith from repentance, the saviorhood from the lordship of Christ, the new birth from discipleship.[16]

But the faith that comes to expression through a true conversion experience is not cheap.

> To those who attacked the evangelical formula of *sola fide* as simply "cheap grace". . . Puritans like Perkins responded with a fuller theology of conversion and rebirth. In the process they rejected the medieval answer to "cheap grace"—semi-Pelagian theology and works righteousness—and instead built their model of conversion squarely on the foundations of Luther and Calvin.[17]

Use #2: As an aid to powerful and balanced preaching of grace.
Perkins's type of covenant theology can give proper balance to the
convicting power of the law, the depth of human sin, the power of
God's grace and the necessity of human response through conversion. God's sovereignty, human inability and the action of humbling
oneself and seeking God's sovereign grace is a powerful model of
coaction that can glorify God as well as satisfy people's need.
Perkins's covenant theology enabled him to follow a consistent line
of coaction that gave strong emphasis to God's sovereign grace in
Christ as the ultimate cause of salvation while at the same time
emphasizing the necessity of human response.

Use #3: As a comfort for those seeking assurance. People in the
church who are insecure in their relationship with God become
knots of neurotic problems, thornbushes of criticism and obstacles
to change. Conversely, Christians who have a deep and satisfying
sense of God's unchanging love for them in Christ and are full of
assurance of their sonship are more able to bear the fruits of the
Spirit and become positive forces in a congregation.

Perkins's practical syllogism states simply how the Spirit con-
vinces the conscience that Christ's benefits and promises belong to
the individual having faith. This tool—an educated and enlightened
conscience that continually issues comforting and approving verdicts
to the soul because of the cross—is the key for enjoying God and
feeling the depth of our security in him. Assured Christians are happy
and productive Christians. Applying the gospel to the conscience is
one of the keys to assurance and happiness in Christ.

Use #4: As a way to promote a believer's church. An emphasis on
conversion provides the church with a way to counsel and to test
the sincerity of a person's confession. We must watch out for
stereotyping, but that should not make us timid about expecting
people to be able to describe some experience of meeting Christ
that is biblical and convincing.

Parents also should be concerned about the salvation of their
children. Teaching children what conversion is all about and guiding them in that process is one of the chief duties of a Christian

parent. We should also teach our children about assurance and how they can know for sure that they are Christians. Perkins can help us on both counts.

Use #5: As a guide to personal evangelism. For a number of years I took part in the evangelistic ministry of my church. Each week we would visit homes and share the good news about Jesus Christ. I remember one time we explained the gospel to a young women who afterward still seemed confused about what it all meant. To my surprise, the friend who was witnessing to this young woman led her in the sinner's prayer and then immediately said, "Welcome to the family. You are now a believer in Jesus Christ." Over the next few weeks it became clear that the woman had *not* accepted Christ and was even angry at what she probably regarded as manipulation on our part.

Perkins's model can guide us in such situations. Don't slide over important aspects of the conversion process, and don't give people false assurance based on a partial conversion. Be sure to include an explanation of a full conversion in your personal evangelism.

Use #6: As a way to renew worship. Assurance of salvation can unleash gladness and joy in God and his redemption, filling public worship with deep affections. Such joy expels the formalism and pharisaism that blight too much worship. The worship of truly converted Christians who sing, pray and drink in the Word from glad and assured hearts is worship of the highest kind, greatly pleasing to God and greatly encouraging to God's people.

In this age of misdirected self-esteem, we need to rediscover that the true foundation of healthy self-esteem is, as Calvin wrote, "a firm and certain persuasion of God's benevolence towards us." For churches that are wrestling with the problems of nominal Christianity, dead orthodoxy and nervous Christians, Perkins's idea that solid assurance is based on a genuine conversion is a great one indeed.

For Discussion

1. Acts 9:1-19 records the conversion of Paul. In 1 Timothy 1:16 Paul claims that his conversion was an example of how God saves.

Read the Acts passage and see if you can spot any or all of Perkins's four aspects of conversion in Paul's conversion.

2. Self-esteem is a major issue. Perkins believes that Christian self-esteem should be based on our assurance of God's love for us in Christ. Do you agree or disagree? Does Perkins's idea need to be qualified in any way?

3. In addition to the applications given here, in what other ways might a sense of full assurance be cultivated in your congregation?

For Further Reading
No full-length published biography of Perkins exists in English, but the article on his life in the *Dictionary of National Biography,* vol. 15 (London: Oxford University Press, 1917), is a good place to begin. Fine selections from Perkins's writings can be found in Ian Breward, ed., *The Work of William Perkins* (Appleford, U.K.: Sutton Courtenay, 1970). I have addressed the topic of this chapter in an article entitled "Drama in the Meeting House: The Concept of Conversion in the Theology of William Perkins," *Westminster Theological Journal* 45 (1983).

5

A VISION FOR WORSHIP
Richard Baxter's Directions for Delighting in God

N o myth exposes the heart of our age more starkly than the story told in Christopher Marlowe's *Dr. Faust*. The protagonist of this sixteenth-century play by a contemporary of Shakespeare is a German doctor of theology who dabbles in the occult. Faust's heart is gradually consumed by the love of earthly learning and the fame and fortune it can bring.

The devil comes to Faust in the person of Mephistopheles and makes a remarkable offer: "Sell your soul to me for eternity and I will give you your earthly desires." Faust wrestles with the eternal implications of this deal. But his love of the world is stronger than his love of God, and so Faust accepts the offer and signs away his soul. Much to Faust's delight, he discovers that the devil is as good as his word. Faust's greedy heart becomes crammed with knowledge, and wealth, women and fame are his.

But time eventually runs out. The devil comes to collect on the debt. At the moment of death, Faust realizes he made a devil's bargain. He acknowledges that he was a fool to exchange eternal pleasures for fleeting ones. But it is too late. There is no way of escape (at least in Marlowe's version). Unable to buy back his soul, Faust is sucked into hell to suffer a life of eternal torment.

A Questionable Exchange

The myth of Faust is the story of our lives. It is a description of the modern world and of modern humanity, whether in New York or Nairobi. Giving up the pleasures of God in exchange for the pleasures of this world is a modern preoccupation.

Christians are not immune to this aspect of the secular spirit. While secularism often wears the mask of skepticism and atheism, it can also wear the mask of religiosity. God is sought not as an end in himself but as a way to achieve secular ends, Faustian ends: wealth, earthly pleasure or fame. Health-and-wealth versions of the gospel come immediately to mind, but more subtle deals with the devil can be made in the pew. We can seek God in order to keep the marriage together, get the kids shined up or find the right job.

The problem is not confined to pew-sitters, however. Those in vocational ministry can also succumb to the spirit of Faust. We are quite capable of waking up one morning to discover that we've been ministering for all the wrong reasons and seeking all the wrong treasures. Decision-makers can be dragged along by the Faustian undertow as well.

Where this secular mindset really touches our lives is in worship. Secularism can create enormous static on Sunday morning. For all of the worship renewal that has been attempted in recent years, no amount of liturgical deck-shuffling can make up for the spirit of Faust in our hearts. An inordinate love for the world erodes public and private worship at the root. We absent-mindedly sing of "sweet hours of prayer" and praise God "from whom all blessings flow" even while our hearts ponder last night's party, the next vacation or the recarpeting of the living room.

How can we renew worship on this most basic level? How can we instill the conviction that the triune God is life's greatest treasure? We all need some ideas, some great ideas, to help us break the bubble of worldly affections and redirect our congregations, classrooms and hearts back toward God.

Christian Hedonism and the Puritan Movement

One of the best antidotes to Faustianism is "Christian hedonism." The term comes from John Piper and his important book *Desiring God: Meditations of a Christian Hedonist.* A hedonist is someone who lives for pleasure. A Christian hedonist is someone who lives for the pleasures of God. For a Christian hedonist the chief end of humankind is to glorify God *by enjoying him forever.* Christian hedonism seeks not to make a god out of pleasure but to make God our highest pleasure and treasure. In fact, Christian hedonism sees increasing delight in God as the essential key to breaking the hold of Faustianism in our churches and our culture and unleashing a new spirit of true worship.

Some Christians have objected to Christian hedonism on the grounds that it deemphasizes traditional Christian virtues such as selfless service, sacrificial love and dutiful obedience. Others have dismissed it as a frothy and superficial approach to worship and Christian living. Critics of Christian hedonism do not always appreciate its roots in one of the most serious and selfless movements of Christian history—the Puritan movement in England and America.

Puritanism, as noted in previous chapters, was a movement within the Church of England (and later in Congregational New England) that began in the 1560s but climaxed in the seventeenth century. It sought to reform worship, piety and morals in accordance with the Scriptures. The Puritan attempt to reform English Christianity and culture was an uphill battle. The seventeenth century, like our own century, was marked by Faustian bargains and countless revolts against the Word of God. Into this secular tempest stepped Richard Baxter. He attempted to counter Faustianism with an emphasis on delighting in God—the pursuit of God as life's most "durable delight."

Baxter is best known for works of piety and pastoral theology such as *A Call to the Unconverted, The Saint's Everlasting Rest* and *The Reformed Pastor.* But the book that will command our attention in this chapter is the *Christian Directory.* In this latter work Baxter offers the contemporary church one of the best ideas in church history—clear advice and direction about delighting in God in Faustian times.

J. I. Packer has called the *Christian Directory* "a landmark. It is the fullest, most thorough, and in this writer's judgment, most profound treatment of Christian spirituality and standards that has ever been attempted by an English-speaking Evangelical author. . . . Baxter is a long way ahead of us here, and we shall do well to try and catch him up."[1] I share Packer's conviction. Baxter's great idea is that *our worship of God is at its best when our delight in God is at its height.* His directions for delighting in God are one of the most powerful antidotes to the Faustian spirit to be found in church history. We need to find out why.

Baxter's Life

The Richard Baxter who wrote the *Christian Directory* and urged believers to make God their supreme delight was a man who knew adversity firsthand. Born in Rowton, Shropshire, in 1615, he grew up in a strict Puritan home, but a home filled with love and affection. His formal schooling ended in 1633, after which he returned home to study theology on his own. He was devastated by the loss of his mother when he was nineteen but found comfort in the company of Puritan ministers. Through their influence he became a nonconformist divine of Presbyterian persuasion, ordained to the ministry in 1638. When the Civil War broke out in England in 1642, Baxter was a pastor in the village of Kidderminster; this was his home until 1660, despite frequent absences to serve as a chaplain for the Parliamentary army during the war.

Baxter came to Kidderminster in fear and trembling. The town's reputation as a "corrupt and unhealthy population of hand-loom workers" was not promising. Yet Baxter's ministry at Kidderminster was a huge success. One key may have been his work discipling families in their homes. This effective strategy is powerfully recorded in his pastoral classic *A Reformed Pastor* (1656). In addition to his daily discipling, Baxter was a conscientious preacher. He ministered the Word to the textile workers of Kidderminster with an intensity that was life-changing. He later wrote that "I preach'd as never sure to preach again and as a dying man to dying men."[2] When George Whitefield visited Kidderminster a century later, he remarked that the effects of Baxter's ministry could still be seen.

After the victory of Parliament in 1647, Oliver Cromwell ruled England as Lord Protector. Baxter was out of favor during Cromwell's reign, having too catholic a spirit to support the extremism that marked English Christianity during the 1650s. When he was asked to preach before Cromwell, Baxter deepened his rift with the Lord Protector by issuing a stern message critical of Cromwell's religious policies.

Charles II was restored to power in 1660, and Baxter was asked to become bishop of Hereford. He declined the offer, asking instead to be restored to Kidderminster. This humble request was denied. The 1662 Act of Uniformity banished men like Baxter from the Anglican Church. From that point on he was a marked man, hounded by the law. The years between 1665 and 1686 were a time of intermittent imprisonments and suffering. During this period he settled in Acton, a small town outside London. There he wrote a number of his most famous books, including the *Christian Directory*. He wrote in the shadow of persecution and trial. "Had Mr. Baxter relaxed in his piety," wrote Adam Clarke, "the rod of the wicked would have ceased from his inheritance; but as he followed Christ in purity and righteousness, this was a crime in the sight of the world which could never be forgiven."[3] Even as he wrote his rules for delighting in God, the London plague swept through Acton, killing hundreds.[4] The toll in London itself was horrific. One hundred thousand were estimated to have died. Baxter escaped from that natural terror only to find himself in the midst of others of a man-made variety.

Most of the 1670s were spent at odds with the authorities. His books made it clear that his religious sympathies were still Puritan, and his occasional preaching broke the notorious laws making unauthorized preaching a crime. In 1681 his wife, Margaret, died, and "with her something died in him too."[5] His heart broken, his vocation taken from him by unjust laws, Baxter struggled with bitterness.

But he had little time for self-pity. Arrested in 1682, Baxter was convicted but released on probation. By 1685 he was back in the courts, charged with libel against the government. After a year in jail, Baxter was released. Though broken in health, he was still an active participant in the major events of his time. He was a conspirator in the overthrow of James II and enthusiastically welcomed the religious toleration brought in by William and Mary in 1688. Baxter died in 1691 at seventy-six years of age, "having endured much persecution, passed through many sufferings, and glorified God in every fire which he permitted his enemies to kindle around him."

Baxter was remembered by friends as tall and slender but somewhat stooped. Clarke wrote, "His countenance was grave and composed, with a cheerful predominant smile. He had a very piercing eye, and spoke with great distinctness." But more than for his appearance, Baxter was remembered as a man of the Word and a powerful preacher. As a writer "his success in enlightening the mind, and affecting the heart, was uncommon."

Baxter's literary output was enormous. He wrote nearly 140 books "and had 60 written against him, but those rather added to, than diminished from his reputation." His masterpiece was not the work on the Trinity over which he labored for years but a compendium of Christian ethics and spirituality that he might never have attempted were it not for the urging of others.

Baxter's *A Christian Directory* was published in 1672. The bulk of the writing had been done in 1664-1665, when he and Margaret were living in Acton. He had been encouraged by the great Bishop James Ussher of Ireland to sum up the Puritan tradition of "practical divinity," roughly equivalent in our day to the three disciplines of spiritual formation, pastoral counseling and ethics. The *Christian Directory* is primarily concerned with exploring the implications of the great commandment: how to love God totally and others equally. The book covers four main areas of Christian living: Christian ethics, Christian economy (family life), Christian ecclesiastics (church life) and Christian politics (duties to our rulers and our neighbors).

Baxter's writing on these important subjects is full of wisdom and prudent advice from someone who had studied the Bible and Christian writers with great care. But what captures the reader's eye in surveying this massive work of Christian faith and practice is the section on delighting in God as the sum and center of holy living. Baxter understood the Faustian spirit and felt he knew a powerful cure. But what did he mean by delighting in God?

Baxter's Directions for Delighting in God

What makes Baxter so useful for understanding Christian hedonism is that he summarized a tradition that goes back to Augustine and even further to Paul—that God is the true object of our deepest longings. For Baxter this is the heart and soul of Christian living and of Christian faith.

Baxter's format in the *Christian Directory* is to ask key questions and then give his answers. Here we'll focus on seven questions raised and resolved by Baxter:

☐ Are love for God and self-love compatible, as Christian hedonists teach?

☐ What does delighting in God actually mean?

☐ How much of this holy delight in God may be hoped for in this life?

☐ What are the dangers of not making delight in God our chief end?

☐ What are the benefits of delighting in God?

☐ What helps has God given to increase our delight in him?

☐ What specific meditations could best stir delight in God and increase my joy and satisfaction in him?

1. *Are love for God and self-love compatible, as Christian hedon-ists teach?* "God is most glorified in us when we are most satisfied in Him." Baxter admits there is a real danger that self-love will deceive the believer: "Be always suspicious," he wrote, "of carnal self-love, and watch against it—for that is the burrow or fortress of sin."[6] Yet he recognized in Scripture a kind of self-love that is consistent with loving God. "Yet it is not a sin to love God for ourselves, and our own felicity, so be it we make him not a mere means to that felicity, as our absolutely ultimate end."[7] Gratitude, commanded everywhere, in Scripture would be impossible without a God-centered self-love whereby we delight to exalt his goodness and beauty. If we were not pleased by these things in God, we would not praise or glorify him. Thus Baxter concludes that "there is no place for the question, whether I must love God or myself," or for the question "whether I must seek God's glory and pleasure, or my own felicity . . . for I must ever seek them both, though not with the same esteem."[8]

2. *What does it mean to delight in God?* If I am required to seek my own good in order to give God glory, what exactly is this "delight" I am supposed to seek and find? Baxter tries to make clear first of all what it is not. Delight in God is not fantasizing about God or having private visions. It is not ecstasy or excitement, some sort of religious shiver that goes up and down the spine. It is not the absence of sorrow or fear, for delight in God can take place in the midst of sorrow and fear. Baxter's life bore eloquent testimony to that fact.

If delight in God is not ecstasy, emotionalism or a painless euphoria, what then is it? For Baxter delight in God is "a solid, rational complacency [satisfaction] of the soul in God and holiness, arising from the apprehensions of that in him which is justly delectable to us."[9] What Baxter means is that delight in God is a state of complete satisfaction of mind and soul in God's moral beauty and love. In simplest terms, delighting in God means being totally satisfied with God in every area of life.

This kind of delight is absolutely necessary for Baxter because "holy delight adjoined to love is the principal part of our religion. . . . When earthly pleasures end in misery, then who would not wish they had preferred the holy, durable delights?"[10] This directly responds to the issues raised by Marlowe in his play about Faust. Delight is not a cheap emotion for Baxter, but the central one. It is the affection that is the mainspring of all human action. "It is not for nothing that God hath made delight and complacency [satisfaction] the most powerful, commanding affection, the end of all other passions which they professedly subserve and seek; and the most natural, inseparable affection of the soul, there being none that desireth not delight."[11] Delight is the most universal and most fundamental habit of the heart.

3. *How much of this holy delight in God may be hoped for in this life?* Even if we admit that delight in God is essential to both God's glory and our need, the question remains how much can we hope to get in a fallen world. After examining a number of Scripture passages, Baxter answers this question in a surprising way: we can expect a lot more delight than we are probably experiencing at the moment. How much can we expect? We can expect (1) enough delight to be happier and more content than the happiest non-Christian, (2) enough delight in God to make thoughts of God and of the life to come pleasant and welcome to us, (3) enough delight to lift us beyond our weariness and depression and make our Christian walk pleasing to us, (4) enough delight to take away our appetite for sinful pleasures, (5) enough delight to make every expression of God's mercy and love to us sweet and satisfying, (6) enough delight to make our suffering more bearable and even enjoyable at times, and (7) enough delight to make the thought of death less terrible.[12]

How much delight in God can we hope for? A lot more.

4. *What are the dangers of not making delight in God our chief end?* Given that commands to praise, delight or rejoice in God are so frequent in Scripture, what can I expect if I take these commands lightly or dismiss them as nonessential? Baxter describes

the spiritual wasteland awaiting me if I remain indifferent to the call to delight in God. I will displease God if I do not experience him as my highest delight.[13] I will not think of God as much, or will not think well of him as much. If God is not my chief delight, my talk of God will be "heartless, forced speech."[14] Since delight is a stronger drive than mere duty, I'll lose my main motivation for obedience if I neglect delight in God. I'll lose my appetite for the rest of life and work as well, since God will withdraw the power of pleasure from those who do not make him their highest pleasure. I will become quarrelsome with other Christians because I am so dissatisfied with my life. I will suffer greater temptations, because failure to be filled with the delights of God makes the pleasures of sin all the more attractive. I will be vulnerable to bouts of depression. I will be more susceptible to apostasy and bad theology. These nine dangers await all who neglect the duty of delight.

5. *What are the benefits of delighting in God?* On a more positive note, Baxter enumerates many benefits of delighting in God. Among the good things that will happen in my life, I can expect the following:[15]

☐ Greater assurance of my salvation, for "delight in God will prove that thou knowest him, and lovest him."

☐ Stronger resistance to materialism, because "prosperity . . . will not easily corrupt thee."

☐ Greater peace in times of trial, because when I am full of eternal delights, "adversity, which is the withholding of earthly delights, will not much grieve" me. To make God my chief delight will mean that "thou hast a continual feast with thee, which may sweeten all the crosses of thy life."

☐ A more alert and alive mind, because "thou wilt receive more profit by a sermon, or good book, or conference, which thou delightest in" than when delight is absent. When I am seeking to delight in God, my mind is awake to every idea that could fuel my passion.

☐ A greater joy in my work, because delight lifts much of the burden from labor. When I am full of delight, I find Baxter's words true: "All thy service will be sweet to thyself, and acceptable to God" (compare Psalm 149:4).

☐ Delight in God increases my joy in just about everything else. "When you delight in God, your creature delight will be sanctified to you, and warrantable in its proper place; which in others is idolatrous or corrupt." God is free to give us more pleasure in things and experiences when he knows we will not make idols of them. Such benefits are strong incentives to seek more of God.

6. *What helps has God given to increase our delight in him?* At this point you may be ready to seek to increase your delight in God. But that raises a practical question: What do I actually do to delight in God? Baxter's response is to point out that God has already done a number of things to help us get over our natural allergy to God and to increase our delight in him. To recognize the many ways he has helped make delighting in him easier is in itself a source of delight in God.

Baxter mentions sixteen ways in which God has helped us to delight in himself; I'm going to mention five of these:

☐ God gives us objects of holy beauty to fix our minds on, such as "his attributes, love, mercy, Son, Spirit, and kingdom." The triune God and his perfections are calculated to inspire praise and delight in our hearts.

☐ God gives us his Spirit, who cultivates a delight in God within us by "mortifying, cleansing, illuminating, and quickening works."

☐ God has given us the cross of Christ, which has purchased joy for his people at the expense of his own sufferings: "having borne our griefs, and being made a man of sorrows, that we that see him not, might rejoice in believing, with joy unspeakable and full of glory."

☐ God gives us his word of command, "again and again commanding us to rejoice, and always commanding us to rejoice."

☐ God gives us his word of promise: "Nor is it vain that he hath filled his word with such matter of delight and comfort, in the gladdest tidings that could come to man and in such free and full and faithful promises."[16]

7. *What meditations will best stir delight in God and increase my joy and satisfaction in him?* Baxter finishes his advice to those who would increase their delight in God by suggesting specific meditations. These "directives" are thoughts we should rehearse in our minds in order to raise our affections. Baxter offers twenty in the *Christian Directory,* of which I've selected ten. To grow in your delight in God, consider the following meditations.[17]

Meditation 1. Think about how much pleasure it gives God to see you happy in him. Baxter observes that "it much hindereth the joy of many Christians, that they think it is against the will of God, that such as they should so much rejoice." We must remember that the ultimate purpose of our delight is not our personal satisfaction but God's exaltation.

Meditation 2. Think about how beautiful the triune God is and therefore how worthy he is to be an object of delight.

He is, 1) Most perfect and blessed in himself. 2) And full of all that thou canst need. 3) He hath all the world at his command for thy relief. 4) He is nearest to thee in presence and relation in the world. 5) He hath fitted all things in religion to thy delight, for matter, variety and benefit. 6) He will be a certain and constant delight to thee: and a durable delight when all others fail.

Baxter's own experience of personal tragedy, having lost everything he loved except his God, gives tremendous credibility to this point.

Meditation 3. Think about how easily negative thoughts can creep in and kill delight. "Take heed of an impatient, peevish, self-tormenting mind, that can bear no cross; and of overvaluing earthly things, which causeth impatience in the want of them." A grumbling or greedy spirit is the enemy of the Christian hedonist. We all get irritable, but we must not let that get in the way of the enjoyment of God.

Meditation 4. Think about how powerful faith is in fueling our delight in God. "It is only a life of faith, that will be a life of holy, heavenly delight; exercise yourselves, therefore, in believing contemplations of the things unseen." Without faith we can neither please God nor be pleased with God. We may look around at our circumstances and see little that inspires delight or gladness. But the eyes of faith can rise above what we see and can focus on the beauty of God's triune family life, or his great grace and love, or his abundant promises. Such exercises of faith give us power to overcome hard times and find joy in God.

Meditation 5. Remember the value of public worship in increasing the enjoyment of God. An ember separated from the fire soon dies, but when joined with others it rekindles its flame. A good worship service with lots of praise and thanksgiving can increase delight in God and banish unbelief and spiritual coldness.

Meditation 6. Think about how all of life's other pleasures can increase your pleasure in God. Determine "that, as soon as the eye, or ear, or taste, perceiveth the delightfulness of their several objects, the holy soul might take the hint and motion, and be carried up to delightful thoughts of him that giveth us all these delights." In contrast to the spirit of Faust, which sees earthly treasure as in competition with eternal treasures, we should let earthly pleasures complement the more "durable delights."

Meditation 7. Remember to use trouble to increase your delight. "The servants of Christ have usually never so much of the joy in the Holy Ghost as in their greatest sufferings. . . . The soul never retireth so readily and delightfully to God, as when it hath no one else that will receive it, or that it can take any comfort from." Baxter's own life illustrates this point. The more he lost his earthly treasures, the more he struggled with bitterness. But God soon filled the void left by the loss of his wife, his work, his health and his freedom. Baxter learned to use trouble to increase his delight in God.

Meditation 8. Think about how the wicked delight in sinful pleasures, and be motivated to delight in God all the more. "Shall hawks, and hounds, and pride, and filthiness, and cards, and dice, and plays, and sports, and luxury, and idleness, and foolish talk, or worldly honors, be so delightful to these deluded sinners? and shall not my God and Savior, his love and promises and the hopes of heaven, be more delightful to me?" The idea here is not to accept the Faustian spirit of the age as normal but to see it as an outrage. We should let the secular world around us produce within us a jealousy for the glory of God that intensifies our delight in him.

Meditation 9. Refuse to let the specter of impending death take away eternal delights. We must overcome fear of death, or else it "will damp [our] joys in the foresight of everlasting joys." Unlike Marlowe's Faust, who came to his senses only after the grip of death was on him, we should use the thought of our impending death to increase our desire for the pleasures that death cannot steal. Against those whose treasures are eternal, death stands impotent.

Meditation 10. Decide to make delight in God the purpose behind all other religious duties. For example, "penitent sorrow is only a purge to cast out those corruptions which hinder you from relishing your spiritual delights. . . . Delight in God is the health of your souls." This is the key to acceptable worship. God is not pleased, nor are we renewed, by a dutiful obedience that is devoid of delight.

"Delight in God is the health of your souls." That sentence sums up Baxter's belief in the centrality of delighting in God. The *Christian Directory* deals with hundreds of additional subjects, but no topic exposes the heart of Baxter's theology as this one does.

The seven questions reviewed here are not the only ones Baxter answers on the subject of delighting in God. Yet they are crucial questions for our day. The counsel that Richard Baxter gives holds great promise for overcoming the temptations generated by a secular society. Each of his answers points in the direction of Psalm 16:11, confirming the truth that "in your presence there is fullness of joy; in your right hand are pleasures forevermore" (NRSV).

But how can we act on these ideas today? Let's wrap up this discussion of Baxter's great idea by making some useful decisions.

Renewing Worship Today: The Uses of Baxter's Great Idea

Baxter's great idea is that *our worship of God is at its best when our delight in God is at its height.* This chapter has reviewed seven questions about delighting in God to which Baxter gives helpful, illuminating answers. What can we do to cultivate this holy delight in those we serve? Let me make three suggestions.

Use #1: Make delight in God an integral part of your own life. There are no shortcuts to integrity. The people we lead, whether they be our children, our students, our church members or our employees, know the difference between plastic praise and genuine delight.

Let me recommend three books to help you make Christian hedonism a genuine part of who you are as a leader. The first is John Piper's *Desiring God,* with its call to glorify God by enjoying him. Reading his book has increased my understanding of how to make this the overriding goal of my life. Second is *The Seven Habits of Highly Effective People.* Stephen Covey says nothing about delighting in God in the book, but he does have a lot to say about redefining success. He writes about success as flowing from "daily private victories," not just public achievements. There's a great need for a character ethic to replace the more superficial personality ethic, for a higher ideal in ministry than mere success. Covey believes that truly successful people "start with the end in view," that is, they view everything they do daily in terms of how it will move them toward their ultimate objective.

I have come to believe that Christian hedonism—the view that God is most glorified in us when we are most satisfied in him—is the highest goal I could possibly pursue. Covey's advice has convinced me that the "daily private victories" I need for success in life involve making delight in God part of the way I think and make decisions. Glorifying God by enjoying him must become, for me, the "end" I start with every day. It must become my measure for success.

A more recent book by Stephen Covey, *First Things First,* written with A. Roger Merrill, shows in even more practical ways how we can make a personal life mission an integrating center of our life. For a serious Christian hedonist, Covey is extremely useful.

My suggestion is to read these three books with a friend, perhaps over the course of a year, and challenge one another to take action on the things you discover together. I am deeply indebted to some good brothers who have done this very thing with me and helped me move ahead in the enjoyment of God. We must decide to internalize this delight before we can effectively cultivate it in others.

Use #2: Make Christian hedonism a part of your counseling ministry. People have problems. The people we serve in our ministry wrestle with marriage problems, kid problems, sin problems, anger problems and a host of other problems. I have come away from more than one conversation with a troubled Christian thinking that part of the problem was that the individual expected too much of the relationship or the church or the school. One way they could reduce their frustration level would be to expect more from God and less from life. If God became their highest treasure, it would reduce some of the unrealistic expectations they have placed on other relationships.

Christian hedonism is not a panacea, but it is crucial "for the health of your souls." To the person who seeks our help over some besetting sin, we need to point out that a passion for the pleasures of God is a powerful way to overcome the passion for sin. We need to teach people to fight pleasure with pleasure and exchange the lesser pleasures of sin for the greater pleasures that come from God. To the person who is seeking our advice about a broken relationship, we need to point out that Christians who are deeply satisfied in God and full of his grace and patience have more resources to heal that broken relationship than if they are full of irritability and a critical spirit. In other words, Christian hedonism is a part of the solution (though not the only part) to every problem that we face.

To tackle any issue empty of God when we could be armed with the power of delight in God is to tackle the issue foolishly. Leaving this truth out of our counseling and teaching would deprive people of a powerful tool for inner healing.

Use #3: Build Christian hedonism into worship services. Those of us who have input into a church's public worship need to make delight in God a crucial component. Duty alone or a spirit of formalism is not acceptable to God. Worship at its heart is delighting in God (Ps 73:25-26). And this delight, to borrow a phrase from Jonathan Edwards, consists primarily in *holy affections.* This means that we need to aim at stirring up love of God and hatred of sin in our worship services. We are not out to entertain people but to inspire them to repentance and praise. We need to encourage the kind of singing, preaching, drama, testimonies, Scripture reading, special music and prayer that arouses not cheap emotionalism but deep delight.

Because it is the special work of the Holy Spirit to produce holy affections (Gal 5:22-23), we need to pray about our worship services as much as we need to pray for missions. But having prayed, we also need to act. An incomparable resource for those who are looking for specific ways to increase enjoyment of God in worship is the series on worship edited by Robert Webber.[18] Volume 3 in particular deals with building creative Sunday worship services calculated to stir delight in God.

When Christopher Marlowe wrote his epic drama on Dr. Faust, he did not realize that he was writing the story of modern humankind. The heart of secularism is the attitude that earthly treasures are more real and valuable than the supposed treasures of God. Like smoke in a burning building, this subtle attitude can choke the life out of the church even before it is directly touched by the flames of open opposition.

I don't know if Richard Baxter ever saw Marlowe's play. I do know that he offers a valuable remedy for the Faust within each of us. "Delight in God is the health of your souls."

For Discussion

1. The psalms are full of exhortations and meditations aimed at increasing delight in God. One of the most important biblical texts for delighting in God is Psalm 73. Note how the psalmist moves

from a Faustian spirit to a new discovery that God is life's greatest source of satisfaction (vv. 25-26). What additional passages in Psalms support this theme of delighting in God?

2. Review Baxter's ten meditations (pp. 104-6). Which of them seem to be the most helpful in producing a Psalm 73:25 experience?

3. What additional uses can you think of for Baxter's directions for delighting in God?

For Further Reading

Besides reading the *Christian Directory*, the person interested in reading more about Baxter should first consult J. I. Packer's *Quest for Godliness* (Wheaton, Ill.: Crossway, 1990) with its tribute to Baxter's piety. Geoffrey Nuttall's biography *Richard Baxter* (London: Nelson, 1965) is a standard life. A more recent study is N. H. Keeble, *Richard Baxter, Puritan Man of Letters* (Oxford: Clarendon, 1982). An appreciative and readable account of Baxter's later years can be found in F. J. Powicke's *The Reverend Richard Baxter Under the Cross (1662-1691)* (London: Jonathan Cape, 1927).

6

A VISION FOR RENEWAL
Jonathan Edwards's Theology of Revival

Side by side in a posh Washington suburb stand two contrasting structures. One is a fashionable community church complete with lighted spire, manicured lawns and well-to-do members. The other is an old fire station recently converted into a shelter for the homeless, operated by another church in town. The community church opposed the firehouse project because its members didn't want the wrong kind of people meeting next to their church.

Travel by the community church on Sunday morning and you will see smiling faces making social contact and listening politely to well-polished sermons. Ride past the firehouse and you will see newly shaven men gathered in a circle, engaging in serious Bible study about new life in Christ.

The community church meets an important social need for most of its members. The firehouse spiritually transforms lives. The community church functions as a chaplaincy for the rat race. The firehouse is an outpost of eternity. The community church offers a secularized Christianity housed in a religious-looking structure.

The firehouse offers an expression of authentic Christianity housed in a secular-looking structure.[1]

The Effects of Secularization

The fire station and the community church are small windows into a big problem—the struggle against the secularizing of the church at the turn of the millennium. Some churches have been more resistant to the forces of secularization than others, but all have felt its strength. Evidence that the winds of secularization have grown stronger is seen in the statistical growth of those who identify themselves as "nonreligious." Where in 1900 less than one percent of the world's population was classified as nonreligious, by the last quarter of the twentieth century over 21 percent of the world's people were so classified. Os Guinness has called this "the most dramatic change on the entire religious map of the twentieth century."[2] According to Guinness, "Atheistic and non-religious peoples now form the second largest bloc in the world, second only to Christians and catching up with them fast."[3]

The net result of secularization in the modern world has been to make "religious ideas less meaningful and religious institutions more marginal."[4] Like the Cheshire cat that bemused Alice in Wonderland, the church is losing its substance and credibility, facing the world with an empty grin.[5] George Gallup Jr. has described what this empty grin looks like. Comparing churched and nonchurched Americans in a number of categories (cheating on taxes, inflating résumés and similar deceitful behaviors), the pollster found "little difference in the ethical views and behavior of the church and the unchurched."[6] Charitable giving of churched and nonchurched who made between fifty and seventy-five thousand dollars a year was virtually the same (1.5 percent of income). Even among conservative Christians Gallup found some surprising statistics. A majority (53 percent) of those who claimed to be conservative, Bible-believing Christians rejected the existence of absolute truth.[7]

The secularizing of the church seems to be fact. But what has all of this got to do with Jonathan Edwards and revival? Much. The acids of modernity have made the question of revival an urgent one. Revivals are times of restoring the church to authentic spiritual life after a period of decline. For this reason Jonathan Edwards's struggles with the secularizing of the church in his day offer some important parallels and pointers for our own.

Secularism was just beginning its long assault on the modern church during Edwards's youth, and its impact was deadening. When God sent a remarkable revival called the Great Awakening, Edwards not only applauded the mercy of the Almighty but also analyzed the movements of the Spirit. The result was the articulation of a powerful theology of revival that can guide the church today as it seeks to tack against the winds of modernity. In the estimate of J. I. Packer, Edwards's theology of revival "is, perhaps, the most important single contribution that Edwards has to make to evangelical thinking today."[8] Sharing Packer's view is D. Martyn Lloyd-Jones: "No man is more relevant to the present condition of Christianity than Jonathan Edwards. . . . He was a mighty theologian and a great evangelist at the same time. . . . He was pre-eminently the theologian of revival. If you want to know anything about true revival, Edwards is the man to consult."[9]

Busy leaders can draw much from Edwards to improve the quality of their decision-making. John Piper of Bethlehem Baptist Church in Minneapolis has seen how this is so. Having encountered Edwards during his seminary studies, he probed his theology deeply. Piper describes the results: "I owe him more than I can ever explain. He has fed my soul with the beauty of God and holiness and heaven when every other door seemed closed to me. He has renewed my hope and my vision for ministry in some very low times. He has opened the window on the world of the Spirit time and again when all I could see were the curtains of secularism."[10]

Edwards has affected my own life in similar ways. When my vision batteries run low and spiritual dullness or despair about the church runs high, Edwards becomes my pastor. I come away from most encounters with Edwards mentally stretched but spiritually renewed. I hope that will be your experience with him as you meet in this chapter.

But beware—Edwards's ideas are in the alpine zone. We'll have to do some climbing in the thin air of the high country. Yet after the trek we'll return with treasures that will justify the effort.

To the decision-makers of today struggling to part the curtains of secularism and open a "window on the world of the Spirit" Edwards offers a great idea, one of the best in church history: *Fight secularism by becoming an agent of authentic revival.* His great idea is a theology of revival proven by both word and experience. This chapter will examine that theology, but first we need to get to know the man.

Edwards's Life

The outward story of Jonathan Edwards's life is easily told. He was born in 1703 in East Windsor, Connecticut, to the Reverend Timothy Edwards and his wife, Esther. Edwards was the only son among the eleven children of the family. When his ten sisters matured and each grew to six feet or more, the congregation joked of their pastor's "sixty feet of daughters." But the height of Timothy's children was less remarkable to family and friends than the depth of his son's intelligence. By seven he was well versed in Latin. At eleven or twelve Jonathan wrote precocious essays on rainbows and spiders that show powers of observation bordering on genius. At thirteen he was off to Yale College. By twenty he had his M.A., and after a short time as a minister in New York and then as a teacher at Yale, Edwards found his true calling as a pastor in Northampton, Massachusetts. In 1727 he began a twenty-three-year ministry there, supported by his wife Sarah and their eleven children.

Two periods of extraordinary awakening, in 1734-1735 and 1740-1742, punctuated Edwards's years in Northampton. But some pastoral blunders, combined with his campaign to require an evangelical testimony as essential to both church membership and participation in the Lord's Supper, brought his Northampton ministry to an end in 1750. The family then moved to the frontier town of Stockbridge in western Massachusetts to become missionaries to the Indians.

In the relative quiet of the Berkshire Mountains Edwards wrote some of the books that would make him famous for centuries, including his greatest work, *The Freedom of the Will*. These seven years of exile came to an end when Edwards was elected president of Princeton College in New Jersey in 1757. What seemed like a new beginning was actually the last act in Edwards's earthly story. After an inoculation for smallpox, Edwards died at fifty-four years of age.

Yet such a summary of Edwards's life hides more than it reveals, for Edwards had a secret not easily understood in our secular century. He was captivated by the adventure of delighting in God, and all his immense intellectual powers were pressed into the service of that adventure. Edwards once wrote that even after we "have had the pleasure of beholding the face of God millions of ages, it will not grow a dull story; the relish of this delight will be as exquisite as ever." One biographer comments that "if he had a secret, it somehow concerned his own capacity for such a delight, while he still had his feet on New England earth."[11] My hunch is that by examining Edwards's theology of revival we will discover this inner story of how he pursued his delight in God.

Edwards on Revival

What is revival, and how can we get it? Given that I'm a Christian living in a secular age, these are the questions that concern me the most. Edwards pondered these questions and gave enduring answers to them. I want to examine his vision of revival as the best way to fight secularism and advance the gospel and then spend some time exploring how decision-makers could use this vision to move their churches down the path of renewal.

Six useful insights summarize this New England Puritan's vision for church renewal. If revival is a time when the church shines against a dark sky like a star, then Edwards's model is a six-pointed star. The star looks like this:

□ The church's spiritual dullness and deadness toward God and spiritual things are the *disease* revival seeks to cure.

□ God and his glory are the *source* and *purpose* of all true revival.

□ Heart-stirring preaching and persistent corporate prayer are the main *methods* by which revival is promoted.

□ Opposition and extremism are the *chronic enemies* of true revival.

□ A spiritually enlightened heart is the *essence* of true revival.

□ The advance of missions through an energized church is the *inevitable outcome* of true revival.

Each of these six insights can move us closer to becoming functional fire stations rather than enculturated social clubs.

The Disease: Spiritual Dullness

The church's spiritual dullness and deadness toward God and spiritual things are the disease true revival seeks to cure. When Gallup notes the decline in traditional Christian belief or charitable giving, he is pointing to symptoms of a deeper spiritual malaise. Edwards looked beyond traditional explanations of the problem such as secularism, prayerlessness, theological drift, immorality and so on to the underlying malady: spiritual dullness.

What did he mean? "Dullness" seems to be for Edwards a time when the realities of God and his gospel grow so dim, and unbelief and worldly affections so strong, that the heart of the church wanders to the lusts and rivalries of a secularized mind. His description of Northampton in the early 1730s is a case in point: a deep-seated boredom with the gospel preceded the renewal of 1734, and in the stony soil of that boredom all manner of sins sprang up.

But dullness is displayed not only by open sin but also by formalism in religion. Though all the right motions be exhibited in worship, the actions may be empty. "The external acts of worship," noted Edwards, "consisting in bodily gestures, words and sounds are the cheapest part of religion, and least contrary to our lusts." Our capacity for spiritual self-deception is almost boundless, for even when "wicked men enjoy their covetousness, their pride, their malice, envy, and revenge, their sensuality and voluptuousness, in their behaviour amongst men . . . they will be willing to compound the matter with God, and submit to what forms of worship you please, and as many as you please."[12]

"Words and sounds are the cheapest part of our religion, and least contrary to our lusts"—quite an indictment of much that passes for true religion even in evangelical circles. The heart that has lost its delight in God and spiritual things is a heart in trouble. The disease that revival seeks to cure, then, is the disease of spiritual dullness seen in both open sin and hypocritical religion.

This is an important insight from Edwards. We might see the problem of secularization primarily in its marginalization of the church and biblical values. In other words, we evangelicals might see the disease to be treated as *cultural and political powerlessness:* evangelical thinking dismissed by leading thinkers, evangelical values rejected by the popular culture. But Edwards reminds us that such marginalization and political powerlessness, while discouraging, are not a life-threatening problem for the church. After all, the church in the book of Acts was politically and culturally marginalized but still vital and dynamic.

Edwards tells us that the real crisis of the church is not external secularism but internal boredom. When the church becomes dull to Christ, to truth, to salvation, to supernatural realities and future hopes, we are in danger. Coldness, not powerlessness, is the crippling malady of the contemporary church.

Edwards helps us greatly, then, in diagnosing the disease. But what is the cure?

The Remedy: God and His Glory
God and his glory are the source and purpose of all true revival. Spiritual dullness does not go unnoticed by God. He who is the fountain of life is treated like a dry and empty cistern by his people. He who is a banquet of life is spurned while his children prefer to "lick the earth." He is not amused by such treatment. Yet God's

response to the personal insult of spiritual dullness is sometimes surprising. He has every right to judge his church for such a sin with an outpouring of wrath. But in extraordinary moments he pours out his grace rather than his judgment and raises up enthusiastic worshipers for his name from the ranks of the dull and dead.

The motive of this gracious redemptive renewal, according to Edwards, is primarily the glory of the triune God:

> In all this God designed to accomplish the glory of the blessed Trinity in an eminent degree. God had a design of glorifying himself from eternity; yea to glorify each person in the Godhead. . . . It was his design in this work to glorify his only-begotten Son, Jesus Christ; and by the Son to glorify the Father (John 13:31-32). . . . It was his design that the Son should thus be glorified, and should glorify the Father by what should be accomplished by the Spirit.[13]

Because God seeks to glorify his triune family, he sends revival to produce a spirit of holy delight in the hearts of secularized sinners and sluggish saints, so that they might praise the divine beauty that they formerly despised.[14]

But God-centered worship produced by the reviving work of the Spirit is not a religious duty that we perform stoically: it is the climax of human satisfaction. Edwards thus espouses a Christian hedonism (so named by John Piper) that echoes back to Richard Baxter. God is most glorified in us when we are most satisfied in him. Because God's happiness comes from having his beauty recognized, and because human happiness comes from being filled with a sense of God's beauty, there is no necessary contradiction between glorifying God and seeking our happiness.[15]

As the church fathers said, our hearts were made for God and cannot be satisfied until they find that satisfaction in him. This is an Augustinian theme that runs through Edwards's writing like a mountain stream. He expresses it clearly in a graceful sermon called "Christian Pilgrims":

> God is the highest good of the reasonable creature; and the enjoyment of him is the only happiness with which our souls can

be satisfied. . . . Fathers and mothers, husbands, wives or children, or the company of earthly friends, are but shadows; but the enjoyment of God is the substance. These are but the scattered beams; but God is the sun. These are but the streams; but God is the ocean.[16]

Thus revivals help fulfill the great end of creation: to glorify God by enjoying him as the great source and end of all things.

This insight, that God is the source and purpose of revival, is important for us today. One of the legacies of secularism is a pervasive human-centeredness that can even seep into our worship and theology. Revivals can be seen as times when attendance improves, or my kids get straightened out, or giving increases, or everybody gets excited about the church again. But such notions are human-centered ways to view revival. Edwards reminds us that revival comes to destroy the malady of spiritual dullness (which often goes hand in hand with excessive focus on human beings and their achievements) and produce a God-centered way of looking at everything. He carefully dispels the notion that revivals are human-generated events that produce religious excitement. Revivals are outpourings of the sovereign Spirit that restore the church to gladness in God and an obsession with his glory and excellencies.

Methods: Heart-Stirring Preaching, Persistent Prayer

Heart-stirring preaching and persistent corporate prayer are the main methods by which revival is promoted. The same God who has ordained an ultimate purpose for redemption and revival has also ordained certain human means to accomplish that end: preaching and prayer. Foremost among revival preachers in the Great Awakening was George Whitefield, the "Divine Dramatist." But it was more than theatrics that gave him his power. Whitefield went for the heart. This was Edwards's aim as well: "I should think myself in the way of my duty, to raise the affections of my hearers as high as possibly I can, provided that they are affected with nothing but truth. . . . Our people do not so much need to have their heads stored as to have their hearts touched and they stand in the greatest need of that sort of preaching, which has the greatest tendency to do this."[17]

In contrast to Whitefield, Edwards has sometimes been described as dull and wooden in his preaching. It is true that he read his sermons, which were written out in manuscript form, and that he used few gestures. But Edwards believed in passionate preaching. An inquirer who wondered if Edwards was eloquent received this response from someone who heard him preach regularly:

He had no studied varieties of the voice, and no strong emphasis. He scarcely gestured, or even moved; and he made no attempt by the eloquence of his style or the beauty of his pictures, to gratify the taste, and fascinate the imagination. But if you mean by eloquence the power of presenting an important truth before an audience with overwhelming weight of argument, and with such intenseness of feeling that the whole soul of the speaker is thrown into every part of the conception and delivery, so that the solemn attention of the whole audience is riveted, from the beginning to the close, and impressions are left that cannot be effaced, Mr. Edwards was the most eloquent man I ever heard speak.[18]

Revival preaching must be intense but does not have to be theatrical; it must be full of truth, though it may not be full of gestures; it must aim to raise affections as high as the truth can take them, even if we speak without shouting; and it must be full of the exposed soul of the speaker, even if it is read from a manuscript. This is anointed preaching, and it is used by God to stir the dull and raise the dead.

Edwards described the kind of preaching that God can use to renew and revive by using the illustration of a burning house:

If any of you who are heads of families saw one of your children in a house all on fire, and in imminent danger of being soon consumed in the flames, yet seemed to be very insensible of its danger and neglected to escape after you had often called to it—would you go on to speak to it only in a cold and indifferent

manner? Would you not cry aloud, and call earnestly to it, and represent the danger it was in, and its own folly in delaying, in the most lively manner of which you [were] capable?[19]
The great subject of this heart-stirring preaching must be Christ and the new birth. Consider the titles of some of Edwards's sermons during the years of revival: "The Justice of God in the Damnation of Sinners," "The Excellency of Christ," "Pressing into the Kingdom," "Justification by Faith Alone," "The·Divine and Supernatural Light," "Sinners in the Hands of an Angry God." These were the great themes preached in the "searching" manner that is a means of revival. The focus of such sermons is human helplessness (rather than self-sufficiency) and God's total sufficiency as redeemer in Christ (rather than our contribution to our own salvation). In Edwards's opinion, both law and gospel are critical to the kind of preaching that can promote revival: "The main work of ministers is to preach the Gospel . . . so that a minister would miss it very much if he should insist so much on the terrors of the law, as to forget his Lord, and neglect to preach the Gospel; but yet the law is very much to be insisted on, and the preaching of the Gospel is like to be in vain without it."[20] These Reformation chords, struck during a time of spiritual dullness and deadness, filled New England (as well as other places) with stirrings of new life and vigor.

But along with intense, affective preaching that focuses on human hopelessness and God's free grace must go persistent and passionate prayer. Edwards presented this necessary means in a book entitled *A Humble Attempt to Promote Explicit Agreement and Visible Union of God's People in Extraordinary Prayer for the Revival of Religion* (1746). The book called for special prayer meetings (preferably on Saturday evenings and "Sabbath days"— Sundays) aimed at the conversion of the world. Edwards was convinced that "if we look through the whole Bible, and observe all the examples of prayer that we find there recorded, we shall not find so many prayers for any other mercy, as for the deliverance, restoration, and prosperity of the church, and the advancement of

God's glory and kingdom of grace in the world."[21] Edwards was convinced that persistence in prayer would bring down God's redemptive blessing on the world, and that if this prayer could be done in concert (with the church praying in unison all over the world at appointed times), the incense of those prayers would fill the heavenly temple and unleash the favors of a deeply pleased God.

Edwards can help us in these two actions of preaching and praying. First, he can help us rediscover revival preaching. In recent years pop psychology has too often been substituted for gospel realities in many evangelical churches. Therapeutic preaching with high entertainment value seems to be more popular than expository preaching with high biblical content. What is needed is *affective* preaching: heart-stirring preaching that speaks in sensory language, using the vocabulary of delight and pleasure but focusing on the great biblical truths of creation, fall and redemption, the light that lifts the curse and that opens up heaven and the durable delights of God. Neither dry exegetical sermons nor lively therapeutic sermons will lift the malady of spiritual dullness, no matter how much they agitate the molecules of human-centered thinking. God-centered preaching that exalts Christ using the language of Christian hedonism is Edwards's sound suggestion for promoting a great awakening of holy delight.

We need to hear Edwards's call to prayer as well. The Concerts of Prayer movement is beginning to gain momentum around the world. Yet it faces a great obstacle within the church: too many of us believe in our heart of hearts that we can produce world evangelism and church renewal if we use the right techniques and push the right buttons. This is the spirit of the church of Laodicea so strongly condemned in Revelation 3:17. Edwards calls us to abandon this spirit of self-sufficiency and recognize our crippling spiritual allergies to the cross. He prods us to cry out for a spirit of prayer as well as a spirit of bold proclamation, so that God's means of revival might be exercised by his church.

Enemies of Revival: Opposition and Extremism

Opposition and extremism are the chronic enemies of true revival.
Edwards paints such a glowing picture of revival's power to cure
the church's maladies that we might conclude that revivals are
times of unalloyed blessings and glorious spiritual success. J. I.
Packer calls this kind of thinking the romantic fallacy. "We fall into
this," he writes, "when we let ourselves imagine that revival, once
it came, would function as the last chapter in a detective story
functions—solving all our problems, clearing up all the difficulties
that have arisen in the church, and leaving us in a state of idyllic
peace and contentment, with no troubles to perplex us any more."[22]

Edwards did not harbor romantic notions about revival. He saw
too much of the dark side of the Great Awakening to ever pretend
otherwise. Many pages in each of Edwards's major writings on
revival (with the exception of his first work, *A Faithful Narrative
of Surprising Conversions*) are devoted to an analysis of corruptions. Packer summarizes Edwards's catalog of revival horrors as
follows:

> They fall into pride, delusions, unbalance, censorious modes of
> speech, extravagant forms of action. Unconverted persons are
> caught up in what is going on; they feel the power of truth,
> though their hearts remain unrenewed; they become enthusi-
> asts, deluded and self-confident, harsh and bitter, fierce and
> vainglorious, cranky and fanatical, quarrelsome and disruptive.
> Then perhaps they fall into spectacular sin, and apostatize
> altogether; or else remain in the church to scandalize the rest
> . . . by maintaining, on dogmatic perfectionist grounds, that
> while what they do would be sin in others, it is not sin in them.
> Satan . . . keeps step with God, actively perverting and carica-
> turing all that the Creator is doing.[23]

To explain the fact that revival brings trouble and tumult, Edwards
used the analogy of springtime, which renews the dead earth
through storm and tempest: "After nature has long been shut up
in a cold dead state, when the sun returns in the spring, there is,
together with the increase of the light and heat of the sun, very

tempestuous weather, before all is calm and serene, and all nature rejoices in its bloom and beauty."[24] Thus we should expect that a powerful work of the Spirit will arouse enormous satanic and worldly opposition. But beyond the storms lies a time of "bloom and beauty."

For this reason Edwards devotes considerable time and space to fighting extremes. He fights extremists who want to reject the revival because of excesses, and then he fights the opposite group of extremists, who want to see the excesses as the true revival. Both are wrong, and both are to be expected in any true revival of God. Old Lights (who oppose revival) and New Light extremists (whose intemperate zeal for revival leads to extremism) cropped up everywhere in the Great Awakening (and, we might add, every subsequent awakening). Time and again Edwards goes back to the need to test religious movements by Scripture. He points to the exaltation of Christ and the evidences of the fruit of the Spirit as the main outward signs of a true work of the Spirit of God.[25] We need to hear this insight from Edwards. When we pray for revival, we are praying for problems.

It is possible to view the church-growth movement around the world (which is largely charismatic in character) as another great awakening. Some reject this interpretation because they dislike the theological anemia or the extremist behavior that attends this global movement. But Edwards warns us against a knee-jerk reaction to excesses and problems. We might find ourselves becoming Spirit-quenching critics of spiritual outpourings because they are filled with carnality and corruption. Our task is to perfect and reform the imperfections of revival, much as Edwards sought to do (through teaching, writing and prayer) and find the middle way between Old Light cynics and New Light fanatics.

Revival's Essence: An Awakened Heart
A spiritually enlightened heart is the essence of true revival. According to Joseph Tracy, writing a century after the event, the great idea of the Great Awakening was the new birth. "This doctrine of

the 'new birth' as an ascertainable change, was not generally prevalent in any communion when the revival commenced; it was urged as of fundamental importance, by the leading promoters of the revival; it took strong hold of those whom the revival affected."[26]

Edwards would have agreed with Tracy. The essence of revival is spiritual enlightenment in the hearts of dead sinners or dull saints, when "a divine and supernatural light" leads them to desire Christ and his moral beauty. What makes this kind of understanding of spiritual things so life-changing? The experience of the heart, which is as different from a purely intellectual understanding of grace as "having a rational judgment that honey is sweet" is from "having a sense of its sweetness."[27]

For those who are spiritually dead this spiritual enlightenment shows itself in a visible conversion which, though varied in each case, involves (1) humbling for sin, (2) complete entrusting of oneself to Christ and (3) an unfolding life of holiness.[28] Edwards's understanding of conversion follows William Perkins's model (discussed in chapter four) with minor modifications. For dull saints the experience of spiritual enlightenment is revealed in a new relish for the realities of salvation and the eternal world.

Thus for Edwards the essence of revival is the Spirit's work of producing or renewing faith. This faith is rooted in the gospel, is a gift of the Spirit, focuses on the moral excellencies of Christ and his mercy, and goes beyond rational conviction based on probability. Reason, as idolized in eighteenth-century Europe and North America, is revealed as impotent before the faith that can penetrate to the essence of God in Christ and the certainty of deliverance that he has accomplished. J. I. Packer is correct in saying that for Edwards "true piety was . . . a supernatural gift, dynamic in character and intensely experimental in its outworking. It was, in fact, a realized communion with God through Christ, brought into being by the Holy Spirit and expressed in responsive affections and activities."[29]

What better defense might we find against today's spirit of secular enlightenment than the sovereign Spirit's work of spiritual enlightenment? What vast changes in our cities and towns, in our politics and media, in our universities and public schools, our churches and parachurch organizations would take place if the vivid and compelling reality of divine things were to sweep over the dead and dull and bring this "sense of the heart" to millions! Edwards has pointed to what must be the main thrust of our striving and yearning—a vast outpouring of the Spirit that produces true faith and its panoply of fruits. This is the heart of the matter.

Outcome: Missions

The advance of missions through an energized church is the inevitable outcome of true revival. Edwards felt that the greatest visible sign of revival is an outbreak of love and service to the world. While expressions of this service will be varied, none can be greater than the spreading of the life-giving gospel, the source of life's highest delights and pleasures.[30] A century before the modern missionary movement penetrated Africa, Edwards foresaw the day when the veil would be taken off the eyes of the nations:

> Then all countries and nations, even those which are now most ignorant, shall be full of light and knowledge. Great knowledge shall prevail everywhere. It may be hoped that then many of the Negroes and Indians will be divines, and that excellent books will be published in Africa, in Ethiopia, in Tartary, and other now the most barbarous countries; and not only learned men, but others of more ordinary education, shall then be very knowing in religion.[31]

What will the great means be to promote this worldwide spread of the gospel? Revivals:

> God by pouring out his Holy Spirit, will furnish men to be glorious instruments of carrying on this work; will fill them with knowledge and wisdom, and fervent zeal for promoting the kingdom of Christ, and the salvation of souls and the propagating the Gospel in the world. The Gospel shall begin to be preached with abundantly greater clearness and power than had heretofore been.[32]

Edwards looked for the day when "a revived American church would serve as a base of the missionary expansion of the Gospel until all the earth was filled with knowledge of the Lord as the waters cover the sea."[33]

Did this vision come to pass? Did the Great Awakening actually produce mission action? A burst of home missions and evangelism followed immediately in the wake of the revival, but spiritual zeal seemed to cool in the 1770s and 1780s. In the 1790s, however, "arose William Carey's missionary endeavors, the forming of the London Missionary Society, the Church Missionary Society, and then, later, the Methodist Missionary Society."[34] Was there a connection between revival and the outbreak of modern missions? Edwards would have said yes without hesitation. Many nineteenth-century missionaries, including Carey, felt that there was an unmistakable connection.

But whatever the actual link between the Great Awakening and the nineteenth-century missions movement, Edwards's insight remains valid: revival should produce outreach. Our concern for church growth and the evangelization of the world (expressed in major missions thrusts like the Lausanne consultations, the A.D. 2000 movement and the "Co-mission" to the former Soviet Union) should not neglect the connection between revival and global outreach. Being a world Christian and seeking revival are necessary corollaries, not separable options. The "latter-day glory of the church" that Edwards wrote about so often will be realized only through awakenings.

Applying Edwards's Great Idea

In a secular century in which the church is fighting for its life, Edwards's theology of revival speaks a relevant word. We have considered Edwards's teaching on true revival: spiritual dullness and deadness as the disease needing cure, God and his glory as revival's source and ultimate end, heart-stirring preaching and persistent prayer as its main methods, opposition and extremism as its chronic enemies, spiritually enlightened hearts as its essence, and the advance of missions through an energized church as its outcome.

But what does Edwards have to say to decision-makers? As a pastor, missionary, teacher, trustee, administrator or staff worker, you may feel that reality forces you into the "tyranny of the urgent" and militates against the "luxury" of long-range vision. Yet George Barna reminds us that the visionary decision-maker can be one of the greatest assets to ministry:

Pastors who actively seek to fulfill God's vision for their ministry are a treasure for the church. They are leaders driven not by a need for self-aggrandizement or ego gratification but by a burning desire to see God's will done to its fullest. They are pastors who have blended their vision for personal ministry with the vision imparted by God for the churches they lead. Their churches will accomplish something unique, meaningful and special because the Holy Spirit has enabled them to capture an image of the future and to chart a course of action to reach that goal.[35]

Edwards can help us become the kinds of leaders who "capture an image of the future and . . . chart a course of action to reach that goal." Edwards's theology shows that we help our people resist secular challenges best when they are experiencing the enlightening ministry of the Holy Spirit.

The major implication of Edwards's theology of revival for decision-makers seems to be that we resist secularization by becoming agents of revival. What is an agent of revival? Two words characterize such an agent: *preparation* and *promotion*. An agent of revival prepares for the coming of revival in ministry and family and then charts a course that will promote revival.

Use #1: Reject the spiritual status quo. Deciding to prepare for revival means first of all rejecting the spiritual status quo. Is your family, ministry or church weighed down by a dullness about God and spiritual things? Do you lack a strong, growing desire for the permanent pleasures of God? John Piper describes the condition in many of our churches when he writes that the enemy of worship is not that our desire for pleasure is too strong but too weak! We have settled for a home, a family, a few friends, a job, a television, a microwave oven, an occasional night out, a yearly vacation, and perhaps a new personal computer. We have accustomed ourselves to such meager, short-lived pleasures that our capacity for joy has shriveled. And so our worship has shriveled.[36]

Enlarging our shriveled capacity for joy is a prerequisite to seeking after revival. Revival is not a time of superfluous spiritual experience but a restoration of what should be normal spiritual experience. Most of the time the church is in a subnormal spiritual state. We must never get used to this state of spiritual dullness. We must fight it as leaders, as heads of families and as individuals.

Use #2: Take some action to restore your passion. Recently my family realized we were going through a time of spiritual dullness. It took us several months to realize we were in a spiritually weak state, but eventually, after having some private conversations with my wife, daughter and son, I called a meeting to discuss the problem. We all admitted to the malady and decided to "restore our spiritual passion," to fight the spiritual status quo and push and pray for a greater experience of God's satisfactions. We found some help in an article by Marlene LeFever, "100 Ways to Take the Yawn out of Your Relationship with God."[37] Each of us made an action plan of four or five things that we would do to get moving again spiritually. Each Sunday night thereafter, we got together to see how we were progressing. Over the course of a month we saw some attitudes change and some atrophied appetites restored.

A church or Christian organization might do well to declare a "Restore Your Spiritual Passion Month" in order to fight dullness and take some useful prerevival action. A spiritual leader prepares for revival by refusing to accept the spiritual status quo.

Use #3: Oppose questionable models of revival. Edwards was not the only Western leader with a vision for revival. A number of theologies of revival emerged in the nineteenth century. Probably the most famous of these models was the one proposed by evangelist Charles G. Finney (1792-1875), a successful revivalist in the early nineteenth century. Some major elements of his model stand in sharp contrast to Edwards's theology of revival. Finney taught a very humanistic view of free will and grace, emphasizing our role in the plan of salvation and minimizing God's grace. He disagreed with Edwards on the divine origin of revivals and insisted that they were humanmade affairs, the results of using the right methods through careful calculation and planning. He believed that a revival occurs when one applies these techniques to generate a high enough level of religious excitement that sinners make instantaneous and emotional decisions. Finney further taught that these emotionally moved sinners should be brought to Christ through public invitations, and that holiness (understood as sinless perfection) is a postconversion experience of perfection that should not be expected of the initial convert.

This model has had an enormous impact in North America and—through the influence of missionaries and traveling evangelists—all over the world, including Africa. I submit that this model is deficient in its view of grace, God's sovereignty, its tendency to manipulate people to make decisions and its incorrect emphasis on holiness as a second stage in the Christian life. Finney accomplished many wonderful things for the kingdom, but his *experience* of revival was better than his *theology* of revival.[38]

The long shadow of Finney's great influence sometimes hides Edwards' better model of revival. The failure rate of so many converts won through the Finney method (and the "burned-over" effect of spiritual hardening that it produces) should make us question methods and theologies of revival that minimize the divine role and maximize the role of human beings.

Edwards is a help to the agent of revival today because he is strong in precisely the areas where we tend to be weak. His model is consistently God-centered, biblically compelling and able to resist the acids of modernity. What kind of model do you present in your preaching and teaching? What definition of revival comes through to your people in your prayers and actions? Decide to

prepare for revival by resisting human-centered versions of renewal and embracing God-centered models.

Use #4: Preach and teach from the heart. In addition to preparing
for revival in the church in the three ways mentioned above
(resisting the spiritual status quo, taking practical action and
avoiding defective models of revival), a visionary decision-maker
needs to make some decisions about the two critical means of
revival—preaching and prayer. Edwards believed that God usually
pours out his Spirit in response to affective gospel preaching and
persistent corporate prayer.

What decisions need to be made in the area of preaching and
teaching? One important decision is to avoid a reactionary spirit
in our preaching. We're aware that the secular humanist worldview is antithetical to the Christian worldview in a number of
ways. Secularism exalts moral relativism; the Christian exalts
biblical absolutes. Secularism is concerned only with earthly and
temporal things; the Christian is concerned with the eternal and
the transcendent. Secularism despises historical facts as a basis
for truth; Christianity depends on historical facts for its truth.
Secularism is naturalistic and pragmatic; Christianity is super-
naturalistic and idealistic.[39] So the preacher or the teacher wanting
to strengthen the believer for the encounter with secularism might
be tempted to become reactionary. Such preaching and teaching
can reduce Christianity to a polemical list of things we are against
rather than providing a vision of life-giving realities that we are
for. We need to preach to the heart, exalting the great truths of
creation, fall and redemption and building a positive Christian
worldview that can support biblical truth and lead to the enjoyment of the triune God.[40]

To avoid reactionary preaching and teaching we would do well
to follow Edwards's model—not by reading manuscripts word for
word, as he apparently did, but by submitting to the dynamics that
gave his preaching so much power. Piper has noted ten of these
dynamics that could promote affective preaching and teaching
today:

☐ Stir up holy affections and longings for God.

☐ Enlighten the mind with truth.

☐ Saturate your people with Scripture.

☐ Employ analogies and images that "make the glories of heaven look irresistibly beautiful and the torments of hell look intolerably horrible."

☐ Use threats and warnings in order to alert people to the dangers of spiritual deadness and dullness.

☐ Plead for a response of love to Christ and repentance from sin and unbelief.

☐ Probe the workings of the heart to expose need and self-deception.

☐ Yield to the Holy Spirit in prayer before preaching.

☐ Be broken and tenderhearted when preaching.

☐ Be intense in presenting the realities and urgencies inherent in the gospel.[41]

Evaluating one's preaching with this ten-point checklist may well be the first step toward promoting the kind of preaching that God has often blessed with revival.

Use #5: Promote revival prayer. What can we do to promote the kind of prayer that results in revival? If we want revival, we may actually need to pray less for revival and more for missions. God's purpose in reviving his church is to promote his great name throughout the earth. Richard Lovelace comments on the need for a new agenda in our corporate prayer: "An increase in the volume of prayer may not be as important as refinement in the agenda. God, as Jesus tells us, is not impressed by the multitude of our words (Mt. 6:7-8). He does respond, however, when we ask those things which are closely related to the interests of the kingdom of his Son."[42]

What kinds of prayer requests would be in the interests of the kingdom of God's Son? Prayers for the advancement of the kingdom of Christ to every people group and every person in the world will lift the church up above the inferiority complex imposed on it by a secular age and will unleash the hopeful worship of the Son who will fill the world with his knowledge. This is why I am so appreciative of the Concerts of Prayer movement. A Concert of Prayer emphasizes adoration, awakening of the church and advancement of the gospel. This is the right agenda. We want to glorify God, and so we pray. We want to spread the fame of his great name around the world, and so we ask him to awaken or revive us to that great task. Such prayers are clearly in the will of God and will bring his blessing.

As of 1993 there were thousands of Concerts of Prayer in North America alone. Young people especially seem keen on missions-oriented prayer because "they get fired up about the greatness of a global God, and about the unstoppable purpose of a sovereign king."[43] Why not work with a few other churches or youth groups in your area to sponsor a Concert of Prayer?

The publication of the fifth edition of Patrick Johnstone's *Operation World* gives the church an improved tool to promote global intercession.[44] *Operation World* contains over six hundred pages of global prayer guidance. Promote this guide for personal prayer, small group intercession and family devotional time. Anything that will encourage a movement of God-glorifying prayer should be advocated by decision-makers. Missions is the prayer agenda that will bring revival because "it flows from a love for God's glory and for the honor of his reputation."[45]

Shrewd decision-makers will see many more applications of Edwards's great idea than I have been able to suggest here. But I trust enough has been said to convince you that Edwards's theology of revival is the most important single contribution that Edwards has to make to evangelical thinking today. And for the Cheshire churches of a secular culture, that is good news indeed.

For Discussion

1. Review Edwards's six insights. A common denominator of all these insights is the need for a new vision of God and his love for us in Jesus Christ. Read Ephesians 3:14-19. To what extent is Edwards's model of revival a commentary on these verses?

2. Pick one of the uses given above and make a plan to put it into practice. Which seems most relevant to your situation? What actions need to be taken to implement the idea?

For Further Reading
Of the many biographies of Edwards, I recommend Ian Murray, *Jonathan Edwards* (Edinburgh: Banner of Truth Trust, 1987), for its sympathetic treatment, although Ola Winslow, *Jonathan Edwards* (1940; reprint New York: Octagon, 1979), is still useful. A judicious selection of Edwards's writing can be found in T. Faust and C. H. Johnson, eds., *Jonathan Edwards: Selections* (New York: Hill and Wang, 1962). A valuable two-volume edition of Edwards's works is available from the Banner of Truth Trust. Perry Miller's biography *Jonathan Edwards* (Cleveland, Ohio: Meridian, 1949) is a classic. In *Seeing God* (Downers Grove, Ill.: InterVarsity Press, 1995), Gerald McDermott explores Edwards's spirituality.

7

A VISION FOR GROWTH
John Wesley's Concept of Discipleship

I maintain that the evangelical church is weak, self-indulgent, and superficial." So writes Bill Hull in *The Disciple Making Pastor.*[1] These are strong words. Just what has gotten Hull's goat? It seems that the main irritant is church growth. What's the problem with church growth? While evangelical churches are filling up with spectators, they are emptying out of disciples. Hull elaborates: "I believe the crisis of the church is one of product, the kind of people being produced." What can we do to improve the quality of the product? "I propose the solution to be the obedience to Christ's commission to 'make disciples,' to teach Christians to obey everything Christ commanded."[2]

Hull is not alone in his concern over the lack of discipleship in the modern evangelical church. Elton Trueblood describes the problem in military terms:

Perhaps the greatest single weakness of the contemporary Christian Church is that millions of supposed members are not really involved at all and, what is worse, do not think it strange that they are not. As soon as we recognize Christ's intention to make His Church a militant company we understand at once that the conventional arrangement cannot suffice. There is no real chance of victory in a campaign if ninety per cent of the soldiers are untrained and uninvolved, but that is exactly where we stand now.[3]

The previous chapter described the revival God sent in the eighteenth century. George Whitefield, John Wesley and Jonathan Edwards were the leading human agents that God used in that revival, a revival that was a powerful force in restoring both church and society. Whitefield is remembered for his transatlantic evangelism. Edwards is remembered for providing the theology that would deepen the quality of the revival. And John Wesley provided the new structures of ministry that would extend the Awakening's impact by discipling the newly converted.

Wesley's great idea was a simple one: *The church changes the world not by making converts but by making disciples.* In order to preserve the fruit of revival and transform society, the church must move beyond making converts and give its attention to bringing converts to maturity.

Wesley's concept of discipleship renewed the ministry of the church, preserved the fruit of revival and was the practical outworking of many Reformation, Anabaptist and Puritan principles. It was one of the great ideas in church history. Decision-makers concerned that today's church is "weak, self-indulgent, and superficial" should give special attention to Wesley's powerful emphasis.

How did Wesley develop this concept of discipleship? What impact did his idea make on his times? Before we can answer these questions, we need to get to know the man behind the idea.

Wesley's Life
A six-year-old boy stared down with terror at his family, huddled together and gazing up at him from the darkness below. He was trapped in an upper-story room as flames consumed the house all around him. Seconds before the roof collapsed, two neighbors

managed to rescue the frightened youth from his smoke-enveloped room. It was a day the boy would never forget. Even in his old age, John Wesley would recall that night and see in it the hand of God. Wesley referred to himself thereafter, using the words of Zechariah 3:2, as "a brand plucked out of the fire."

Why was he spared? What did God have in mind? In retrospect we can say that God spared him in order to save England—both the church and the nation. Both were in need of such help. Consider the situation in early eighteenth-century England.

Contemporary observers describe an England that was sliding into moral and intellectual rebellion against Christianity. Deism had taken its toll even though the apologetics of churchmen like Joseph Butler had temporarily slowed its progress. Butler described the other challenges facing the church in the early eighteenth century:

> It is come, I know not how, to be taken for granted, by many persons, that Christianity is not so much a subject for inquiry; but that it is, now at length, discovered to be fictitious. And accordingly they treat it as if, in the present age, this were an agreed point among all people of discernment; and nothing remained, but to set it up as a principal subject of mirth and ridicule, as it were by way of reprisals, for its having so long interrupted the pleasures of the world.[4]

The bishop of Cloyne, George Berkeley, added that evil was so rampant in English society that it "threatens a general inundation and destruction of these realms."[5]

Writing on the English Awakening of the eighteenth century, A. Skevington Wood documents the moral, spiritual and theological sterility of both the Church of England and the dissenting churches. Though there were undeniable bright spots, the theology of latitudinarianism and the moralism and rationalism of clergy like Archbishop Tillotson rendered the Church of England unequal to the task of stemming the flood of irreligion. Meanwhile, nonconformity was so riddled with Arianism and spiritual deadness that with the exception of godly men like Isaac Watts, no hope for renewal could be expected from that quarter.

John Wesley's early life and education prepared him for his calling as an evangelist, a reformer and a disciplemaker. If there was a recurrent theme in his upbringing, it was the importance of discipline and order. Born in 1703 as the fifteenth child of the Reverend Samuel Wesley, an Anglican rector at Epworth, Wesley grew up in a home in which every child had to pull his weight. His mother, Susannah, taught her son that the secret of success was "to have a place for everything and everything in its place." This passion for order and discipline ran deep. Wesley's grandparents had been Puritan nonconformists, and by the time Wesley was sent off to Oxford he was convinced that sloth and superficiality were two of the greatest enemies of the soul, while spiritual success could be earned through discipline. Wesley believed he could help thwart moral and spiritual laxity by following in his father's footsteps. He was made a deacon in 1725 and was ordained in 1728.

While awaiting ordination, Wesley became a fellow at Lincoln College, Oxford, in 1726, and he received his M.A. in 1727. But his life was consumed by something more than academics. It was during those years as a teacher that Wesley read William Law's *A Serious Call to a Devout and Holy Life*. The impact of this book was profound. Wesley felt drawn to an ascetic life in order to find God by the path of self-denial and self-discipline. He proved the strength of his conviction by assuming the leadership in a religious society founded by his younger brother Charles and dubbed in mockery "the Holy Club." The club's rules called for strict personal discipline, a rigorous devotional life and significant charitable work among the poor.[6]

The Holy Club was not unique. Religious societies like it were multiplying all over England. The roots of this small group movement lay within the *collegia pietatas* of German Pietism. A Lutheran pastor, Philip Spener, had encouraged the formation of these fellowships of prayer and piety in his book *Pia Desideria* (1675). In England, Anthony Horneck attempted to put Spener's idea into practice in 1678 by founding a society for young Anglicans.

By the early 1700s there were scores of these small groups.

Wesley submitted to the rigorous rules of the Holy Club for a simple reason: he wanted to save his soul by becoming free of all sin. In a 1734 letter to his father he wrote, "My one aim in life is to secure personal holiness."[7] Wesley believed that if he could reach a state of complete holiness and purity, he might find salvation. He looked for additional opportunities to polish his soul.

In 1735 such an opportunity presented itself. Wesley had a chance to become a missionary to the newly founded colony of Georgia. John and his brother Charles met Colonel James Oglethorpe, the proprietor of the colony, and Oglethorpe recruited them for Georgia. John would work as missionary to the Indians, and Charles would be personal secretary to the colonel.

Soon they were off for America. During the rough journey across the Atlantic, Wesley became impressed by the piety of a group of Moravians who were fellow passengers. Under the leadership of the godly David Nitschumann, these German Pietists exhibited humility, loving service to others and fearlessness even in the face of death. Wesley felt that they manifested a degree of faith in God and Christlikeness that he himself did not possess.

Wesley was right about both issues. Georgia, as a place to find salvation through service, was a complete bust. He never did get to the Native Americans. Instead he worked as a priest in a parish church and soon ran afoul of the people. Wesley fell in love with an attractive settler named Sophy Williamson and dreamed of marriage. He was stunned when she abruptly married a rival who had little use for religion and none at all for Wesley. Wesley retaliated by barring her from Communion. He fled Georgia when a lawsuit was brought against him, and returned to England overwhelmed by a sense of failure. In his journal he lamented, "I went to America to convert the Indians but, O, who will convert me?"

Back in England, Wesley's despair reached a new low. He found some relief by talking to Peter Böhler (1712-1775), who led a Moravian group in England. Böhler spoke to Wesley about the idea of an instantaneous conversion experience based on faith in Christ alone. Wesley's lifelong obsession with salvation through perfection stood in sharp contrast with Böhler's view that salvation was a radical and immediate work of grace that produced a justifying faith. It was too much for Wesley to accept.

But a few weeks later, on May 24, 1738, Wesley had his famous Aldersgate experience. "I felt my heart strangely warmed," he wrote in his journal. "I felt I did trust in Christ, Christ alone for my salvation. An assurance was given me that he had taken away my sins, even mine, and saved me from the law of sin and death." Wesley now experienced what Böhler had tried to describe.

Wesley's doctrinal understanding was still weak, and because of this his emotions were erratic. Eight months after Aldersgate he wrote, "I affirm I am not a Christian now. . . . I received such a sense of forgiveness of sins as till then I never knew. But that I am not a Christian at this day I as assuredly know as that Jesus is the Christ." Yet a work of grace had begun that would transform him from a defeated perfectionist to a preacher of grace.

Part of that transformation took place through the help of George Whitefield. Whitefield had been a member of the Holy Club but had undergone an evangelical conversion before Wesley. His powerful open-air evangelism had created a great stir in London as well as in Bristol. Whitefield was due to leave England for an evangelistic tour of the American colonies and needed someone to take over his outdoor preaching ministry. In March 1739 Whitefield recruited a reluctant John Wesley to preach in the open air to the coal miners of Kingswood in Bristol.

Wesley was at first offended, feeling that "saving souls [is] a sin if it had not been done in a church." He finally overcame his distaste for the "vile method" and preached to the attentive colliers on the text "The Spirit of the Lord is upon me." There was a good response to his message. Surprisingly, Wesley also found his own evangelical convictions growing as he proclaimed them to others. Böhler had encouraged him to "preach Christ until you have faith." Wesley's conversion was now complete. Not only was he born again, but he had also found his life purpose: "to reform the nation, particularly the Church and to spread scriptural holiness over the land."

Wesley was an extraordinary evangelist. He developed a lifelong pattern of evangelism centered on the cities of London, Newcastle and Bristol. Though he occasionally preached in Ireland and Scotland, he never returned to America. Methodism, as his movement was called by his critics, would be spread to the New World by the work of others. In 1784 Wesley personally ordained Thomas Coke to superintend the work across the Atlantic. When he died in 1791 at the age of eighty-seven, he had spent a life preaching to a nation, covering 250,000 miles, mostly on horseback, and delivering an estimated 40,000 messages.[8]

Wesley's Convictions About Discipleship

One secret of Wesley's success is sometimes overlooked. Beyond his work in evangelism, Wesley was a fierce champion of radical disciplemaking. He had strong convictions about grounding new converts in the faith, and so he established his Methodist societies with their classes, bands and special societies to preserve the fruits of evangelism. Though his methods for producing disciples were not new, they were immensely effective.

Wesley's concept of discipleship can be broken down into four supporting convictions: (1) the necessity of discipleship, (2) the necessity of small groups for discipleship, (3) the necessity of lay leadership for discipleship and (4) the necessity of making holiness and service the double goal of discipleship. Each of these convictions deserves closer scrutiny.

1. The Necessity of Discipleship

Early in his evangelistic career Wesley saw the need to follow up those who professed conversion. Many would leave his meetings only "half-awakened." Some sort of aftercare was need to bring the baby Christian to maturity. The more he traveled as an evangelist, the more convinced he became about the necessity of discipleship. Consider this extract from his journal of March 13, 1743, written in Tanfield:

From the terrible instances I met here (and indeed in all parts of England), I am more and more convinced that the devil himself desires nothing more than this, that the people of any place should be half-awakened and then left to themselves to fall asleep again. Therefore I determine, by the grace of God, not to strike one stroke in any place where I cannot follow the blow.[9] Wesley's theology played a role in producing this desire for disciples rather than converts. Not that his theology was all that different from other revivalists'. Though Wesley rejected Calvinism, he still stressed many of the same things that Whitefield and Edwards preached: the necessity of the new birth, justification by faith, and the unmerited grace of God. What gave Wesley his particular burden for discipleship was his theology of holiness. His great uniqueness lay in his stress on Christian perfection and the development of methods to achieve that end. Halfhearted, nominal converts do not seek radical holiness. Wesley could never rest with such a state of affairs.

Later in his ministry he reaffirmed the centrality of discipleship to the Methodist revival when he calculated that in one town where discipleship had been neglected "nine in ten of the once-awakened are now faster asleep than ever."[10] Wesley pledged himself to avoid this evil by giving himself as fully to the work of discipleship as he did to evangelism. Discipleship was a necessity.

2. The Necessity of Small Groups for Discipleship

As early as 1739 Wesley began to organize his converts for discipleship. The Foundery, Wesley's London headquarters, became the center for his program of discipleship. When he saw the large number of converts in London and the inability of his traveling preachers to attend to their spiritual care, he resolved to do something about it, and he organized a Methodist "society." In 1743 Wesley defined what these societies were all about: "Such a society is no other than 'a company of men having the form and seeking the power of godliness, united in order to pray together, to receive the word of exhortation, and to watch over one another in love, that they may help each other to work out their own salvation.' "[11] The societies were not substitutes for the local church. Members of a Methodist society could be expelled if they failed to attend their local church faithfully.

There was no theological or denominational requirement for membership in a society. The only qualification was a "a desire to flee from the wrath to come, to be saved from their sins."[12] Wesley was sure every true desire for salvation would show itself by an ongoing desire to be free from all sin.

How could this holiness be attained? Discipline was the key. To help advance the cause of holiness he added three kinds of small groups to his societies: classes, bands and select societies. Wesley was far from original. The Moravians, Whitefield and a host of others had pioneered some of these techniques. What was unique was the intensity with which Wesley perfected the small group structure in order to create the radical disciple.

Classes were the most basic small group structure of a Methodist society. When Wesley observed that a number of his converts were falling away and backsliding into sin, he turned to classes as a way to rehabilitate the new convert from the habits of sin built up over a lifetime. His classes were not what the term might lead us to believe. These were not gatherings for academic learning. The class was a small group composed of twelve to twenty members under the direction of a lay leader. The class met weekly in the evening in order to avoid conflicting with either work or church attendance. The purpose of the class was mutual confession of sin and accountability for growth in holiness. Money was also collected to distribute to the poor. Tickets were given quarterly to admit each person to the society's love feasts as well as the next quarter's class meetings. If members showed repeated spiritual and moral laxity, they were not given tickets. If they repented, however, they could resume attending.[13]

For chronic offenders even more severe discipline was meted out. In 1748 Wesley purged the Bristol society and classes, expelling 170 from the movement for such sins as sabbath breaking, selling liquor, habitual lying, evil speaking, idleness, smuggling and carelessness. In 1747 he had examined the classes at Gateshead and also insisted on massive discipline. "The society," wrote Wesley, "which the first year consisted of above eight hundred members, is now reduced to four hundred but according to the old proverb, the half is more than the whole. We shall not be ashamed of any of these when we speak with our enemies in the gate."[14]

In addition to the classes, which all members of a Methodist society were expected to attend, Wesley initiated a second kind of small group called the band. This structure was really a version of two small group experiences Wesley had had before his conversion: the Holy Club, with its strict rules and accountability, and the Fetter Lane Society, which Wesley led just after his conversion. What Wesley had learned firsthand from his own small group encounters he applied to the band. A typical band was composed of between five and ten members (either all women or all men) who gathered for pastoral care and mutual accountability. Bands were more demanding than classes. Howard Snyder estimates that perhaps 20 percent of the members of a Methodist society belonged to the bands.[15]

The band had six rules: (1) meet weekly, (2) be punctual, (3) begin with singing and prayer, (4) "to speak each of us in order, freely and plainly the true state of our souls, with the faults we have committed in thought, word or deed, and the temptations we have felt since our last meeting," (5) end meetings with prayer for each, and (6) "to desire some person among us to speak his own state first, and then to ask the rest, in order, as many and as searching questions as may be, concerning their state, sins and temptations."[16] The questions that members were expected to ask one another were probing: Any known sins since last week? Any temptations? How were you delivered? Any doubtful thoughts, words or deeds?[17]

Beyond bands were the select societies. These most specialized of small groups were the nurseries of future leaders. Select societies were expected to (1) hold to extreme confidentiality, (2) give

absolute submission to the leader in things indifferent and (3)
contribute all money beyond necessities to a common fund. The
group life on this third level was intense, but out of this deep
accountability came many of the disciples who helped reform both
church and nation.

3. The Necessity of Lay Leadership in Discipleship
Wesley soon found that he needed a small army of leaders to
maintain the system of discipleship through small groups. Snyder
estimates that by the year 1800 the Methodist small groups had
one hundred thousand members with ten thousand leaders. The
selecting and training of such an enormous number of leaders
required a Herculean effort.

The Methodists cared little about the background of leaders.
Much to the amusement of Methodism's critics, barbers, black-
smiths and bakers were chosen to shepherd the budding small
group movement. Traveling lay preachers looked after societies
and classes, supervising discipline and training leaders. The job
description of the typical itinerant included the duty to preach,
teach, study, travel, meet with bands, classes, "exercise daily and
eat sparingly."[18] Women could become lay preachers, and many
were involved in classes and bands. The significance of this massive mobilization of lay leaders should not be missed:

> One hears today that it is hard to find enough leaders for small
> groups or the other responsibilities in the church. Wesley put
> one in ten, perhaps as many as one in five, to work in significant
> ministry and leadership. And who were these people? Not the
> educated or the wealthy with time on their hands, but laboring
> folks with little or no training, but with spiritual gifts and
> eagerness to serve.[19]

Discipleship through small groups would have been impossible
with this massive mobilization of the laity. Wesley was convinced
that it was necessary and showed that it worked. Here was an
application of the Reformation principle of "the priesthood of all
believers."

4. Holiness and Service as the Goals of Discipleship

What was the outcome of such intense discipleship? What was the impact on church and nation? Wesley's small group movement produced a new kind of citizen. In 1777 he described what these new citizens looked like:

> This revival of religion has spread to such a degree, as neither we nor our fathers had known. . . . Multitudes have been thoroughly convinced of sin; and, shortly after, so filled with joy and love, that whether they were in the body, or out of the body, they could hardly tell; and, in the power of this love, they have trampled under foot whatever the world accounted either terrible or desirable, having evidenced, in the severest trials, an invariable and tender goodwill to mankind, and all the fruits of holiness.[20]

Godliness and goodwill, spirituality and service to others: these were the goals of Wesley's evangelism and discipleship, goals that he saw being fulfilled before his eyes.

Wesley believed in Christian perfection. He has been criticized, I believe rightly, for the questionable theological basis for this teaching. What should not be overlooked, however, is that *the pursuit of sinlessness is a biblical goal.* The positive byproducts of this pursuit are many: Christian social action, family renewal, a reduction in crime and immorality, and so on. Stress on personal *and* social holiness kept the Wesleyan small group movement from becoming ingrown and quietistic. When holiness and justice are the goals of discipleship, a tough-minded Christian can be produced, one who can truly reform both church and nation.

How to Use Wesley's Idea in Decision-Making

We have examined Wesley's belief that the church changes the world not by making converts but by making disciples. Four convictions provided the foundation for this great idea: the necessity of discipleship, the necessity of small groups for discipleship, the necessity of lay leadership in discipleship, and holiness and service as the necessary goals of discipleship. The question we must now face is how to put these convictions into action.

Use #1: Make small group life a priority in your church, organization and home. Today small groups are everywhere. Bible studies abound on campuses and in company cafeterias. Covenant groups, fellowship groups, affinity groups, support groups, recovery groups, teen groups and mission groups are a critical part of the biggest churches in North America and abroad. Not long ago I visited America's largest church, the fifteen-thousand-member Willow Creek Community Church in Barrington, Illinois. It happened to be the Sunday focusing on the small group ministry of the church. I had often wondered how a church of fifteen thousand builds community and trains disciples. I found out that Sunday. Over one thousand small groups make up a significant part of Willow Creek's body life. Seeker services may draw people in, but small groups are what build them up.

The principle that applies to churches, whatever their size, is that small groups provide the best setting for the growing of disciples.

Use #2: Train others to do the work of disciplemaking. Ironically, while large churches are big on small groups, many other churches are undecided. Some churches that once focused on small groups have moved away from them. One contributing reason is lack of leadership. Small groups are labor-intensive, demanding constant training and upkeep. Wesley knew this well but was willing to pay the price. The big job of recruiting, training and guiding small group leaders is well worth the effort.

For several years the Serendipity ministry of Lyman Coleman has held regional workshops on small group leadership across the United States. Books like Jim and Carol Plueddemann's *Pilgrims in Progress: Growing Through Groups* (Shaw), InterVarsity Press's *Good Things Come in Small Groups,* and *Navigator Guide on How to Lead Small Group Bible Studies* (NavPress) are excellent resources which could be used to train leaders of small groups. Similar books are available in the United Kingdom, Australia and other countries.

Use #3: Adopt the Three C's strategy: Celebrations + Congregations + Cells = Church. Some churches marginalize disciplemaking by arguing that their focus is on worship, Sunday school, missions or some other worthy aspect of the church's life. Discipleship is seen as a rival emphasis. My answer is that healthy churches don't isolate one element to the neglect of disciplemaking. Instead they integrate discipleship into their overall church life and whatever additional emphases they may have. A church that focuses on renewing worship should bring that emphasis down to the small group level and disciple people to worship. Churches with a strong doctrinal emphasis should move beyond the pulpit and bring the discipling of the mind down to the small group level.

I like the formula Peter Wagner offers for a healthy growing church: Celebrations + Congregations + Cells = Church.[21] Celebrations are the public worship services of the church. Congregations are the midsized group meetings, such as adult Sunday school. Cells are small groups of six to twenty where significant relationships can develop and people can be truly known and discipled.

A fine example of the integration of celebrations, congregations and cells is Peninsula Community Chapel in Newport News, Virginia. Under the leadership of Tom Kenney, who planted the church in the early 1980s, creative, seeker-sensitive worship services are only the most visible aspect of the church. Children's programs and adult Sunday school provide an additional level of Christian ministry at the congregational level. About 80 percent of the members and regular attenders of PCC attend neighborhood "satellite groups," where serious Bible study, creative worship, deep community and a strong missions emphasis help to shape balanced believers. Kenney and his group leaders meet with individuals from their groups regularly for more intense discipleship. Kenney also gathers satellite leaders every other month for feedback and training. Every elder of PCC is a satellite group leader. Along with teaching and missions, discipleship is a major emphasis of PCC and is integrated into everything the church does.

Use #4: Renew evangelism in your church by adding a disciple-

making side. One of the missing pieces in much contemporary evangelism is discipleship. Wagner stresses the need for evangelism that moves beyond professions of faith to disciplemaking:

Our intended objective in evangelism and church is, we reaffirm, to make disciples. Bringing a person to a decision to accept Christ and to counsel and pray with that person is important as one of the means toward making a disciple. But if the person does not eventually make a commitment to the Body of Christ, usually validated by baptism and church membership, there is little to suppose that a disciple has been made.[22]

I was involved for years in the "evangelism explosion" program of my local church. The results were exciting. A number of decisions were made for Christ. Yet I look back on that experience convinced that I did not do enough follow-up. While some converts have gone on to maturity, others were left to flounder. Forming support groups for new Christians, developing personal relationships of prayer and accountability with the newly converted, integrating each infant believer into a fellowship group for care and feeding—I would try to do all these things with more determination the next time around. I encourage you as a decision-maker to brainstorm ways to add a stronger disciplemaking emphasis to your current efforts at evangelism.

These uses of John Wesley's great idea may well bring those we lead further down the path of Christian maturity. "This is the great work," Wesley wrote: "not only to bring souls to Christ but also to build them up in our most holy faith."[23]

Wesley calls the church to wage war against cheap grace. Dietrich Bonhoeffer explains why such a war must be fought:

Cheap grace is the preaching of forgiveness without requiring repentance, baptism without church discipline, communion without confession, absolution without personal confession. Cheap grace is grace without discipleship, grace without the cross, grace without Jesus Christ, living and incarnate. . . . Costly grace is the Gospel which must be sought again and again. . . . Such grace is costly because it calls us to follow, and it is grace because it calls us to follow Jesus Christ. It is costly because it costs a man his life, and it is grace because it gives a man the only true life.[24]

For an evangelical movement that has grown "weak, self-indulgent, and superficial," the costly grace of disciplemaking is truly the way forward.

For Discussion

1. Romans 12 is an important text on the anatomy of a disciple. Note particularly the "one another" references in verses 10-16. How does Wesley's concept of discipleship through small groups help the church to obey these commands?

2. How might some of Wesley's ideas help the small group movement in your church or ministry?

3. What suggested uses strike you as valuable? Which ones would you seriously consider putting into practice? Why?

For Further Reading

Many fine biographies of Wesley exist. I recommend A. Skevington Wood's *The Burning Heart: John Wesley Evangelist* (Minneapolis: Bethany Fellowship, 1978). Howard Snyder's fine study *The Radical Wesley* (Downers Grove, Ill.: InterVarsity Press, 1980) takes an insightful look at Wesley's methods for making effective disciples. The eight-volume 1938 edition of John Wesley's *Journal* (London: Epworth) is a key primary source for Wesley's own thoughts and actions. Numerous single-volume editions of the *Journal* are also available.

8

A VISION FOR THE LOST

William Carey's Model of Mission

I used to think the world was getting smaller, but now I'm not so sure. In an age of CNN, e-mail and jumbo jets the world does seem to be shrinking. Yet in light of Christ's command to disciple the nations I now feel that the world is getting *bigger.*

Paul Borthwick mentions eleven different worlds that are crowded into our little planet. Consider the following galaxy of worlds that make up our globe:

□ the Chinese world, made up of one out of every five people on earth

□ the Hindu world, concentrated in India but also including many New Age movements in several continents

□ the Buddhist world, which occupies much of South Asia

□ the Muslim world of the Mideast and Africa

□ the communist world, with its boundaries shrinking since 1989

□ the illiterate world, with its three thousand languages without the Bible

□ the nominal Christian world (mostly in the West), where Christianity is merely a tradition and no longer a vital personal reality in people's lives

☐ the world of the poor with their one billion hungry, crowded into the slums of the globe

☐ the world of children under fifteen, who compose nearly 33 percent of the Third World

☐ the urban world, composed of three hundred world-class cities with populations of over one million

☐ the tribal world, where many of the twelve thousand so-called hidden people groups live with no witness to the gospel in their own culture[1]

These multiple worlds present a great challenge to the contemporary church. I sometimes wonder how much Western church members care about these eleven worlds and the command of Christ to disciple them. In the early 1990s the number of missionaries sent from North America declined dramatically.[2] The seventy-five thousand North American Protestant missionaries of 1988 had dwindled down to about forty-five thousand by 1992. How could we lose thirty thousand missionaries in a six-year period? In light of these numbers I have to wonder if we have the will and wisdom to make an impact for Christ in these eleven worlds.

Despite the rise in Third World missionaries who help offset the decline in North American numbers, I am convinced that the Western church needs to catch a vision for the world once again. I am also convinced that the rising Third World missions movement needs better models of mission to follow as its leaders formulate their strategies and tactics.

William Carey, Man of Vision
A man who can help us today on both fronts is someone who started a missions revolution two centuries ago. William Carey was a practical visionary. His role in promoting modern missions has been exaggerated by enthusiastic evangelicals, yet it is true that while before Carey evangelicalism was indifferent to missions, after Carey it became obsessed with missions. Carey was not the

only agent of change, but he was probably the most important one.

There is much to criticize in the life and work of Carey. He was accused of having an autocratic spirit that frustrated younger colleagues. The Baptist Mission Society complained of his lack of accountability for his finances and work. He was accused of insensitivity and neglect as a father and husband. His evangelism and church planting were sometimes ineffective. His translations were criticized by other scholars. Yet despite these shortcomings, Carey's concept of mission is one of the greatest breakthroughs in church history.

William Carey changed the way the church did missions by presenting a powerful model that inspired the "Great Century of Protestant Missions," as Kenneth Scott Latourette characterized the nineteenth century. At the heart of Carey's model was a great idea. In the words of Ian Murray, Carey's missionary life and work embodied the truth that "faith in the Word of God is the great means by which Christ advances his kingdom through human instrumentality."[3] For Carey the great task of missions was to root the Word of God in human cultures by the application of seven principles:

1. Effective mission is based on a biblical theology that produces both prayer and action.

2. Effective mission is facilitated by parachurch agencies committed to the Word of God.

3. Effective mission must focus on the translation and dissemination of the Word of God.

4. Effective mission is furthered by a visible unity among believers in the Word of God.

5. Effective mission depends on national churches and indigenous leaders discipled in the Word of God.

6. Effective mission must display a cultural sensitivity consistent with the Word of God.

7. Effective mission flows out of a lifestyle modeled on the incarnate Word of God.

Carey and his colleagues were so convinced that these principles were critical to the success of the missionary enterprise that they incorporated many of them in a covenant that they reviewed repeatedly throughout their lives. Carey gave his life to advancing these principles. His success in India, and the success of missions whenever these principles have been followed throughout the world, argues for their relevance today.

Carey's Life

In 1790 an estimated 174 million people out of a world population of 734 million were professing Christians. The vast majority of the world was outside the Christian faith. The two largest blocs of non-Christians were the 430 million pagans and 130 million Muslims.[4] Despite these statistics, the Protestant church seemed unmoved. Little was being done outside of Moravian and Roman Catholic circles. William Carey, shoemaker and preacher, became incensed by Christian indifference to the lost around the world.

Carey was an unlikely champion of world missions. His own upbringing was simple and provincial. Carey was born in 1761 near Northampton, England. His family was religious in a formal sense, but the idea of a personal relationship with God such as Wesley was preaching throughout England never seemed to penetrate his home. His father was a parish clerk and schoolmaster who may have been disappointed when his fourteen-year-old son left home to become an apprentice shoemaker. In the small village of Hackleton, Carey heard the gospel for the first time through a fellow apprentice.[5] After more than a year of resistance, Carey gave his life to Jesus Christ as his Lord and Savior.

Carey's church connections were with the Particular or Calvinistic Baptists, the heirs of John Bunyan. Theological controversy was all too common among the Particular Baptists. One bone of contention was the offer of the gospel to the nonelect. If Christ died for the elect only, what right did the church have to offer the gospel indiscriminately to all? Some even concluded that evangelism was questionable and missions suspect. Unable to agree with such a position, Carey gravitated toward the teaching of Robert Hall Sr., who became his spiritual and theological mentor.

Carey discovered his "system of divinity" in Hall's *Helps to Zion's Travelers*.[6] This system can be called "evangelical Calvinism." Inspired by the writings of Jonathan Edwards, Hall's system of divinity affirmed that God is sovereign in salvation; at the same time he asserted that the gospel should be offered to all of fallen humanity, who should be encouraged to seek after the salvation offered in Christ. God is sovereign to save, the church is obligated to preach, and fallen humanity is responsible to respond. Of Hall's book Carey later wrote, "I do not remember ever to have read any book with such raptures as I did that. If it was poison, as some then said, it was so sweet to me that I drank it greedily to the bottom of the cup; and I rejoice to say, that those doctrines are the choice of my heart to this day."[7] This evangelical Calvinism of Hall and Carey's friend Andrew Fuller gave the young Christian a dynamic theological foundation for his growing interest in world missions.

Shortly after his baptism in 1783, Carey became a part-time preacher. In 1786 he became pastor of Moulton Baptist Chapel. Carey finally left shoemaking completely in 1789, when he became pastor of the Baptist Church in Harvey Lane, Leicester. During much of the 1780s his love for the global mission of the church was nurtured by a new prayer movement in the pastors' fellowship in which he regularly participated. Jonathan Edwards's book *A Humble Attempt to Promote Explicit Agreement* made a great impact on the Northamptonshire Baptist Association of which Carey was a member. Edwards called churches all over the Christian world to pray regularly for the fulfillment of the Great Commission and predicted that the day when "the earth shall be filled with the knowledge of the glory of the Lord" was near at hand:

If the Spirit of God should be immediately poured out, and that work of God's power and grace should now begin, which in its progress and issue should complete this glorious effect, there must be an amazing and unparalleled progress of the work and manifestation of divine power to bring so much to pass by the year 2000. . . . And would it not be wonderful if in the next whole century, the whole heathen world should be enlightened, and converted to the Christian faith, throughout all parts of Africa, Asia, America and Terra Australis.[8]

As Carey meditated and prayed on Edwards's vision of a global Christianity, he began to take practical action. Maps and charts filled with statistics decorated the walls of his home. He began gathering material for a booklet that would urge the church to put feet to its prayers and actually send missionaries to foreign lands. In 1792 this booklet was published under the title *An Enquiry into the Obligations of Christians to Use Means for the Conversion of the Heathens*. It proved to be a catalyst for missions beyond Carey's wildest dreams.

In that same year Carey addressed the Baptist Association on Isaiah 54:2, "Enlarge the place of thy tent." Carey chided the church of his day for being "supine" (indifferent) about missions. The church had allowed the tent of the gospel to become small and shriveled. The stakes of the church needed to move beyond England and Europe. The ropes of grace needed to be stretched across the globe. The church needed to "expect great things from God and attempt great things for God." Those who heard the message were convicted of the "criminality of our supineness in the cause of God."[9]

On October 2, 1792, the Baptist Mission Society was formed, "the first foreign missionary society created by the Evangelical revival."[10] In 1793 Carey left for India with his wife, Dorothy, and a coworker, John Thomas. He would never see England again.

The first year in India was a hard one. Carey and Thomas soon ran out of funds and found themselves destitute in Calcutta. The British East India Company was opposed to missionary work and thwarted Carey in every way possible. The hardships rendered Thomas completely ineffective, and he soon became a missionary dropout. Carey persevered. In desperation he became manager of an indigo factory near Madras, a position he held from 1794 to 1798. It proved to be a godsend. Carey was required to work for only three months each year and could devote the rest of his time to the study of Indian languages.

In 1798 Carey completed a partial translation of the Bible into Bengali. In order to distribute it he started a printing press. He also established a school to teach literacy. But Carey was really not a one-man show. He worked best in a team. Thomas was gone, and Carey's wife was slowly descending into total insanity. Team members were in short supply.

When an opportunity came to move from British-controlled India to the Danish coastal colony of Serampore, Carey jumped at the chance. The Danish colony afforded more freedom for his work. In 1800 he was joined by capable partners, Joshua Marshman and William and Hannah Ward. Carey, Marshman and Ward became the "Serampore Trio." One of the most remarkable expressions of their partnership was a covenant they formulated in 1800 (and later expanded in 1805). This covenant, or "Form of Agreement," as it was called, made eleven promises about the way the trio would conduct their missionary labors:

1. To set an infinite value on men's souls
2. To acquaint ourselves with the snares which hold the minds of the people
3. To abstain from whatever deepens India's prejudice against the gospel
4. To watch for every chance of doing the people good
5. To preach "Christ crucified" as the grand means of conversion
6. To esteem and treat Indians always as our equals
7. To guard and build up "hosts that may be gathered"
8. To cultivate their spiritual gifts, ever pressing upon them their missionary obligation, since Indians only can win India for Christ
9. To labour unceasingly in biblical translation
10. To be instant in the nurture of personal religion
11. To give ourselves without reserve to the cause, "not counting even the clothes we wear our own"[11]

This remarkable document was to be read publicly three times a year, and each missionary was expected to recommitment himself to its resolutions.

With the covenant in place, Carey, Ward and Marshman began their work. They engaged in new translation projects and planted a number of mission stations in and beyond Bengal. God greatly blessed this new partnership when on the last Sunday of 1800 Indian Christianity was given its first convert in the person of Krishna Pal, who followed Christ faithfully thereafter until his death in 1821.

Despite the conversion of Krishna Pal, Carey soon realized that he was a poor evangelist and church planter. His colleagues were much better at this than he was. He made a decision to concentrate on his areas of strength, namely, language and translation work. In 1801 Carey completed the New Testament in Bengali. The whole Bible was finished by 1809.

In 1819 Carey helped to establish Serampore College, where he became professor of languages. He was convinced that "it is only by native preachers we can hope for the universal spread of the Gospel though this immense continent."[12] By 1824 Carey (with the help of Marshman) had translated and printed portions of the Bible in thirty-seven other languages, including six complete translations.[13] In addition to the translation work Carey wrote and published numerous grammars and dictionaries, his greatest achievement being the Bengali dictionary of 1815.

In 1828-1829 Carey played a key role in passing legislation to abolish *suttee* (widow burning). He lobbied against the Hindu practice of infant sacrifice. He worked to establish a leper hospital, to end the practice of burning lepers. By word and deed Carey was changing India.

Carey faced a number of difficult trials in his life and work. There were times when he felt that he "had descended a mine and lost all contact with those who were supposed to be holding the ropes."[14] He lost Dorothy in 1807. Their final years together had been difficult due to her mental illness. A happier second marriage ended in his second wife's death after twelve years. Conflicts with the Baptist Mission Society were often bitter and discouraging. Younger colleagues sometimes complained about the difficulty of working with the three pioneers.

Yet despite their limitations and failures, Carey and his colleagues were convinced that the gospel could not fail. In spite of their weakness the grace of God would give them power to plant the Word of God in the soil of India. Even in death, Carey proclaimed his belief in the sufficiency of God's grace to overcome one's frailties. He died in 1834 in India at age seventy-three, and his tombstone read: "William Carey, born August 17, 1761; Died June 9, 1834. 'A wretched, poor and helpless worm, on thy kind arms I fall.' "

Carey's success as a missionary was not by chance. He was convinced that the Word of God contained the principles of successful missions. In both his earlier writing and preaching in the 1790s as well as in the historic "Form of Agreement," Carey affirmed principles that can lead to effective mission. Seven of these, listed earlier in the chapter, are summarized in figure 5.

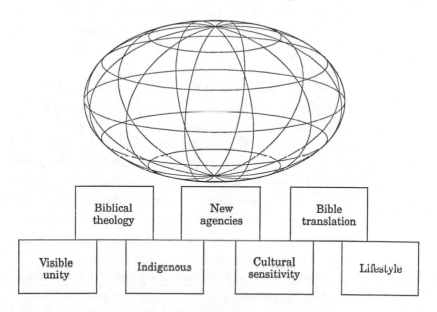

Figure 5. William Carey's model of missions

1. A Biblical Theology for Prayer and Action
You may have heard the famous story that the young Carey was rebuked for his interest in missions by a hyper-Calvinist who said

that if God wanted to save the heathen he would do it without our help. Carey was an ardent Calvinist but a practical one, and he believed that the God who had ordained that the kingdom of his beloved Son would spread throughout the world had also ordained means to that great end. Carey also believed that the Great Commission outlines some of the means by which the redemptive rule of Christ would be realized: preaching, discipling, baptizing. He was no systematic theologian, but his life and work as a missionary did depend on certain theological foundations about human need, Christ's sufficiency and God's sovereignty.

Carey believed in the "infinite value" of human souls and the eternal punishment that awaits those who die in their sins. Without this "awful sense of the value of souls, it is impossible that we can feel aright in any other part of our work, and in this case it had been better for us to have been in any other situation rather than in that of a Missionary." Carey wanted to be motivated by "the dreadful loss sustained by an unconverted soul launched into eternity."[15]

If human need burdened Carey, Christ's sufficiency in salvation filled him with hope. "He who raised the sottish and brutalised Britons to sit in heavenly places in Christ Jesus, can raise these slaves of superstition, purify their hearts by faith, and make them worshippers of the one God in spirit and in truth."[16] This miracle of transformation would come, however, through the preaching of Christ. "It would be very easy for a missionary to preach nothing but truths, and that for many years together, without any well-grounded hope of becoming useful to one soul. The doctrine of Christ's expiatory death and all-sufficient merits has been, and must ever remain, the grand means of conversion." Carey pointed to Paul's practice of preaching "Christ crucified" as support. He also pointed to the Moravians. "It is a well known fact that the most successful missionaries in the world at the present day make the atonement of Christ their continued theme."[17]

Finally, Carey based his mission on a third powerful truth—the sovereignty of God. "We are firmly persuaded," wrote Carey and his brethren, "that Paul might plant and Apollos might water, in vain, in any part of the world, did not God give the increase." Yet "we cannot but observe with admiration that Paul, the great champion for the glorious doctrines of free and sovereign grace, was the most conspicuous for his personal zeal in the work of persuading men to be reconciled to God."[18]

These truths of the Word of God led Carey to a life of prayer. In the decade before he left for India, Carey participated in the weekly prayer meetings of his ministerial association, which were focused on missions. Carey had read Edwards's *A Humble Attempt,* with its call for global concerts of prayer for the evangelization and discipleship of the world. As a missionary in India, Carey and his colleagues continued to make prayer central to their life and work.

Carey's theology produced not only prayer but also action. What is remarkable in his thought is the balance between divine empowerment and practical action. He believed in the sovereignty of God in extending without fail the kingdom of his Son around the earth. At the same time, he believed the church should act in practical ways to realize that goal of history. This balanced theology of mission was aptly summarized by Carey in his Isaiah 54:2 sermon: "Expect great things from God; attempt great things for God." One emphasis without the other would lead to an unbalanced mission and possibly the end of missions. God is the source of all mission through his Word, work and Spirit. We are to respond to the grace of pardon and power that he infuses within us by giving our lives fully for his service and mission. This is the kind of theology for mission needed by every generation of the church.

2. Parachurch Agencies Committed to the Word of God

Carey worked out some of the practical considerations of his theology of mission in a booklet that has been called "the first and still the greatest missionary treatise in the English language." In 1792 Carey published the eighty-seven-page *Enquiry into the Obligations of Christians to Use Means for the Conversion of the Heathens.*[19] This booklet, coupled with Carey's belief that divine sovereignty was compatible with human responsibility, led to the formation of the Baptist Mission Society, the first modern mission society, in that same year. "It was Carey who then first proposed a 'free market' approach to missions which 'proposed the formation of a company of serious Christians, laymen and ministers, with a committee to collect and sift information, and to find funds and suitable men.' "[20] The mission agency was based on the capitalist model of a trading company with shareholders:

> When a trading company have obtained their charter they usually go to its utmost limits; and their stocks, their ships, their officers and men are so chosen and regulated as to be likely to answer their purpose; but they do not stop here, for encouraged by the prospect of success they use every effort, cast their bread upon the waters, cultivate friendship with everyone from whose information they expect the least advantage.[21]

Carey sketched out for his readers the implications of this model for missions:

> Suppose a company of serious Christians, ministers and private persons, were to form themselves into a society, and make a number of rules respecting the regulation of the plan, and the persons who are to be employed as missionaries, the means of defraying the expense, etc., etc. This society must consist of persons whose hearts are in the work, men of serious religion, and possessing a spirit of perseverance; there must be a determination not to admit any person who is not of this description, or to retain him longer than he answers to it.

Widely imitated, this new structure helped create the modern mission movement. Andrew Walls has written,

> The voluntary society, of which the missionary society was one early form, was to transform the nineteenth century church. It was invented to meet a need rather than for theological reasons, but it undermined all the established forms of church government. In the first place it made possible ecumenical activity. Churchmen and dissenters or seceders cut off from church business could work together for defined purposes. It also al-

tered the power base in the church by encouraging lay leadership. Ordinary Christian men, and later women, came to hold
key positions in the important societies. And again the best
societies made it possible for many people to participate. . . . The
nineteenth century missionaries and the societies which called
and directed them were a major factor in transforming Christianity into a world church—perhaps the most important fact
about it in the past century.[22]

3. Translation and Dissemination of God's Word

The Serampore Trio, in article 9 of their Form of Agreement,
determined "to labor with all our might in forwarding translations
of the sacred Scriptures in the languages of the Hindoostan."[23] Why
this emphasis on Bible translation? "It becomes us to use all
assiduity in explaining and distributing the Divine Word on all
occasions, and by every means in our power to excite the attention
and the reverence of the natives towards it, as the fountain of
eternal life, and the Message of Salvation to men."[24] Carey was
convinced that the Bible was the only source book for the gospel.

Carey was not the first to emphasize the importance of translation work, but he was the greatest of the early practitioners. The
scope of his achievement was remarkable: learning, translating
and printing the Bible into over thirty-seven languages and dia-
lects. Literacy work was a necessary corollary to this work of
translation and distribution. "The establishment of native free
schools," wrote Carey, "is also an object highly important to the
future conquests of the Gospel."[25]

The translation of the Scriptures into Bengali and related languages proved to be a decisive force in the raising up of an
indigenous Christianity that also affected the wider culture. The
spiritual impact of the translations was their most direct and
important fruit, but a notable secondary impact occurred as well.
John Watts explains: "Carey's writing and printing of Bibles and
other books in Bengali, as well as his dedicated teaching of this
language in the Fort William College, gave the language and the

culture a standing both in the eyes of the British and in the eyes of the Bengalis themselves which they had never had from their Hindi overlords."[26]

The impact of this translation work in raising up an indigenous church and transforming Bengali culture was enormous. Carey's principle is relevant for the church today in view of the estimated three thousand languages that remain without a Bible.

4. Visible Unity Among Believers

For Carey, missions benefited from true ecumenicity. In a letter to Andrew Fuller of the Baptist Missionary Society he called for a world conference of all missions to be held in 1810 in Cape Town, South Africa, a crossroads of East and West. He was convinced that in terms of mission strategy and arousing interest and motivation in the churches "we should understand each other better in two days than in two years of correspondence." Fuller dismissed the idea as Carey's "pleasing dream," and nothing came of Carey's dream until after his death. In 1910 an international conference of missions was held in Edinburgh—a meeting that launched the ecumenical movement.

Carey's vision of pluriformity through parachurch mission agencies has become one of the great facts of our time and one of the most hopeful expressions of Christian unity. The great evangelical conciliar movement of the late twentieth century seen in such meetings as Lausanne in 1974 and Manila in 1988, the emergence of the A.D. 2000 movement and the Co-mission venture in the Commonwealth of Independent States are instances of a vision first promoted by Carey. Missions can be advanced by the visible unity among believers in the Word of God.

5. National Churches and Indigenous Leaders

Before Henry Venn's famous strategy of forming self-governing, self-supporting and self-propagating churches, Carey and his colleagues boldly championed the indigenous principle. In the "Form of Agreement" the trio stated, "We think it our duty, as soon as possible, to advise the native brethren who may be formed into separate churches, to choose their pastors and deacons from amongst their own countrymen, that the word may be statedly preached, and the ordinances of Christ administered, in each church, by the native minister, as much as possible, without the interference of the missionary."[27]

Why this strong emphasis on national leadership? Carey and his team were convinced that "it is only by means of native preachers that we can hope for the universal spread of the Gospel throughout this immense continent."[28] Serampore College was founded in order to train such "native preachers." It was a great success. So much of the paternalism and Western domination of churches that have marred the missionary record in the late nineteenth and early twentieth centuries could have been avoided if Carey's principle of indigeneity had been more closely followed.

6. Cultural Sensitivity

In the "Form of Agreement" Carey, Marshman and Ward mention a number of ways in which they might win a hearing for the gospel. Three expressions of cultural sensitivity stand out. First, they resolved to learn all they could about the Indian people, "to know their modes of thinking, their habits, their propensities, their antipathies, the way in which they reason about God, sin, holiness, the way of salvation, and a future state." This sensitivity was not based on the idea of religious pluralism, however. Hinduism was clearly regarded as "idolatrous worship." But the gospel itself produced a spirit of cultural servanthood. Carey realized that without a serious grasp of Hindu culture he and his coworkers would appear as "barbarians" in the eyes of the Hindu.[29] As an expression of this principle Carey and Marshman gathered and published a collection of Hindu stories depicting aspects of Indian culture and history, *Itihasmula* ("garland of stories"). The two friends also collaborated on a translation of major sections of the Indian epic *Ramayana*.

Second, Serampore Christians were encouraged to keep their traditional names and dress. Carey refused to give converts Christian names, even when the convert's name was that of a Hindu god. The first convert, Krishna Pal, was encouraged to keep his traditional name. Carey was criticized by other missionaries for this stand, but he refused to bend. Conventional dress was similarly preserved. In a radical contrast with the British colonial attitude toward India, Carey "believed that culture should be baptized rather than destroyed."[30]

Third, Carey and company displayed cultural sensitivity in their pledge to "abstain from those things which would increase their prejudices against the Gospel." This included giving up "those parts of English manners which are most offensive to them." It also included avoiding "cruelty to animals." More important, this pledge to avoid giving offense meant that Hinduism should not be attacked. "Nor is it advisable," Carey wrote, "at once to attack their prejudices by exhibiting with acrimony the sins of their gods; neither should we upon any account do violence to their images, nor interrupt their worship." Why this cautious approach? "The real conquests of the Gospel are those of love."[31] Cultural sensitivity was an act of love that would earn a hearing for the gospel.

7. A Lifestyle Modeled on the Incarnate Word of God

Carey, Marshman and Ward advocated what has been called "integral mission." Bruce Nicholls defines this as "social justice and the renewal of society integrated with compassionate service, universal education, fearless evangelism and church planting."[32]

The integral model was breathtaking in its scope: Bible translation, evangelism, church planting, medical work, social justice (opposing *suttee*), education and leadership training. Different gifts were needed to make this total approach work. Carey was weak in evangelism and church planting, but Ward and Marshman were strong there. Carey was strong in social justice issues and translation. The integral model of mission produced a team approach to missions.

The integral approach required a broad encounter with the culture. The Serampore Trio has sometimes been criticized for their lack of statistical gains and geographic penetration (though by 1813 there were an estimated eleven Bengali churches, twenty native evangelists and five hundred baptized believers). But what should not be missed is that "it was his evangelical zeal that led Carey to explore the world of India in its religious, linguistic, botanical, and social diversity. No barrier of unfamiliarity, no obstacle of ignorance or suspicion was great enough to restrict what he considered the universal range of the gospel."[33]

The task of the Great Commission, for Carey, was to raise up a church that would take possession of the culture for Christ. Such a total and integral ultimate goal of mission required integral and multifaceted means of mission. Carey gives a corrective to the one-dimensional liberal strategy of mission with its essentially material and cultural approach and the equally one-dimensional pietistic approach of evangelism and church planting.

The integral model of missions, however, involved more than just keeping busy on a variety of fronts. It also included the character and Christlikeness of the missionary. The integral approach to mission bridged the gap not only between evangelism and social action but also between being and doing. In the "Form of Agreement" the Serampore Trio resolved to be "instant in prayer, and the cultivation of personal religion." What they had in mind in particular was "prayer, secret, fervent, believing prayer," which "lies at the root of all personal godliness."[34]

Along with fervency in prayer came total commitment to the cause. "Let us continually watch against a worldly spirit, and cultivate a Christian indifference against every indulgence," Carey wrote. "Rather let us bear hardness as good soldiers of Jesus Christ and endeavour to learn in every state to be content."[35] Carey and his coworkers admitted that "we are apt to relax in these active exertions, especially in a warm climate; but we shall do well always to fix it in our minds, that life is short, that all around us are perishing, and that we incur a dreadful woe if we proclaim not the glad tidings of salvation."[36]

Such was the integral model of missions. It combined a wide

spectrum of ministry with deep devotion and spiritual commitment. Effective missions flow from such a Christlike lifestyle.

Putting Carey's Model to Work

William Carey's missionary life and work embodied the truth that "faith in the Word of God is the great means by which Christ advances his kingdom through human instrumentality." How might this great idea and its principles promote a fresh vision for missions? What kind of classic decision-making might flow from Carey's model?

Use #1: Review Carey's principles periodically. If you are a missions executive, a missions pastor or a missionary on the field, consider reviewing Carey's principles periodically and evaluate your own ministry or missions program in light of his model. Have we displayed the same cultural sensitivity he did? Have we emphasized Scripture translation? Have we paid close enough attention to lifestyle issues? Do we have a sufficient theological foundation for our mission? It may well be that an annual or biannual retreat for the missions committee, the leadership team or you and a few trusted colleagues would be the best forum for such a review.

Use #2: Cultivate world Christians in your home, church or organization. Tom Sine put his finger on a malady that affects many of our people: "We all seem to be trying to live the American Dream with a little Jesus overlay. We talk about the lordship of Christ, but our career comes first. Our house in the 'burbs comes first. Upscaling our lives comes first. Then, with whatever we have left, we try to follow Jesus."[37] Our families, our agencies, our churches need to have a focus that transcends ourselves and our little agenda. They need to become world Christians with a faith focused on what Jesus is doing globally and not just locally.

Conferences, magazines, seminars, tapes and books abound to help cultivate a world Christian mentality. Two books by Paul Borthwick might be good places to start. His *Mind for Missions* and *How to Be a World Class Christian* are full of practical suggestions for becoming part of God's global action.[38] Encourage people to read the books with a friend or workmate. Use them for family devotions if your kids are old enough. Teach them in a Sunday-school class. If you live in North America, another suggestion is to take the Perspectives in World Missions course produced by the U.S. Center for World Mission. It is offered at hundreds of locations and can be an important consciousness-raising tool.

World Christians are made, not born. Use your power as a decision-maker to build a few more.

Use #3: Rebuild the theological foundations of mission. Not long ago I was asked to speak at a church's mission conference. This was a strong, evangelical church with excellent leadership and an outstanding commitment to missions. What surprised me was the topic I was asked to address. "Could you speak about the necessity of faith in Christ for salvation? Quite frankly, not all of our people believe this anymore." I was stunned by this confession. I agreed to come, and I did indeed speak on the necessity of faith in Christ for salvation.

Carey's strong emphasis on the lostness of humankind, the uniqueness and sufficiency of Christ and the sovereignty of God made possible his pathbreaking missionary career. We will not be able to sustain a missions thrust in our churches where these three themes are allowed to atrophy. Bible studies on the uniqueness of Christ and strategic preaching on this topic are needed to counter the growing confusion in evangelical circles about whether Christ is the only way.

A strong presentation of the necessity of faith in Christ is given in John Piper's *Let the Nations Be Glad: The Supremacy of God in Missions.*[39] A discussion of this book and particularly of the chapter on Christ might be the place to begin in renewing the mission theology of your family, church or organization.

Use #4: Formulate a mission vision and strategy for your church. Tom Telford, a missions consultant for scores of North American churches, says that most churches he visits "have a very erratic approach to ministry. They're like the guy who shoots an arrow into the wall and draws a bull's eye around the arrow. He then claims that he hit the target."[40] One of the things that impress me most about Carey and his comrades is how careful they were to plan their work and then work their plan. The "Form of Agreement" laid down the basic vision and strategy that the Serampore Trio would follow for the rest of their lives. It gave each of them a focus that helped them achieve more for God.

ACMC (Association of Church Mission Committees), a mission consulting agency, publishes a number of helps for churches that want to formulate a vision and strategy for missions. ACMC can be contacted at P.O. Box ACMC, Wheaton, IL 60189.

Use #5: Send your people around the world. For some things "seeing is believing." I wouldn't recommend that approach when it comes to biblical truth, but it does have some value when it comes to geography. The horizons of my family have grown because we have traveled to many parts of the world. It's hard for me to imagine that my children, Anne and Jonathan, will easily slip into a provincial mindset as they grow to adulthood. They've lived overseas for much of their lives. We've had exchange students live in our home. They've gone on missions trips. We've visited a number of foreign countries.

Carey's vision for the world began with geography. He learned about the new lands that Captain Cooke had discovered in his epic voyages. He learned about the religious and cultural characteristics of India. By encouraging decision-makers and others in your family, church or organization to travel overseas, you are promoting a world Christian mentality.

Use #6: Promote mission-focused prayer. "A local church can develop fantastic programs and channel hundreds of thousands of dollars into world missions, yet if it is not first a praying church, its efforts and dollars are minimally effective." So declares a recent missions manual. Why will prayerlessness compromise our effectiveness in missions? "God will not share his glory with anyone . . . and prayerless efforts on the part of a local church indicate an independent spirit, one that does not acknowledge that God alone brings about spiritual change in people's lives."[41]

Revitalize missions prayer by adding it to the morning worship service, lacing it throughout the midweek prayer meeting or spreading it out among the small groups of your church. Organize a regional Concert of Prayer for missions. Use Patrick Johnstone's *Operation World* as an individual or as a family. Find ways to make prayer happen. Nothing is more crucial for effective missions. As Andrew Murray said decades ago, "Prayer, more prayer, much prayer, very special prayer, should first of all be made for the work to be done in our home churches on behalf of foreign missions."[42] Carey would agree.

Maybe the world is getting smaller. I'm not convinced it is. For me it seems to be getting bigger and more complex. How can we reach the eleven worlds that surround us? Will boomers and busters be able to rise to this challenge? The need of the hour is a fresh vision for the world. Carey's vision ignited his generation for missions. If given a chance, his great idea might just do it again.

For Discussion

1. In John 20:21 Christ told his disciples that "as the Father has sent me, I am sending you." As you review Carey's seven principles, do any of them reflect Christ's own style of ministry while he was here on earth? What are the similarities and differences?

2. Imagine yourself on the mission committee of your local church. Which of the uses mentioned above would you recommend be put into practice? Why?

For Further Reading

A fine biography of Carey has been written by Timothy George, *Faithful Witness: The Life and Mission of William Carey* (Birmingham, Ala.: New Hope, 1991); Carey's *Enquiry* is reprinted as an appendix. Key articles on Carey have been gathered by Bruce Nicholls in *Evangelical Review of Theology* 17, no. 3 (July 1993). The full text of Carey's "Form of Agreement" may be found in George Smith, *The Life of William Carey* (Edinburgh: T & T Clark, 1885).

9

A VISION FOR JUSTICE
William Wilberforce's Model of Christian Social Action

The year 1994 was in many ways a bleak year for the human race. Between the rape and murder in Bosnia and the slaughter and genocide in Rwanda, the year seemed to yield a bumper crop of hatred. According to one newsmagazine, it was a year that seemed to hold up the motto "Hate thy neighbor."

Yet despite violence in the Balkans and death in Central Africa, there was a significant ray of hope in that year, and it came from an unlikely place. In April 1994, after fifty years of apartheid, multiethnic and multiparty elections were held in South Africa. Nelson Mandela, freed in 1990 after twenty-six years of imprisonment, led his African National Congress to victory, becoming the first black president in his nation's history.

The collapse of apartheid and the successful transition to a more just and representative government was a great hour in South Africa's history. It was also a great hour for evangelicalism. After decades of relative silence on the subject of racial injustice, evangelicals in that land actively supported the end of apartheid and the beginning of a new day of democracy for their nation. The turning point for evangelicalism had occurred in 1986, with the publication of *Evangelical Witness in South Africa: A Critique of Evangelical Theology by Evangelicals Themselves.*[1] A group calling themselves "Concerned Evangelicals" was responsible for this document. They repented of evangelical indifference to matters of social justice and pledged to follow the example of their Lord and work on the side of the poor and oppressed. Pentecostals soon followed with a similar statement against injustice. Partly due to this shift within evangelicalism, by 1990 popular support for apartheid had withered away among white South Africans. President F. W. de Klerk, sensing that white minority rule was doomed, dismantled the structures of apartheid and freed Mandela from prison, thus setting in motion the series of events that culminated in the April 1994 elections.[2]

Evangelicalism's recovery of a social conscience in South Africa reminds me of another hour of greatness in evangelicalism's history. In the early 1800s a group of British evangelicals concluded that slavery was inconsistent with the gospel. The slave trade that they chose to attack was big business, with its transatlantic traffic of over one hundred thousand slaves per year in the late 1700s. It was also "thought to be inseparably associated with the commerce and welfare, and even the national security of Great Britain."[3] Slavery "had been legalized by charters (1631, 1633, and 1672), by an act of parliament (1698), and by treaty (1713, 1725, and 1748); and even more significantly, it had flung its far-reaching tentacles around the interests and ambitions of multitudes of ordinary folk."[4] William Wilberforce and his influential friends who formed the "Clapham Sect" swam against the tide of public opinion in their opposition to slavery. "The Evangelical emphasis on the value of the human soul, and hence, of the individual" lay behind their protest.[5] For much of his life, Wilberforce worked to show that Christ was on the side of liberation. He and his friends were able to turn the tide in England and bring an end to the evils of slavery.

Evangelicals today struggle with the issue of social justice.

Critics accuse evangelicalism of an escapist spirituality that cares little about the needs of the poor and oppressed. In the eyes of its critics, it is simply a religious expression of the "me generation" of the 1970s. Yet the roots of evangelicalism are deeply implanted in movements that refused to separate personal and social transformation. One thinks of the balance between the gospel and social justice in Calvin's Geneva, Puritan England, Wesley's Methodism, Edward's theology and Finney's revivalism.[6]

In our own time younger evangelicals in North America, South America, South Africa and Europe have sought to reclaim this heritage. Despite these hopeful signs, however, "the enlarging bulk of Evangelicalism" remains silent about many social injustices.[7] What can get us moving again in this area? How can we oppose injustice in a way that honors Christ and advances his cause? How do we find the middle way between the extremes of social inaction on the one hand and a secularized social gospel on the other? My conviction is that William Wilberforce found that middle way and can help us do the same.

Wilberforce's model of Christian social action represents one of the best ideas in church history. Let's explore his concept that *vital Christianity fights for the personal freedom and betterment of those who suffer using the weapons of persuasion, education and legislation.*

Wilberforce's Life

William Wilberforce was born in 1759 to a prominent merchant family in the British port city of Hull. The death of his father when young William was still in grammar school brought him under the temporary influence of his Methodist aunt, much to his mother's chagrin. His small size was a handicap in school, but the diminutive Wilberforce survived by his eloquence. James Boswell later described him as the "shrimp" who, when he spoke, "swelled into a whale."[8]

In 1776 Wilberforce entered Cambridge University. His years there were spent pursuing games instead of grades. Wilberforce

later summarized his Cambridge experience to his son Samuel:
The first night I arrived at Cambridge I supped with my tutor
and was introduced to two of the most vicious gambling characters perhaps in all England. There was also a set of Irishmen of
this sort to whom I was introduced. There I used to play cards
a great deal and do nothing else and my tutor who ought to have
repressed this disposition, if not by his authority at least by his
advice, rather encouraged it.[9]
His time at university was not a total waste, however. Wilberforce
did gain a smattering of the classics before leaving Cambridge.

Somewhere along the line Wilberforce also developed a social
conscience. There is a charming story about the fourteen-year-old
Wilberforce writing a letter against slavery to a Yorkshire newspa-
per. Unfortunately the story belongs more to myth than to history.[10]
There is evidence, however, that prior to his election to Parliament
in 1780 Wilberforce had confided to a friend that he hoped to "do
something on behalf of the slaves."[11] In Parliament, Wilberforce
soon gained fame for his eloquence and was dubbed "the nightin-
gale of the House of Commons."[12] In 1784 he switched his seat to
Yorkshire, where he served until 1812. At that time he moved to a
safe seat, which he held until his retirement in 1825.

The spiritual turning point in Wilberforce's life came in 1784. In
that year he went on a tour of the European Continent accompa-
nied by Isaac Milner, an old school chum from Hull. Milner was an
evangelical and engaged the young Wilberforce in conversations
about Christianity. On their trip they read together Philip Dod-
dridge's *Rise and Progress of Religion in the Soul*. Wilberforce was
greatly moved by this book and professed a personal faith in Christ
as a result. He spent much of the rest of his life seeking to become
a disciplined follower of Jesus Christ, although food, drink and
sloth were constant temptations. He wrestled with opium addiction after a doctor prescribed it for an illness. One of the side affects
of the opium was depression.[13] The burden of the abolitionist cause
nearly broke his health from time to time. Yet his faith sustained
him.

What eventually gave him power to persevere was his delight in God, the kind of delight described by Richard Baxter (chapter five). Wilberforce felt that joy in Christ was a powerful apologetic for the Christian faith. "My grand objection to the religious system still held by many who declare themselves orthodox Churchmen," he said, was that "religion is made to wear a forbidding and gloomy air and not one of peace and hope and joy."[14] Joy in God became characteristic of Wilberforce's faith. This bent toward joy is seen in his love of children. His adult friends sometimes complained when Wilberforce, bored with adult conversation, would excuse himself, grab a ball and go play with the children out in the garden.[15] Hannah More, however, saw this attribute of joy as a gift from God that enabled him to attract non-Christians to the gospel. She encouraged him to look "on joy as one of the choicest fruits of the Spirit."[16] Another friend wrote of Wilberforce that "by the tones of his voice and expression of his countenance he showed that joy was the prevailing feature of his own mind, joy springing from entireness of trust in the Saviour's merits."[17]

Whether Wilberforce's Christian hedonism was influenced by the writings of Richard Baxter is not clear. We do know that he had a high regard for Baxter (who had condemned slavery in 1680) and praised his writings on the spiritual life: "The writings of few, if any uninspired men, have been the instruments of such great and extensive benefits to mankind as those of Mr. Baxter."[18] Whoever influenced his Christian hedonism, one thing is certain: Wilberforce's conversion gave him a new energy with which to fight against slavery and injustice. The joy of the Lord would be his strength.

As the century came to an end, Wilberforce intensified his attacks on two of England's most serious problems—nominal Christianity and social injustice. In 1797 he published the theological foundations for his social activism in a book entitled *A Practical View of the Prevailing Religious System of Professed Christians*. His publisher, a Mr. Caddell, was nervous about the project. Religious literature did not sell well in Enlightenment

England. He thought he might sell five hundred copies. Within six months, however, he had sold seventy-five thousand.[19] Wilberforce had struck a nerve. Though his book was primarily an attack on nominal Christianity, Wilberforce also sought to show that Christianity was the key to justice and prosperity in a nation:

If any country were indeed filled with men, each thus diligently discharging the duties of his own station without breaking in upon the rights of others, but on the contrary endeavouring, so far as he might be able, to forward their views and promote their happiness; all would be active and harmonious in the goodly frame of human society. There would be no jarrings, no discord. The whole machine of civil life would work without obstruction or disorder, and the course of its movements would be like the harmony of the spheres.[20]

This new world order of peace and justice would not come simply through human effort. Christian truth and a vital experience of union with Christ were both necessary to produce the kind of person able to work for this new political vision. Wilberforce warned against the "fatal habit" of separating "Christian morals" from "Christian doctrine."[21] Only truly converted persons could be counted on to work for a "general peace and prosperity."[22]

Though Wilberforce may have exaggerated the political benefits of "vital Christianity," his views were widely influential. A *Practical View* was a bestseller and went into numerous editions in Wilberforce's lifetime. It remains in print to this day.[23]

Armed with a changed heart, a joyful spirit, a practical theology and high-placed patrons such as William Pitt (prime minister 1783-1801; d. 1806), Wilberforce had almost all the components he needed to launch a successful attack on slavery. One thing was lacking: he needed kindred spirits to sustain him. This last need was soon met. Wilberforce became a central figure in a group of like-minded high-born evangelicals whom history later dubbed the Clapham Sect, though they were not a sect, nor did they all live in the London suburb of Clapham.[24] Associated with names like Henry Thornton, John Venn, John Newton, Hannah More, Thomas

Henry Thornton, John Venn, John Newton, Hannah More, Thomas Clarkson, Zachary Macaulay, James Stephens, Granville Sharp and Charles Simeon, the Clapham Sect championed a wide variety of humanitarian and religious causes. They founded a number of voluntary societies to advance their reforms: the Church Mission Society (1799), the British and Foreign Bible Society (1804) and a colony for freed slaves in Sierra Leone (1787). Even in such glittering company, Wilberforce was the brightest star, "the very sun of the Claphamic system" as one of them later exulted. It was no surprise that the Claphamites' greatest cause would become the same as Wilberforce's—the abolition of slavery.

Despite the impressive spiritual and human resources that Wilberforce brought with him into battle, the first victory against slavery took time. Wilberforce's bill for the abolition of the slave trade became law on March 25, 1807, twenty years after his first legislative attempt.

Emancipation could not be far away. Yet Wilberforce surprised many by arguing for delay. He felt there were dangers in pressing too quickly for total liberation. Time was needed to prepare all the parties for the implications of emancipation. By 1833 that time had come. Though Wilberforce had resigned his seat in 1825, his mantle had fallen onto the capable shoulders of Thomas Buxton. Wilberforce remained active behind the scenes, often encouraging Buxton to press forward.

On July 26, 1833, a bill for emancipation of slaves in British possessions passed the House of Commons. What was amazing to most observers was that the "British people, in a time of national stringency, laid upon themselves a tax of £20,000,000 to give freedom to the Negroes."[25] Even Wilberforce was stunned. He rejoiced that he had "lived to witness a day in which England is willing to give twenty million sterling for the abolition of slavery in England."[26] He was even more grateful that he had lived to see the day in which "real religion is spreading; and, I am persuaded, will increasingly spread, till the earth is filled with the knowledge of the Lord, as the waters cover the sea."[27]

his biographer, "proof that a man may change his times, though he cannot do it alone."[28]

Wilberforce's Model of Christian Social Action

How did Wilberforce change his times? To answer that question, let me point out seven attractive features of Wilberforce's model of Christian social action.

Feature #1: Reject radicalism. Side by side with Wilberforce in Parliament were political radicals such as Cobbett, who opposed almost everything Wilberforce stood for. Wilberforce witnessed the radicalism expressed across the Channel in France in 1789. The French Revolution promoted a human-centered deism that was the antithesis to all that Wilberforce believed. He saw how the revolutionary "Declarations of the Rights of Man" produced mass murder, anarchy and the reign of terror. He rejected all utopian solutions largely because he believed the sinfulness of humankind renders all such schemes impossible.

Because Wilberforce believed the only real hope for the betterment of nations lay in Christianity, he could not agree with any ideology that rejected Christian faith. When Tom Paine's *The Age of Reason* was published in England, advocating the ideas that had so unsettled France, Wilberforce opposed the book and its message. For Wilberforce, to be at war with Christianity was to be "at war with the morality and happiness of mankind."[29] He was certain that "if material and mental progress became the only criteria the nation would lose its spirit."[30] Radical politics was a path to misery.

Feature #2: Reject reactionary conservatism. Wilberforce was more than just a critic of radicalism. He also rejected the errors of the political right. In the decade after 1789, the English ruling class was so frightened by the "Terror across the Channel" that they opposed even the slightest movement toward democracy or social change. "Paris had clearly demonstrated," wrote one historian, "that reform, even well-intentioned reform, was of its own evil momentum irresistibly carried to chaos, and that the only safety lay in grateful acquiescence in the existing order, and swift and ruthless measures with every would-be reformer."[31] So extreme did the political right become that "the hard won liberties of the past were discarded, . . . tyranny was dressed in ermine, and oppression broadened down from precedent to precedent."[32]

Some scholars have argued that Wilberforce's reforms were themselves expressions of a conservative panic that sought to "ameliorate the kind of abuses which brought about the French Revolution and even to subdue the lower classes."[33] This view overlooks the fact that two years before the French Revolution and fresh from his conversion experience, Wilberforce had already started his campaign against slavery. It further overlooks the fact that antirevolutionary conservatives did not support Wilberforce and the Clapham group but rather blocked and attacked their initiatives.[34]

Wilberforce rejected the right-wing extremism that seized many decision-makers in Georgian England. His faith in God and his rule through Jesus Christ kept him from panic. The promises of the Word of God convinced him that a God-honoring pursuit of justice from within the system would not degenerate into anarchy. History proved him right.

Feature #3: Stress the practical nature of true Christianity and the new birth. Many in Wilberforce's England objected to evangelical Christianity on the grounds that it was mere "enthusiasm," that is, emotionalism without any moral or social backbone. Wilberforce knew better. His own experience was a testimony that the new birth animated a person with a powerful love for God and others. In Wilberforce's own words, the regenerate person is energized with a sense of duty and service: "Let him still remember that his chief business while on earth is not to meditate, but to act; . . . that he is diligently to cultivate the talents with which God has entrusted him, and assiduously to employ them in doing justice and shewing mercy, while he guards against the assaults of any internal enemy."[35]

Wilberforce's own life was testimony to the fact that "the servants of Christ, animated by a principle of filial affection, which renders their work a service of perfect freedom, are capable of as active and as persevering exertions, as the votaries of fame, or the slaves of ambition, or the drudges of avarice."[36] The genius of evangelical conversion is that it produces "a life at the same time useful and happy."[37] Wilberforce would undoubtedly chide today's evangelicals for restricting the animating power of the gospel by privatizing the faith to a dangerous degree. A full experience of the new birth, such as William Perkins pioneered and Wilberforce described in *A Practical View,* inevitably produces a new creature who finds "doing justice and shewing mercy" his or her joy and crown.

Feature #4: Use the means of persuasion, education and legislation. Wilberforce was not a conversionist who believed that the only answer to social problems was to lead people to salvation. He certainly believed that a religious awakening that produced huge numbers of transformed men and women would change the face of England. He said as much in his *Practical View.* But Wilberforce went beyond the conversionist model of social change. He believed that political and charitable action could accomplish much good in and of themselves. For his thirty-five years in Parliament he worked tirelessly to pass legislation that would improve the lot of the poor and oppressed. He further believed that the way to get such legislation passed was to use "all the known methods of moving the masses, all the expedients of the politician, all the tricks of the party campaign."[38]

He started voluntary societies such as the Society for the Relief of the Manufacturing Poor. He encouraged More in her writing about social causes, particularly the simple tracts that she wrote for the masses. He advocated schemes for inoculating citizens against smallpox and promoting the growing of potatoes, all in an attempt to alleviate the suffering of the lower classes. He advocated "educating our people up to our newspapers, if I may use the expression: by which they may be less likely to become the dupes of designing and factious men."[39]

Many of Wilberforce's schemes backfired. He supported the

disastrous Corn Laws of 1815. He was not always consistent with his own principles. He unwisely supported the repeal of habeas corpus laws during the war with France.[40] But in spite of miscalculations and inconsistencies, Wilberforce held to his belief in the great triumvirate of persuasion, education and legislation. These were useful means for accomplishing the will of God in society.

Wilberforce would have great trouble understanding the anti-government mood that pervades many Christians in North America today. He would probably encourage us to return to constructive social action through persuasion, education and legislation as the best way to bear witness to God's kingdom of justice.

Feature #5: Display patience and persistence in promoting justice. While Wilberforce rejected the idea that slavery should be allowed to wither away gradually, he also rejected the impatience of some abolitionists who would force it through at any price. He believed in emancipation, but he also believed in due process. Wilberforce spent his whole life opposing slavery, and though he often grew weary, he never fainted. He knew that public opinion turns not on dimes but on decades.

When Wilberforce began his campaign, the prevailing view in Parliament was that nothing could ever dislodge public support for the slave trade. Edmund Burke was "afraid to make the trade an issue lest it should ruin his party."[41] Even John Wesley in his *Thoughts upon Slavery* stated his belief that it could not be overturned by law. When Wilberforce introduced his first bills against the trade in slaves in the late 1780s, they were defeated. Lord Penrhyn spoke for the majority in Parliament when he declared that it would be absurd to "abolish the Trade . . . [on which] two-thirds of the commerce of this country depended."[42] Against the odds, Wilberforce continued patiently opposing slavery, slowly eroding the logic of its supporters, gradually exposing the horrors done to its victims, persistently appealing to enlightened consciences. Victory finally came. Slow and steady won the race.

As evangelicals address the many social and economic evils of our own era, Wilberforce's example of patience is crucial. Violent acts such as the killing of proabortion doctors may win a battle, but they lose the war by discrediting protest. Patience and persistence in promoting the cause of reform is the path of permanent change and eventual victory.

Feature #6: Rely on Christian community and voluntary societies. How do we get the stamina to persist patiently in promoting justice, especially in the face of stiff opposition? Wilberforce's answer is Christian community. The circle of friends that gathered at Henry Thornton's estate in Clapham gave Wilberforce the encouragement and support to carry on in the darkest of times.

While I have stressed Wilberforce's role in the abolition of slavery, he was not alone. The Clapham Sect was there at every point. He used the legal talents of James Stephens. He employed the writing ability of Thomas Clarkson. He tapped the financial resources of Henry Thornton. He depended on the spiritual advice of John Newton. He sought the encouragement of Hannah More. Together these friends started societies for the promotion of missions, the settling of freed slaves, the abolition of slavery, the publication of Bibles and the reform of prisons and factories. The life of Wilberforce illustrates the principle that great change can occur when the resources of Christian community are channeled to the area of need by efficient voluntary societies.

Feature #7: Identify the practices that obscure humanity's God-given dignity and contradict the gospel, and then oppose them with all your might. The chief diagnostic tool Wilberforce used to determine the social evils that most needed to be addressed was a theological one. As E. M. Howse has written, the abolition movement in England "sprang out of a new doctrine of responsibility toward the unprivileged, a doctrine which received its chief impulse from the Evangelical emphasis on the value of the human soul, and hence, of the individual."[43] Wilberforce and his friends did not oppose poverty, slavery, ignorance and injustice out of some vague idealism. Their impetus was a certain view of human beings, a view that comes from the opening chapters of Genesis, in which humanity is made in the image of God. Only consciences trained to recognize the divinely given dignity of human beings can be sufficiently moved to action by the horrors of injustice. The very concept of what is unjust is tied to a certain view of the worth of the human being.

Though Wilberforce was no systematic theologian and hated the hair-splitting that he associated with the theologically minded, he nonetheless based his entire social program on a theological point. Any practices that obscure the divinely given dignity of humankind and contradict the gospel must be opposed with all one's might.

Applying Wilberforce's Model

We've been exploring Wilberforce's vision for justice, a model of Christian social action with a number of attractive features for evangelical Christians today. The model of Wilberforce is built around a great idea: *the vital Christianity that flows from the experience of a new birth compels Christians to fight for the personal freedom and betterment of those who suffer using primarily the weapons of persuasion, education and legislation.* But how can we make meaningful decisions based on this idea?

Use #1: Fight for justice from the inside. Charles Colson contends that "as a general strategy, we will be more effective" in promoting righteousness in society "when we penetrate behind the lines, influencing the culture from within."[44] This is consistent with the commission of Christ in Matthew 5:13 to be "the salt of the earth." This means that "Christians are to be 'rubbed' into culture, penetrating every aspect of life and preserving and seasoning the society in which we live."[45]

Fighting for justice from the inside means infiltrating areas of need. Aaron Johnson was not only North Carolina's first African-American secretary of corrections when he was appointed in 1984; he was also the only ordained minister in the United States in such a position. Johnson used his position to purge the prison systems of pornography and profanity.[46] When Tom Phillips was CEO of Raytheon Corporation, he established an ethics office that "reviewed company policy and offered guidance to managers and employees on a confidential, case-by-case basis." Phillips's message to his employees was uncompromising: "Even if you think you are serving your company by bending the rules, let me be absolutely clear: Don't do it. Don't even think about doing it."[47]

Fighting from the inside may also mean relocating to an area of need. Raleigh Washington and Glen Kehrein live in inner-city Chicago. From their interracial friendship has come Rock of Our Salvation Church and Circle Urban Ministries. What does it mean to be salt and light in a decaying multiracial neighborhood in Chicago? Through the work of these men and their ministries, former crack dens, rundown tenements and vacant lots are being transformed into senior citizen housing, low-rent apartment complexes and shelters for the homeless.[48] By relocating to the area of need, they were able to work from the inside.

Wilberforce used his calling as a Christian politician to fight from the inside as salt and light from God. Christian CEOs, lawyers, public-school teachers, journalists, contractors and civil servants today should follow his lead and work from the inside to alleviate all that contradicts the gospel and obscures the image of God in human beings.

Use #2: Work for reformation rather than revolution. Everybody seems to love the word *revolution.* Fewer people like the word *reformation. Time* magazine's Man of the Year for 1995 was U.S. Speaker of the House Newt Gingrich. He was chosen for his role in the "Republican Revolution" of 1994-1995 when the Republican party gained majorities in both the House and Senate and instituted a new "Contract with America." *Time's* award reminds me how we overuse the word *revolution.* One reason we overuse it is that we consumption-oriented Americans want what we want and we want it now. Revolutions are "quick and dirty."

Reformation is not nearly as popular a word or concept as *revolution.* Yet the slow and patient work of reformation is far more effective over time than is revolution. It is also more consistent with the Christian worldview. Since the French Revolution of 1789, revolution has meant radical and violent change. This concept of change is deeply anti-Christian. Albert Wolters tells us why:

Revolution in this sense is characterized by the following features, among others: (1) necessary violence, (2) the complete removal of every aspect of the established system, and (3) the construction of an entirely different societal order according to a theoretical ideal. The biblical principle of "reformation" opposes each of these three points. In the first place, reformation stresses the necessity of avoiding violence both in the ordinary sense of harming individuals with physical or psychological forces and in the historical sense of wrenching and dislocating the social fabric. No matter how dramatic the new life in Jesus Christ may be, it does not seek to tear the fabric of a given historical situation. In the second place . . . it recognizes that no given societal order is *absolutely* corrupt; thus, no given societal order need ever be totally condemned. And in the third place, it does not place its confidence in blueprints and conceptions of the ideal society that have been arrived at by scientific or pseudo-scientific speculation. Instead, it takes the given historical injunction to "test everything [and] hold fast to what is good" (1 Thess. 5:21).[49]

Wilberforce rejected the revolutionary model because he believed in the goodness of creation and culture as made by God. In a fallen world, creation and culture are misdirected toward idols and ideologies rather than the glory of God, but they can be redirected by God's grace and power. The Christian never gives up on people, or the business world, or Hollywood, or the state. No matter how badly distorted those areas of creation have become, they are never beyond reform and redemption. Fundamental to effective Christian social action, then, is the commitment to work for reformation and not revolution.

Use #3: Work through the sodalities of voluntary societies. Rather than trying to do everything themselves, local churches and Christian families should take Wilberforce's example to heart and work through existing voluntary societies to promote justice. We need to let the Lord guide individuals and groups within the church to establish voluntary societies that channel people and resources constructively, just as we have developed partnerships with mission agencies to promote global evangelization.

Prison Fellowship is a sterling example of a parachurch agency that has focused on one crucial area of social justice (the criminal and his transformation) and has produced measurable results to show that Christ can change those whom the courts have called incorrigible. Prison Fellowship has excellent training programs that equip members of local churches to minister effectively to prisoners, ex-offenders and their families.[50]

Or consider the case of Emmanuel Gospel Center in Boston. Emmanuel was founded in 1938 to help the poor in the name of Christ. For over thirty years Doug and Judy Hall have directed this work. Emmanuel provides legal service for the poor. Its Starlight Homeless Ministries takes the love of Christ to street people. Its Urban Research department fosters united evangelical action for evangelism, church planting and urban development. I suppose I could wander into Boston and try to do some of these things on my own, but it would make a lot more sense for me to work through Emmanuel.

I think also of a retired pastor friend of mine, David Madeira, who spends many of his Saturdays in Providence, Rhode Island, hammering together homes for the homeless through Habitat for Humanity. Hundreds of specialized parachurch ministries exist to channel money and volunteer help to the place of need.

Wilberforce had a wide justice agenda. He worked for prison reform, factory reform, missions and economic reform. Yet Wilberforce never lost his central mission—to free the slaves in the name of Christ. Christian voluntary societies are most effective when they focus on a single issue—the family, the unborn, the prisoner or the poor. Your church or family may choose to work through a number of voluntary societies for the promotion of justice. Generally, however, choose voluntary societies that have a single cause.

Use #4: Remember the pattern of the cross—win through losing. Wilberforce lost more battles than he won, but the way he lost made possible his final victories. The pattern of the cross is relevant here. We don't need a new Constantinian Christianity in which the state enforces theology and church attendance. In the long run such a repressive Christianity betrays the essence of the faith—personal trust in the crucified Christ of the Gospels, not the politically imposed Christ of the state. Republican revolutions, Democratic victories and Fortune 500 partnerships will not bring us what we want. Loving enemies, blessing those who despitefully use us, persistently acting as salt and light, insisting on the use of spiritual and not carnal weaponry—these are the tactics that will produce long-term results. Good Fridays of opposition and even apparent defeat, if borne in faith, will lead to Easter Sundays of change and transformation in the world around us.

Use #5: Witness to the coming kingdom; don't try to build it. There is a great difference between engaging in works of justice in order to bear witness to what the rule of Christ is like and trying to actually establish the rule of Christ on earth. Bearing witness means being content with persuasion and suffering. Establishing kingdom structures requires power and money. Bearing witness humbly recognizes that the coming kingdom is just that—a future and glorious reality that can never be embodied in any current humanmade structure or movement.

Avoid the temptation to confuse our transient witness to the kingdom with the glorious reality of the kingdom. History is full of examples of the cruel injustices done by the church when it confused its theocracies with the reign of God on earth. We need effective witnesses of the kingdom (Acts 1:8), not presumptuous counterfeits.

Use #6: Recognize that spiritual renewal and social action are necessary partners. Richard Lovelace has demonstrated in *Dynamics of Spiritual Life* that spiritual revival and social justice are not enemies but useful partners in advancing the work of God. Both the First and Second Great Awakenings in America produced a mighty river of social action.[51] The work of Wilberforce and the Clapham Sect would be difficult to imagine without the work of

Wesley and the Methodist movement. Timothy Smith broke new historical ground many years ago when he demonstrated the connection between Methodist perfectionism and abolition and other reforming movements in early nineteenth-century American history.[52]

What must not be missed in these examples is the partnership between spiritual renewal and social justice. Modern evangelicals have not always been very good at holding these two things together. Commenting on the decline of Evangelicals for Social Action, Lovelace offers a compelling picture of the way forward:

Some of its younger troops are still learning to combine the spiritual dynamics essential to evangelical awakening with the deep concerns which are driving them toward social witness. They have caucused together for political reasons, but they have done little praying and sharing together and have experienced little complementary repentance and sanctification. Consequently they have been sitting ducks for the divisive tactics of Satan. But if a whole generation of young evangelicals can mature in their spirituality, and if older evangelical leaders can expand their vision, we have the potential for a new level of evangelical impact within the church and on society.[53]

As Wilberforce taught in his *Practical View*, vital Christianity compels the Christian to fight for justice. The separating of social action from spiritual passion, like the separation of a live coal from the fire, will cause it to cool and die.

Though hate seemed strong in 1994, the story of justice breaking through in South Africa shone like a light in the darkness. Evangelicals in South Africa, like their spiritual ancestors in Wilberforce's England, ended up on the correct side of that struggle. As we face the future darkness, we need to borrow these old torches. They are still bright enough to light the road ahead.

For Discussion

1. One of the most powerful biblical statements Jesus ever made about social justice is found in Matthew 25:31-46. In what ways

does Wilberforce's model shed light on these commands of our Lord?

2. What are the specific social evils that Christians need to address today? Look over the uses mentioned in this chapter. Which ones might help you take the next step toward serving "the least of these"?

For Further Reading
John Pollock's *Wilberforce* (1977; reprint Tring, U.K.: Lion, 1986) is a well-written and well-researched biography. For a look inside William Wilberforce's own mind and heart, read *A Practical View of the Prevailing Religious System of Professed Christians in the Higher and Middle Classes in This Country Contrasted with Real Christianity* (1797; reprint London: SCM Press, 1958). For a look at Wilberforce's place in the Clapham Sect I recommend Ernest Marshall Howse, *Saints in Politics: The "Clapham Sect" and the Growth of Freedom* (London: George Allen and Unwin, 1953).

10

A VISION FOR FELLOWSHIP

Dietrich Bonhoeffer's Principles of Christian Community

Do you remember those *Indiana Jones* movies of the 1980s? The hero always thwarted the Nazis—everybody's favorite bad guys. Whether it was finding the lost ark or searching for the holy grail, "Indy" always found a way to undermine the Nazis' dastardly schemes. The movies were escapist cinema at its most entertaining. After all, the Nazis were long gone, and who could take them seriously any more?

But the *Indiana Jones* movies may have been prophetic. The ghosts of fascism, tribalism and neo-Nazism reared their ugly heads just as the twentieth century began to close. Ethnic cleansing reappeared in Bosnia and Rwanda. White supremacists bombed the federal building in Oklahoma City, killing hundreds. Muslim fundamentalists bombed the World Trade Center. A right-wing extremist assassinated the Israeli prime minister in the name of Jewish nationalism. The world is breaking into a thousand tribes, many of which are willing to kill in order to get their point across. The spirit of Nazism—ethnic or cultural supremacy at any price—is everywhere. Everybody's favorite bad guys seem to be making a comeback. We could use an Indiana Jones.

Tribalism and Postmodernity

This new political tribalism parallels a new cultural and intellectual tribalism. When the Berlin Wall came crashing down in 1989, it signaled more than the symbolic end of communism. It was also the symbolic end of modernity.

Modernity had grown out of the eighteenth-century Enlightenment. Central to the faith of modernity was belief in human progress. This secular gospel taught that utopia was just around the corner: all that was needed to realize heaven on earth was the systematic application of reason to the social, economic and political ills of humankind. This belief system made a religion out of "secular humanism." Communism was this secular religion's most extreme expression. When the wall fell, it was thus a testimony to the world that the arrogant humanism of the Enlightenment had failed. Modernity was dead as a belief system. Rising from the ruins of modernity was a new world order for the twenty-first century—the postmodern world.

This brave new world of postmodernity at first appeared to be a positive development for the Christian cause. Postmodern criticisms of secular humanism sounded a lot like Christian complaints. Gene Veith explains:

> If the "modern" age is really over, Christians have every reason to be glad. Ever since the battles between "modernists" and "fundamentalists" (and before), Biblical Christianity has been bludgeoned by the forces of modernism, with its scientific rationalism, humanism, and bias against the past. Today the assumptions of modernism, including those that have bedeviled the church in this century, are being abandoned. Christians can rejoice at the dawn of a postmodern age.[1]

Modernity is dead. Long live postmodernity.

But there is another side to postmodernity. Postmodernity comes with an ideological attachment called postmodern*ism*. This new ideology is in many ways antagonistic to Christian faith. For example, postmodernism opposes the very concept of objective and absolute truth. Postmodernism is therefore as hostile to Christian truth claims as it was to Enlightenment truth claims. In the place of absolute truth, postmodernism preaches the gospel of relativism. A Hunter college student captured the essence of postmodern relativism when he claimed that since "all beliefs are subjective; one should believe only what makes one feel good. What is true for oneself is what makes one feel good."[2]

"Feel-good" thinking produces very little consensus. What it does produce is a thousand "me first" ideologics, insulated from any meaningful common truth or shared values. As one journalist observed, "Society is splintering into hundreds of subcultures and designer cults each with its own language, code and life-style."[3]

Behind this radical relativism is something even more sinister than simple selfism. Behind the relativism is the familiar face of fascism. Veith explains:

Many of the ideas that came together in the fascism of the 1930s survived World War II and continued to develop in postmodern thought. Fascism taught that reality is a social construction, that culture determines all values. Particular cultures and ethnic groups therefore constitute their own self-contained worlds, which should be kept uncontaminated, although these groups will often compete with each other. Individuality is a myth; particular human beings can only find fulfillment when they lose themselves in a larger group. "Humanistic values" are a myth; there are no absolute transcendent moral laws by which the culture can be judged. These are "Jewish"—i.e., Biblical— ideas that are responsible for alienation, guilt, and instability of Western culture. Strength, not love and mercy, must be the true expression of a culture's will to power. Collective emotion, not abstract reason (another "Jewish" contribution), must be cultivated as the culture's source of energy. . . . Hitler may have failed because he was ahead of his time.[4]

These are chilling words, but they possess the ring of truth. The movie *Cabaret* chronicled the rise of Nazism in the decadent years of the Weimar Republic. As the movie showed, the excessive individualism, immorality and despair of Germany in the 1920s created the cultural soup that made Hitler's fascism possible. Nazi tribalism was seen as a way of cultural salvation for a German culture sinking into relativism and selfism. Veith's earlier study *Modern Fascism: Liquidating the Judeo-Christian Worldview* (1993) led him to the conclusion that there are numerous links between postmodernism and fascism. What looked like an ally now looks like a formidable new foe. Veith concludes that "postmodernists and the fascist intellectuals of the 1930s both embrace a radicalism based not so much on economics but culture. They both reject individual liberty in favor of the will to power. They reject reason in favor of irrational emotional release. They reject a transcendent God in favor of an impersonal, mystical nature."[5] The "Raiders of the Lost Ark" are rising from their graves.

How ready is the Christian church to contend with the forces of postmodernism? It doesn't look good. Just when the church needs to bear effective witness to a new generation, it seems to be compromising with the relativism and tribalism of postmodernism. According to a recent poll, "53 percent of those who identify themselves as evangelical Christians believe there are no absolutes."[6] The rejection of universal absolutes means the creation of "arbitrary absolutes" that define the boundaries of the new tribalism.[7] I sometimes feel about the state of the church the way historian Arthur Schlesinger Jr. feels about the state of America: "We have too much *pluribus* and not enough *unum*."

The old selfism that we complained about in the 1980s has changed. It joined up with a radical tribalism in the 1990s. Party politics, spiritual consumerism and an emphasis on "feeling good about oneself" are producing subcultures within the church that seem to reflect the values of postmodernism more than the gospel. Birds of a feather are, unfortunately, flocking together. Real Christian community, where genuine love and relationships can exist among different age groups, genders, interest groups and even people who don't like each other, is threatened by a postmodern Christianity in which I hang around only with "my kind of people." The vision of body life described with such power by Paul in 1 Corinthians 12, of unity within diversity, seems to be sinking beneath the waves of postmodernity.

How can the church navigate the troubled waters of the postmodern world? Of the many pilots who have sought to steer the church through similar storms, German theologian and pastor Dietrich Bonhoeffer was one of the most successful. In the Hitler-crazed Germany of the 1930s, when nationalism became vicious and the German Christian churches bought a party card, Bonhoeffer turned to the resources of genuine Christian community to guide the church. In ways that he could not foresee, Bonhoeffer also laid down a theology of Christian fellowship that can help us combat both the selfism and the tribalism of the postmodern world.

Bonhoeffer's blueprint for community is found in his book *Life Together*. Where many recent evangelical writers on issues of fellowship and discipleship have focused on techniques, Bonhoeffer focused on truth. Those who focus on techniques are vulnerable to takeover by rival ideologies. Bonhoeffer's theological sensitivity guarded the church from these rival ideologies even as it guided the church toward a rich experience of mutual love and deep relationships. Though some have questioned Bonhoeffer's theological soundness in other areas, I am convinced that Bonhoeffer is a reliable guide in the area of Christian community.

What was his great idea? Let me phrase it as follows: For Dietrich Bonhoeffer, *the key to Christian community is learning to let Christ be the mediator of our relationships.* Properly understood, such an idea can help liberate the church from the selfism and tribalism of postmodern times.

Indiana Jones isn't around today. No one person is able to sweep away, with a few swashbuckling exploits, the neo-Nazi assumptions that pervade much of postmodernism. No single crack of the whip can restore the fragmented relationships and broken communities that litter our landscape. Yet Bonhoeffer's blueprint might take us a long way toward renewing genuine Christian community and recapturing the postmodern world for Christ. Such a promising blueprint deserves a closer look.

Bonhoeffer's Life

The architect behind this blueprint was born in 1906 in Breslau, Germany. Dietrich Bonhoeffer grew up in a close family of seven children. His father was a noted physician and psychiatrist, and also a nonbeliever mildly skeptical of Christianity. His family remained on the fringes of Christianity. "The Bonhoeffers were not a church-going family in the sense of active membership of and participation in the life of a congregation," wrote Bonhoeffer's biographer and brother-in-law, Eberhard Bethge. "The children were not sent to church, and the family did not go to church even on the high festivals."[8] Yet through the influence of Dietrich's mother, the Bible and its stories were kept alive within the home.

By the time young Bonhoeffer was fourteen, he surprised his family by announcing his decision to become a minister and study theology. His brothers and sisters attacked his decision and told him that the church was "a poor, feeble, boring, petty bourgeois institution." Dietrich's reply to the attack on the church was simple: "In that case I shall reform it."[9]

In 1923, at seventeen years of age, Bonhoeffer entered the University of Tübingen. After a year of study, in which he absorbed much of the liberalism of the day, he transferred to the University of Berlin, where he completed his theological studies. Just prior to his transfer to Berlin, a visit to Rome impressed him with the power and solidarity of Roman Catholicism. This visit instilled within him the desire for the visible unity and communion of the church that would later mark his mature theology.

The University of Berlin was the home of some of the great liberal theologians of the early twentieth century. Adolf von Harnack was still teaching there in the 1920s. Karl Holl taught church history. Reinhold Seeburg lectured in systematic theology. But the most profound influence upon Bonhoeffer was a professor who touched him through his books—Karl Barth. Barth broke with the liberal theology championed by Friedrich Schleiermacher (1768-1834), which made humankind and human experience the starting point and reference point of theology. For Barth only the Word of God, which is fundamentally antagonistic to human thinking and experience, could be the true starting point for theology. Bonhoeffer's discovery of Barth changed the course of his life.[10]

In 1927 Bonhoeffer received his doctorate from Berlin. His dissertation was on the communion of the saints. Bonhoeffer defined the church as "Christ existing as community." For Bonhoeffer "God, though distant, was close," and through "concrete encounter with one's fellow" the believer could live a true life of faith. Faith was defined as "tying oneself in with the community." He concluded that "living a human life was possible through fellowship."[11] Bonhoeffer, perhaps caught up in the spirit of his times, overidentified Christ with the church. These early ideas would later be modified and corrected. What is crucial at this stage is that Bonhoeffer had discovered the theme that would dominate his life.

Between 1928 and 1933 Bonhoeffer was on the move. He pastored in Barcelona, Spain, and then briefly in Berlin. In 1930 he spent a year at Union Theological Seminary in New York, making contact with Reinhold and H. Richard Niebuhr. He left New York with a lifelong love of African-American spirituals and a concern for the plight of the African-American in a racist society. By 1931 Bonhoeffer was back in Berlin, lecturing at the university. But he found that Berlin had changed since his student days. At the heart of most of the changes was a new political and cultural movement called National Socialism, led by Adolf Hitler. Within two years Nazism would become the most popular political party in Germany.

On February 1, 1933, two days after Adolf Hitler had come to power, Bonhoeffer addressed the nation over the radio on the subject of the "Younger Generation's Changed View of the Concept of the Führer." Bonhoeffer warned his listeners not to allow any leader "to succumb to the wishes of those he leads, who will always seek to turn him into their idol." A leader who succumbs to this temptation becomes a "leader who makes an idol of himself and his office, and who thus mocks God."[12] Before Bonhoeffer could finish his talk, his microphone was switched off.

Within a few weeks the Reichstag was burned to the ground under suspicious circumstances, and Hitler declared a state of emergency, making himself dictator of Germany. By March, Hitler was assuring the churches that "Christianity [provided] the unshakable foundations of our people's ethical and moral life."[13] Everyone breathed a sigh of relief.

In April 1933 a number of German pastors gathered to declare their agreement with the "Führer principle." They also endorsed the idea of Aryan supremacy with its corollary of anti-Semitism. In keeping with these policies, the pastors voted to exclude Jewish Christians from their churches. This was the beginning of the German Christian movement. Bonhoeffer, Barth and others were shocked at these new policies and vowed to fight them.

By 1933 the Gestapo were arresting Lutheran pastors who dissented from the German Christian movement. Certain that he was next, Bonhoeffer left Germany and became pastor of a German-speaking congregation in England. Even from London he continued to remain active in the protest movement in his homeland. Bonhoeffer issued a pastoral letter in May 1934 calling for the confessing churches to issue an "ultimatum" to the compromising German Christian leaders. This culminated in the Barmen Declaration, with Karl Barth as its principal drafter. The declaration (which was endorsed by Bonhoeffer, although he was not in attendance at Barmen) rejected the "false doctrine that the Church, as the source of its proclamation, could and should, over and above God's one Word, acknowledge other events, powers, images and truths as divine revelation." It further declared that the church had no right to "set up or allow herself to be given, special leaders with sovereign powers."[14] Christ alone was Lord.

Bonhoeffer returned to Germany in 1935. His task was to help the confessing church establish a seminary at Finkenwalde. Under Bonhoeffer's headship the twenty-five residents of the seminary shared a common life. Bonhoeffer wanted the young men at the seminary to learn not only a passion for the Word of God but also "how to lead a communal life in daily and strict obedience to the will of Christ Jesus, in the humblest and highest service one Christian brother can perform for another; they must learn to recognize the strength and liberation to be found in brotherly service and communal life in a Christian community."[15] From these quiet years of Christian community came two of Bonhoeffer's greatest works, *The Cost of Discipleship* and *Life Together.*

After the Gestapo closed the seminary in 1937, Bonhoeffer turned his attention to writing about his experience in community. In 1939, the year that Germany began World War II with the invasion of Poland, he published *Life Together* in order to summarize his insights about Christian community in a hostile world. It would become the most widely read of Bonhoeffer's books during his lifetime. "Here," according to Bethge, "were the outlines of a living Protestant community."[16] After the publication of *Life Together,* Bonhoeffer visited the United States. Though friends urged him to stay, he returned to Germany.

From 1940 onward Bonhoeffer was deeply involved with the Resistance movement within Germany. In the winter of 1942-1943, as the tide of war turned against Germany, the Resistance hatched two plots to assassinate Hitler. Both failed. Eventually Bonhoeffer's role in the conspiracy was discovered. He was arrested in 1943.

During his prison years Bonhoeffer continued to write. He began to speak of "religionless Christianity" and "a world come of age." Both phrases have been the subject of much debate. Bonhoeffer apparently believed that secularism, while godless and destructive, was a sign that God was once again drawing near to history because his most powerful work is done under the veil of apparent weakness. Clarifying the phrase "a world come of age," he wrote from prison: "I don't mean the shallow and banal this-worldliness of the enlightened, the busy, the comfortable, or the lascivious, but the profound this-worldliness, characterized by discipline and the constant knowledge of death and resurrection."[17] Luther's theology of the cross thus shaped the ideas that occupied Bonhoeffer's final years.

Bonhoeffer never made it out of prison. Just a few weeks before the Allies liberated his compound, he was killed. On Monday, April 9, 1945, after conducting worship the previous day (and preaching on Isaiah 53:5, "with his stripes we are healed"), Dietrich Bonhoeffer was executed by hanging. His last words were "This is the end, but for me it is the beginning of life."[18] The camp doctor, who had watched men die for fifty years, wrote of Bonhoeffer, "I have hardly ever seen a man die so completely submissive to the will of God."[19]

If there is a continuous thread that runs through Bonhoeffer's life and work, it is the centrality of Christian community in a world full of discord. In a series of paradoxes worthy of Luther himself, Bonhoeffer sought to penetrate to the heart of Christian community. Bonhoeffer's discoveries in *Life Together* may be summarized by the following six principles.

Community as a Gift

Principle #1: In a hostile world the gift of Christian community is a great treasure from God not to be despised. Life Together is an extended meditation on Psalm 133:1: "Behold, how good and how pleasant it is for brethren to dwell together in unity." This simple celebration of Christian fellowship must not be taken for granted. Consider, for example, how the simple pleasures of Psalm 133:1 evaded the Lord Jesus Christ: "Jesus Christ lived in the midst of his enemies. At the end all his disciples deserted him." If our Lord lived a life of warfare against the world, "so the Christian too belongs not in the seclusion of a cloistered life but in the thick of foes."[20] The modern world with its secularism and idolatry provides just that kind of setting for the Christian. If in the midst of the hostilities the Christian finds genuine fellowship, it should not be despised. In a fallen world Christian fellowship is a gift of grace to be treasured, and not an achievement for which the church can take credit.

Yet the failure to treasure Christian community is often the very first violation of true fellowship in Christ. "That which is an unspeakable gift of God for the lonely individual," writes Bonhoeffer, "is easily disregarded and trodden under foot by those who have the gift every day." In times of relative peace it "is easily forgotten that the fellowship of Christian brethren is a gift of grace, a gift of the Kingdom of God that any day may be taken from us, that the time that still separates us from utter loneliness may be brief indeed." Because of the turbulent times in which we live, "let him who until now has had the privilege of living a common Christian life with other Christians praise God's grace from the bottom of his heart. Let him thank God on his knees and declare: It is grace, nothing but grace, that we are allowed to live in community with Christian brethren."[21] To treasure the gift of community is thus the beginning of true fellowship.

Christ as the Mediator

Principle #2: In a self-reliant age, Christian community must be mediated by Christ alone. Christian fellowship requires more than gratitude to be experienced. It needs a mediator. The minimum number for Christian life together is not two but three. Who is the third party in relationships that are genuinely Christian? "Christian community means community through Jesus Christ and in Jesus Christ."[22] But isn't Christ just a mediator between God and humanity? For Bonhoeffer, Christ mediates our relationship with both God and our fellow believers. How does Christ mediate between my brother or sister and me? Bonhoeffer's reply is that Christ is the mediator of Christian fellowship in two ways. "It means, first, that a Christian needs others because of Jesus Christ. It means, second, that a Christian comes to others only through Jesus Christ."[23]

First, Christ as our mediator leads us into community. No Christian can have Christ alone, apart from his body. I need Christ to save and justify me. Only he is able to do that. But for the faith to believe in Christ I need community.[24] As Christ draws me to himself, he first draws me to the community in which his name is proclaimed, his Word is believed and his Spirit is active. Because I need Jesus, I need others who can bring me to Jesus. Thus Jesus mediates Christian community by creating within us a need for the fellowship that will draw us closer to the mediator.

Each of us needs others because "the Christ in his own heart is weaker than the Christ in the word of his brother; his own heart is uncertain, his brother's is sure."[25] What this means is that my own confession of Christ as Savior and Lord will seem weaker to me than my brother's confession of Christ. When I speak of Christ, I am conscious of my internal doubt, fear, hesitations, sin and unbelief. The knees of my soul knock in trembling uncertainty when I speak of Christ. But when my brother speaks of Christ, I cannot feel his fear or see his trembling heart or sense his struggling faith. I can only hear his words, and they penetrate to my soul with a confidence and certainty that my own words never could. Therefore my search for faith in Christ leads me to Christian community where "the Christ in my heart," weak and tentative though it may be, is made strong by the "Christ in the word of my brother." I need others because of my need for Christ.

This leads to a second way in which Christ is the mediator of Christian fellowship. Not only do I need others because I need Christ, but also I need Christ in order to truly come into fellowship with others. I need Christ to stand between me and my brother or sister.

But surely this is an exaggeration. If I want a little Christian fellowship, I just get off my duff and head down to the local church or call up a believing friend and go out for coffee. Isn't it as simple as that? Bonhoeffer says no. "Without Christ we should not know God. . . . But without Christ we would also not know our brother. . . . The way is blocked by our own ego." What this means is that even though I may be in physical and even relational proximity to my fellow believer, there is an inward barrier that keeps us apart. I am too worried about my own ego, how I appear to him, what he must think of me and so on to ever really know him or be truly known by him. I keep tripping over my ego. But the picture is completely different when I am with my brother and consciously recognize the presence of Christ.

When I sense a brother's criticism, contempt or rejection, it does not have to hit me directly. Christ stands between us. He put this relationship together and absorbs my brother's criticism of me. When I become critical of my brother and find myself filled with accusation and anger, Christ confronts me and reminds me that he is the advocate for my brother. He commands me to pour my anger and accusation not on my brother but on his own head. He absorbs my criticisms of my brother and shields my brother's criticisms of me. No matter how deserved such criticism of one another may be, they are distorted criticisms if they leave Christ out of the equation.

Thus Christ is the mediator not only between God and human beings but also between one human being and another. "Our community with one another consists solely in what Christ has done to both of us."[26] If Christ is allowed to mediate my relationships within the church, he will lead me to a variety of people in ways that will surprise me, thus averting the kind of tribalism that would lead me to associate only with "my kind of people."

Losing the Ideal

Principle #3: In a world addicted to ideology, Christian community must not be based on an ideal of community. Bonhoeffer issues a warning to believers who try to bring into their fellowship pleasant dreams of past community. "Someone who wants more than what Christ has established does not want Christian brotherhood. He is looking for some extraordinary social experience which he has found elsewhere." If I enter a church fellowship and complain about the coldness of the people or the lack of greeters at the door or the absence of anyone I can really pour out my heart to, I have done something that is far more destructive than being cold or failing to show friendliness. I have created an idol of past experiences of fellowship, and without letting Christ mediate an entirely new experience of Christian community, I have condemned the new situation with all the arrogance of a Pharisee. Beware the acids of idealism, warns Bonhoeffer, for "he who loves his dream of a community more than the Christian community itself becomes a destroyer of the latter, even though his personal intentions may be ever so honest and earnest and sacrificial."[27]

Bonhoeffer even goes as far as saying that there is value in being initially disappointed by the quality of Christian fellowship in a church. Christ may be leading us to that experience of disappointment in order to dethrone the idols of community that we have forged from memory or from theory. "Thus the very hour of disillusionment with my brother becomes incomparably salutary, because it so thoroughly teaches me that neither of us can ever live by our own words and deeds, but only by that one Word and Deed which really binds us together—the forgiveness of sins in Jesus Christ."[28] Disappointment with my fellow believers forces me to seek the mediator of genuine, satisfying Christian life together, Jesus Christ.

Human Love Is Not the Basis

Principle #4: In a humanistic age Christian community must not be based on human love. Bonhoeffer was suspicious of the love he saw in the Nazi movement—love of country, love of power, love of one's own kind. Such tribal love may appear at first to be a thing of beauty, but over time its ugliness is revealed. For this reason Bonhoeffer distrusted direct fellowship between believers based on human love alone. What this means is that any fellowship that is based merely on mutual attraction or mutual benefit and not mediated by Christ is sub-Christian. Such fellowship will eventually be destructive for one of two reasons. Either it will exclude others who are not sufficiently attractive or beneficial, or it will fail over time as fellow believers lose their attractiveness or apparent benefit to me. Human love will not do.

Another kind of love is needed that comes from above—a love for the unlovely mediated by Christ.

In the community of the Spirit there burns the bright love of brotherly service, *agape;* in human community of spirit there glows the dark love . . . of *eros.* In the former there is ordered, brotherly service, in the latter disordered desire for pleasure; in the former humble subjection to the brethren, in the latter humble yet haughty subjection of a brother to one's own desire.[29] Bonhoeffer is concerned about the possibility of personality cults if an unmediated relationship with one's brother or sister is sought. He saw too much of this in the German Christian movement to regard it as merely a theoretical threat:

In the community of the Spirit, the Word of God alone rules; in the human community of spirit there rules, along with the Word, the man who is furnished with exceptional powers, experience, and magical, suggestive capacities. There God's Word alone is binding; here, besides the Word, men bind others to themselves. There all power, honor, and dominion are surrendered to the Holy Spirit; here the spheres of power and influence of a personal nature are sought and cultivated.[30]

In genuine Christian community the Spirit governs with innocence and simplicity, but where misdirected human love governs, it is through psychological techniques and manipulation that dehumanizes.[31]

We can be easily deceived by human love, imagining it to be the love of Christ. This happens because human love often "surpasses genuine Christian love in fervent devotion and visible results. It speaks the Christian language with overwhelming and stirring eloquence," but it is the love condemned by Paul in 1 Corinthians 13:3.[32] The true evil of human love is its desire to push Christ to the sidelines of fellowship in order that I may connect directly with the brother or sister.

Human love is directed to others for their own sake; spiritual love loves them for Christ's sake. Human love seeks direct contact with the other persons; it loves them not as free persons but as those whom it binds to itself. It wants to gain, to capture by every means; it uses force. It desires to be irresistible, to rule.[33]

When the selfish agenda and manipulative techniques of one's Christian brother and sisters are discovered, as they eventually will be, the fellowship is destroyed. We withdraw in distrust from Christian community, fearing that intimacy will mean exploitation.

The only salvation for the Christian community when the masquerade of human love has been exposed is to return to Christ as the mediator of our relationships.

Jesus Christ stands between the lover and the others he loves.
. . . Because Christ stands between me and others, I dare not desire direct fellowship with them. As only Christ can speak to me in such a way that I may be saved, so others, too, can be saved only by Christ himself. This means that I must release the other person from every attempt of mine to regulate, coerce, and dominate him with my love. . . . Because Christ has long since acted decisively for my brother, before I could begin to act, I must leave him his freedom to be Christ's; I must meet him only as the person he already is in Christ's eyes.[34]

Fellowship is his to maintain or dissolve as he bids. Christ is the bridge to others but also the barrier preventing fallen *eros* from devouring one another.

Because of Jesus Christ we must not allow fellowship to be sundered by a separatistic spirit: "Life together under the Word will remain sound and healthy only where it . . . understands itself as being a part of the one, holy, catholic, Christian church, where it shares actively and passively in the sufferings and struggles and promise of the whole church." Because Christ stands between me and the church, he leads me to suffer with it in its weakness and to work patiently for its healing and reformation.[35]

Individualism in Community

Principle #5: In an age of selfism and tribalism, the only individualism that is safe is in Christian community, and the only Christian community that is safe is that which allows individualism. Bonhoeffer has a prescription that seems tailor-made for postmodern times. In postmodern culture a radical self-centeredness leads one to seek a subculture where the self can "truly belong." But often the tribe demands a high price for belonging. Frequently the individual must give over her individuality to the group—or retain her individuality and leave the group.

Christian fellowship must never succumb to these twin dangers of an arrogant individualism and an oppressive communalism. When Christ is consciously asked to mediate our experience of Christian fellowship, he leads us to a third way. Bonhoeffer describes this alternative path.

"Let him who cannot be alone beware of Christian community."[36] We must be able to be alone with God through Christ and find our needs satisfied in him, or else we become a burden and parasite on the Christian community, sucking the life out of fellowship because we have made it an idolatrous substitute for God. We must learn to be alone with Christ, to find our sufficiency in him, before we can become a constructive and contributing member of the fellowship.

But there is another side to this third way: "Let him who is not in community beware of being alone."[37] This is the necessary corollary to the above rule. An independent spirit that needs no one and prefers self-reliance to radical reliance on the body of Christ is a spirit that is in danger. Thus "only in the fellowship do we learn to be rightly alone and only in aloneness do we learn to live rightly in the fellowship."[38]

Disciplined Humility

Principle #6: In an arrogant age, the Christian community must humbly practice the disciplines that will make it strong in Christ. Christ alone is able to lead us to this balance between a holy individualism and a holy communalism. As in all of the five principles of Christian community, Christ alone is the key. But what specific disciplines should I practice to live out these principles and bring Christ into the center of community? Bonhoeffer gets very practical in *Life Together* and describes a wide variety of disciplines that will cultivate, prepare for, deepen or heal the fellowship. I can only list these twenty disciplines, but you should get the idea that's there is a great deal we can do, in glad dependence on Christ, to promote Christian fellowship.

In chapter two of *Life Together* Bonhoeffer mentions six corporate disciplines that cultivate Christian community: (1) Christ-centered meditation on the Psalms, (2) Scripture reading, (3) singing together, (4) praying together, (5) eating together and (6) working together. In chapter three he lists five personal disciplines that should be practiced in solitude to prepare us for community: (1) solitude and silence, (2) meditation, (3) private prayer, (4) intercession for others and (5) private affirmation of the community in solitude (whereby one affirms the others in one's heart and before the Lord when they are not present).

In chapter four Bonhoeffer lists seven interpersonal disciplines that deepen Christian community: (1) the ministry of holding one's tongue, (2) the ministry of meekness, (3) the ministry of listening, (4) the ministry of helpfulness, (5) the ministry of bearing and sustaining one another, (6) the ministry of proclaiming the Word to one another and (7) the ministry of authority, whereby we submit to leaders who practice the other six ministries for the good of the community.

Finally, in the closing chapter of *Life Together* Bonhoeffer talks about two additional disciplines that serve a special function. Beyond the disciplines that cultivate Christian community and the disciplines of solitude that prepare us for community, there are two disciplines that repair Christian community: confession of sin and Communion.

"In confession the breakthrough to new life occurs. Where sin is hated, admitted, and forgiven, there the break with the past is made."[39] Such confession of our sins one to another is based on the theology of the cross. Because "the cross of Christ destroys all pride," we will not be able to "find the cross of Jesus if we shrink from going to the place where it is to be found, namely, the public death of the sinner. And we refuse to bear the cross when we are ashamed to take upon ourselves the shameful death of the sinner in confession."[40]

When we have confessed to God and one another, we can turn to the final and most joyous of all the disciplines of community: Communion.

The day of the Lord's Supper is an occasion of joy for the Christian community. Reconciled in their hearts with God and the brethren, the congregation receives the gift of the body and blood of Jesus Christ, and, receiving forgiveness, new life and salvation. It is given new fellowship with God and men. The fellowship of the Lord's Supper is the superlative fulfillment of Christian fellowship. . . . Here the community has reached its goal. Here joy in Christ and his community is complete.[41]

In light of Christ and his cross, which alone can produce true community, even a love for one's enemies, Bonhoeffer feels constrained to paraphrase Psalm 133:1: "Behold, how good and how pleasant it is for brethren to dwell together *through Christ.*"[42] Only when Christ stands between us are we safe from the ravages of our own egos, agendas, idealism and fears. "Through him alone do we have access to one another, joy in one another, and fellowship with one another."[43]

Using Bonhoeffer's Concept of Community

Though he was no Indiana Jones, Dietrich Bonhoeffer helped steer the church through the selfism and cruel tribalism of the Nazi era by laying out a plan for genuine Christian community. We have explored that great idea in this chapter. I repeat it once again: For Bonhoeffer, *the key to Christian community is learning to let Christ be the mediator of our relationships.* The question now is, how do we make use of this idea and its principles in building our fellowship?

Use #1: Practice the disciplines of Christian community. Richard Foster's bestselling *Celebration of Discipline* testifies to the hunger that exists within the Christian community for more disciplined lives.[44] The success of the Promise Keepers movement points in the same direction. Groups and classes within the church would do well to study *Life Together* and examine in detail Bonhoeffer's twenty disciplines of Christian community. I once taught at a seminary that required first-year students to study *Life Together* in small groups led by faculty members. It was my first exposure to the book, and it is an experience I'm glad I didn't miss. Something similar may benefit your church, organization or family.

Use #2: Appropriate the good and fight the bad within postmodernism. Christians can learn from postmodernism. The postmodernist believes that reason is inadequate. So does the orthodox Christian. The postmodernist feels that everyone should have a voice in a world without consensus. This means that Christian orthodoxy has a right to be heard. Postmodernism has a new openness to history, something that was not true about the old modernity. Christianity is rooted in history and has a strong orientation to history. These are areas of agreement that should be nurtured.

We must, however, oppose the fragmentation and tribalization of community that are a necessary outcome of postmodern ideas. We must reemphasize a biblical model of community, as Bonhoeffer attempted to do, if we are going to survive the balkanization of culture and society occurring around us.

This may mean revisiting old and trusted ideas of ministry. For all the good in church-growth ideology, we must develop more critical skills in applying its program. The most questionable of its methods is the homogeneous unit principle.[45] The idea that we should create monocultural churches may have been safe advice in the more or less unified 1950s and 1960s. But in the tribalized 1990s that advice must be critically reexamined. We can get away with tribalized churches only for a short time, and then we experience the law of diminishing returns. We begin to look exactly like the world and can offer no hope or redemptive alternative.

Decision-makers may forge creative small group strategies to meet the needs of particular groups of people in the church. But above these small groups must be unifying congregations and celebrations, as Peter Wagner recommends.[46]

Use #3: Renew the theological foundations of community. Gene Veith recommends this strategy to the church, calling it the "confessional option."[47] Its roots are in Germany's confessing church of the 1930s: "The churches that resisted the regime of Adolf Hitler, that first postmodernist state, referred to themselves as the 'confessional' churches. They confessed their faith against a syncretic church and against the police state, taking their stand on the Word of God and Christian doctrine, as expressed in their historic confessions of faith."[48]

While admitting that a new emphasis on doctrinal Christianity could backfire, Veith believes the advantages outweigh the disadvantages:

Confessionalism should not mean "dead orthodoxy," the insistence on some kind of doctrinal purity at the expense of a warm, personal faith. The goal should be "live orthodoxy," a faith that is both experiential and grounded in truth, with room for both the feelings and the intellect. At times in church history doctrine has been overemphasized, but that will hardly be a danger in a society whose every tendency is to deny truth altogether.[49]

We need to restore more than just theological systems. We need to recover an authentic theology of the cross that penetrates our hearts. Erwin Lutzer reminds us that "the battle is not so much between church and state as it is within our own hearts. If Christ has all of us, if the Cross stands above politics and the world as Bonhoeffer has reminded us, we shall overcome regardless of the cost."[50] Luther's theology of the cross, described in an earlier chapter, can help us recover this perspective.

A resource that decision-makers can use for raising the theological literacy of their people is CURE (Christians United for Reformation). Under the leadership of Michael Horton an impressive and entertaining series of books, tapes, magazines and videos have been produced to help restore just the kind of confessional Christianity that seems most needed to face the challenge of postmodernism.[51]

Use #4: Restore biblical literacy as an aid to community. George Lindbeck has observed that "until recently, most people in traditionally Christian countries lived in the linguistic and imaginative world of the Bible."[52] Not only did this biblical literacy serve a redemptive function; it shaped the entire culture of the West. The decline of biblical literacy has created a consequent crisis in literature, political discourse and popular culture. We have lost the common imagination, common language and common pool of values previously provided by the Bible. We have lost the language of community. "Whether a society can survive under these conditions," muses Lindbeck, "is open to question."[53]

The church must relearn the Bible in order to be faithful to its Lord as well as a renewing cultural force in society. "God has promised to be with his people as judge and savior both in the catacombs and on the throne," writes Lindbeck, "and for either of these destinies believers need a mastery of their native tongue which is at the moment fast disappearing." Lindbeck concludes that if the church is to be renewed and make an impact on postmodern culture, "relearning the language of Zion is imperative."[54]

This may involve overhauling the Sunday-school curriculum of the church. Individual believers should be encouraged to read the Bible through in a year. The popular Walk Through the Bible seminars should be encouraged at your church. Biblical literacy is crucial for the renewal of Christian community as well as cultural preservation.

Use #5: Engage in civil disobedience. In *Hitler's Cross* Erwin Lutzer meditates on the lessons today's American church can learn from the churches under Nazism. One of the most important concerns the limits of patriotism:

> We must support our government, but we must be ready to criticize it or even defy it when necessary. Patriotism is commendable when it is for a just cause. Every nation has the right to defend itself, the right to expect the government to do what is best for its citizens. However, if the German church has taught

us the dangers of blind obedience to government, we must eschew the mindless philosophy "My country, right or wrong."[55] In mounting a movement of civil disobedience, the principles of passive resistance must be adhered to. There is no place for violence in the name of Christ. We also must avoid the temptation to identify the cause of Christ with any political party or agenda. Lutzer warns,

> Some political activists have filled the Christian bottle with a strategy for political reform. Salvation, it appears, is selecting conservatives to national and local office. Important though this might be, we must always remember that God is neither Republican nor Democrat. When the Cross is wrapped in the flag of a political party, it is always distorted or diminished.[56]

Use #6: Revitalize the celebration of the Lord's Supper. Whether you are from a high-church or low-church background, there is value in rediscovering the Lord's Communion. We don't need more ritual, but we do need more depth of experience and insight into the meaning of this communion with Christ and one another. As Bonhoeffer believed: "The fellowship of the Lord's Supper is the superlative fulfillment of Christian fellowship. . . . Here joy in Christ and his community has reached its goal."[57]

East Glenville Community Church, under the leadership of the Reverend Ron Sylvester, changed its monthly Communion service. During this simple service the traditional message is set aside, and a time of mutual confession and praise prepares the people for the pledges of forgiveness and new life to be given in the Lord's Supper. The celebration of the Lord's Supper has taken on new meaning.

In the last Indiana Jones movie the object of the quest is the holy grail, the cup that Jesus Christ used in that first Communion. Both the Nazis and Jones want the cup because of its healing powers. Near the end of the movie, Jones's father is shot by a Nazi officer and lies dying. Jones finds the grail and brings it back to his father. He fills the grail with water and pours it on his father's wound. Miraculously, the wound fades away and his father's life is saved.

In postmodern times, when the wounds within our culture and

our institutions are deep and perhaps terminal, the power of the sacrificial death of Christ, symbolized by both Christian Communion and Christian community, can be a medicine for great healing. Let's pour it on and watch the weary wounds of a postmodern world fade before the healing wounds of Christ.

For Discussion
1. Read Matthew 18:20, which talks about Christ's presence in the midst of believers. I have often taken Christ's presence in Christian community to be that of a passive observer. Bonhoeffer has challenged me to see Christ present as an active mediator of Christian community. Which of Bonhoeffer's principles point to this truth?

2. Which of the six suggested uses might enable your church to experience Christ more powerfully as the active mediator of Christian community? What additional applications do you see of Bonhoeffer's principles? What steps could be taken to implement these ideas?

For Further Reading
The most authoritative life of Bonhoeffer is Eberhard Bethge, *Dietrich Bonhoeffer* (New York: Harper & Row, 1977). Bonhoeffer's ideas on Christian community are presented in his *Life Together* (San Francisco: Harper & Row, 1954). A classic of Christian living that also contains wisdom about living in community is Bonhoeffer's *The Cost of Discipleship* (1937; reprint New York: Macmillan, 1963).

EPILOGUE
From Vision to Decision

Firstirst Presbyterian Church, Quincy, made a series of decisions in the late 1960s that led it to growth and health in the decades that followed. The words Stephen Brown spoke to the church in 1967 are still valid today: "Every church, at one time or another, stands at the crossroads of its church life. One road leads to mediocrity, frustration and failure. The other leads to greatness, fulfillment, and the advance of the Kingdom of God. I believe that now is our time of decision."[1]

The decisions that we make in our churches, our families and our organizations will determine which of these two roads we travel. The path of mediocrity, frustration and failure needs no atlas. The failure to think, plan, wrestle with the Word or evaluate automatically puts us on the path of mediocrity. This book has sought to map out the other road. The path of "greatness, fulfillment, and the advance of the Kingdom of God" comes by making decisions that are based on the best ideas available. Great decisions flow out of great ideas.

But one question remains to be addressed before we conclude

this study. How do you take great ideas, such as we have looked at in this book, and make them live in your home, church or organization? Richard Neustadt and Ernest May in their provocative *Thinking in Time: The Uses of History for Decision Makers* advise decision-makers to identify a few useful mini-methods rather than find an elaborate twelve- (or twenty-) step process to make "bulletproof" decisions. "We make no pretense of organizing a capital-M Methodology," they write. For busy leaders a better approach is to define some "mini-methods" that are "intended to be easily remembered and applied for short times on short notice, as befits men and women at work."[2]

I'd like to suggest seven mini-methods to help busy leaders and heads of families use the ideas of church history to make better decisions. Though the methods I will suggest are generally different from those suggested by Neustadt and May, my methods and theirs are based on a methodological common denominator: "Enlightening questions are the point of every method we propose." If these mini-methods slow you down long enough to use a little more imagination, a little more theology, a little more analysis in your decision-making, then they will have served their purpose.

The point is not to turn you, the decision-maker, into the managerial equivalent of a Babe Ruth or a Ted Williams. But even marginal improvement in decision-making, like marginal improvement in baseball, can lead to a big payoff. There is only a 10 or 12 percent difference between a baseball team that wins the pennant with ninety wins and one that finishes in the mediocre middle with eighty wins. Just one more win in every fifteen games can separate the great team from the mediocre one. If these mini-methods offer you even marginal improvement in your decision-making, then, they may mean the difference between spending your time on the "path of greatness" and spinning your wheels on the road to "mediocrity, frustration, and failure."

Mini-method #1: Put First Things First
Identify God's mission for your family, church or organization. In

an earlier chapter I quoted Tom Telford on the folly of leading without an overall plan. Do you remember his words? Leading without a clear mission statement is "like the guy who shoots an arrow into the wall and draws a bull's eye around the arrow. He then claims that he hit the target." The way to avoid that kind of leadership style is to start out with a written mission statement that embodies God's call for your church, agency or home.

Stephen Covey tells the story of Viktor Frankl, an Austrian psychologist who survived Hitler's death camps. As Frankl watched the inmates around him and wondered where they got their will to live, he made an important discovery that would shape his own future as a psychologist. He concluded that health, vitality, family life, intelligence and survival skills, as important as they may be, were not the most important factors in determining survival. "The single most significant factor, he realized, was a sense of future vision—the impelling conviction of those who were to survive that they had a mission to perform, some important work left to do."[3] Covey concluded from this that formulating a personal or organizational vision statement is one of the most powerful things decision-makers can do to help the people they lead. When that vision is shared and treasured by others in the group, wonderful things can happen. Individual strengths can be directed toward a common goal, and tremendous synergy can be unleashed.

As our family of four has traveled back and forth from Africa over our career as missionaries, it has not always been easy to define where home is. Each of us feels the occasional pangs of rootlessness. One thing that has helped us develop alternative roots is our family mission statement. We discuss this mission periodically. Every so often we update it in light of what God seems to be telling us as a family. When decisions must be made, we review our mission statement to see which course of action fits best. It has given us a higher sense of purpose and direction than we would otherwise have had. It has helped me guide the family in the direction that we all feel God has called us.

Identify God's mission for your family, church or organization. The mission statement is one of the best tools a decision-maker can have.[4]

Mini-method #2: Think Classic

Put the ten great ideas into four classic categories and move forward. The church down through the ages has often used four classic marks to describe what it is to be and do in the world. By "classic" I don't mean "old and moldy." I mean that which is always relevant and never out of date. The true church, the ancients said, is *one, holy, catholic* and *apostolic,* and I believe the best decision-making is based on these four classic marks. These marks have been understood in a host of different ways down through church history. The best explanation I can give of them is that they describe four different ways of loving God and others.

Oneness speaks of loving God's people, using our gifts to minister to one another in the name and power of Christ. It also involves an interdependent relationship with like-minded churches.

Holiness means loving God's person. This involves delighting in God as life's greatest treasure and pleasure. Its supreme expression is found in "being satisfied with all that God is for us in Jesus."[5] From this delight and satisfaction in God flows a life of worship and righteousness.

Catholicity means loving God's mission. The church has no right to be local, parochial or tribal. Since God's salvation is for all people in all places in all ages, his church must embrace the same diversity. *Catholic* means "whole" or "general" as opposed to that which is narrow and exclusive. To be catholic is therefore to be evangelistic and mission-oriented. It means loving God's mission to save the lost and gather his church.

Apostolic means loving God's truth. This involves believing, professing and proclaiming that Christ is Lord over sin, death and redemption. This fourth mark is not just one alongside the others. It is the master mark that gives shape to all the others, as figure 6 illustrates.

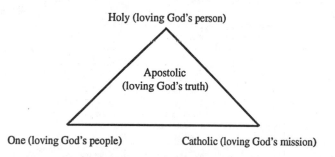

Holy (loving God's person)

Apostolic
(loving God's truth)

One (loving God's people)   Catholic (loving God's mission)

Figure 6. **The four marks of the church and the centrality of apostolicity**

Classic church growth occurs when a church moves forward in each of these four marks. Church history can be a valuable ally in this growth, because it presents examples of the four marks in action. The ten ideas explored in this book are all ways of moving ahead in one or more of the marks. The ideas that stress apostolicity have slightly more significance due to the fact that apostolicity shapes the other marks: the gospel creates the church. The table on page 220 relates the ten ideas to these four classic marks.

Classic decision-making involves planning activities and choosing options that will move the church forward in one or more of the four marks. The ten ideas represent specific ways to do that. As you develop a mission statement for your organization or church, think of ways to incorporate the four marks in the wording. By using such classic categories you are choosing an approach that helps you connect with the great ideas of the past. Thinking in classic terms is another powerful tool for the decision-maker who wants to head down the path of greatness.

Mini-method #3: What's the Story?
Learn to ask, "What's the story?" not "What's the problem?"[6] We can make better decisions if we learn to ask better questions. When a crisis occurs, we're generally tempted to ask, "What's the problem?" The answer we get to this question is not always an accurate description of the problem. More often than not it will be some-

Mark of the church	*One:* loving God's people (fellowship, mutual ministry, cooperation with other churches)	*Holy:* loving God's person (worship) and law (morality)	*Catholic:* loving God's mission to the world (evangelism, missions, discipleship and service)	*Apostolic:* loving God's truth (preaching, teaching, believing the gospel)
Biblical basis	Burroughs on denominationalism; Bonhoeffer on community; Wesley on discipleship	Calvin on Christian life; Baxter on delighting in God; Edwards on revival	Wilberforce on social action; Carey on global missions	Luther on the cross; Perkins on conversion and assurance
Appropriate activities	Small groups, one-on-one discipleship, Sunday school, youth groups, support and recovery groups, regional fellowships, denominational fellowships, decision-making, planning, leading, organizing	Public worship, family worship times, devotional disciplines, spiritual retreats, prayer concerts, days of repentance and confession	Voluntary societies, marches and demonstrations, mission festivals, Bible translation work, education, crosscultural evangelism, training leaders	Preaching, teaching, evangelism, writing theological education, counseling, exhorting group Bible study, personal Bible study, reading Christian literature

body's suggestion for action.

If the Smiths leave the church and you ask Mr. Smith what the problem was, you might get a little discourse on how you should have preached better, visited more often or been better with the youth. But if you ask a better question like "What's the story?" you may get a more illuminating answer. Mr. Smith may describe a sequence of events that led up to the departure of his family. One event in that sequence—the rebellion of his teenage son—may illuminate the real reason for the departure and guide you in deciding what to do regarding the Smiths.

Before you can adequately determine which of the ten great ideas relates most directly to the needs of your church or organization, you need to have a sense of the "story" that has preceded you. Make a time line of key events. Ask the six journalist questions—who, what, where, when, how, why. List the "cast of characters" who have shaped what your church is today. Such a historical understanding of the "little story" of your situation will help you decide which of the "big stories" of church history is the most relevant to current needs.

Mini-method #4: The Power of Prayer Goals

Set annual goals for prayer and action. Praying is one of the most important things a decision-maker can do. To focus your prayer in a way that harnesses the power of your mission statement and thinks in terms of the classic marks, establish prayer goals for your organization for the six- to twelve-month period ahead. By spending a few hours with your leadership team you can generate a list of very focused goals for classic growth that can become a regular agenda for prayer and action.

Use the four marks as categories. Keep your list balanced. Think of the key areas of your life or agency. Do you have goals that cover most of these areas, or are all the goals bunched around one or two chronic areas? Keep the list to ten or fewer if you can. Too many goals may be unwieldy, and less may actually get done.

My friend Randy MacFarland used this mini-method effectively as both a pastor and a seminary dean. He would gather his leadership team at a retreat center once a year and would pray and brainstorm about the prayer goals for the year. The lists that emerged would be typed up and put on cards to be kept at hand for prayer and guidance in decision-making. I have tried to follow his practice and feel that it has helped me make better, more prayerful decisions.

Mini-method #5: Baby Steps to Greatness

Use a weekly worksheet. Do you remember the Bill Murray movie *What About Bob?* Murray's character becomes the psychiatric patient of the doctor played by Richard Dreyfus, whose claim to fame is a new form of therapy summarized by the title of his runaway bestseller, *Baby Steps.* In ridiculous ways Murray applies the therapy of taking small steps to overcome paralyzing fears.

There is something I like about the wacky "baby step" philosophy lampooned in the movie. It contains a kernel of conventional wisdom that is hard to argue with: "Success is easy by the inch but hard by the yard." If you intend to make classic decisions and move your people along the path of greatness, you need a mechanism to help you do it inch by inch.

Stephen Covey mentions just such a mechanism in *First Things First*. He calls it the weekly worksheet. The basic idea is simple. Don't just plan your time; plan your priorities. As you make out your schedule for the week, ask yourself the following question: "In light of my life mission, what one or two things could I do this week in each of the key areas of my life that would bring the most quality results?" Plan those activities and build your week around them as much as possible. It will make you a better decision-maker.

Mini-method #6: Classic Crisis Management

Keep on track when the bottom falls out. At this point you may be thinking, *These mini-methods are great in theory, but he obviously doesn't know our church [or organization or family]; we spend so much time putting out fires that we don't have time for all this planning and goal setting.* I confess that I have felt that way myself. How can I work at getting a better handle on Luther, Edwards or Bonhoeffer when I've got papers to grade or a weekend retreat to plan and lead?

The key once again is your life mission or your organization's mission. In light of your mission statement and the wisdom of the four marks, determine whether this crisis is an opportunity to move ahead. If conflict breaks out in the congregation, couldn't that be an opportunity to work on one of the four marks? Could Bonhoeffer's concept of community give you any ideas to help you sort out the problem and move your people toward oneness? Crises don't have to be barriers to quality decision-making. They can also be bridges along the path of greatness.

Mini-method #7: The Splendor of Synergy

Affirm the differences and the problems. What all these mini-methods are aiming at are better results. We want better churches, better organizations, better families. When Christ brings together talented people, great ideas and moments of providential opportunity, surprising results can occur. Synergy can come about. *Synergy* "means that the whole is greater than the sum of its parts."[7] Synergy is the fruit of creative cooperation. Results exceed expectations when synergy takes place. Synergy occurs when two loaves and five fishes are swept up in the Master's hands and consecrated to God. "Synergy is the highest activity in all life."[8] Wise decision-makers know that synergy is not so much made as discovered.

When God brings together different people with different talents and personalities, friction can run high, but the potential for synergy also shoots up. Synergy means that a Wilberforce chooses not to work alone but to mix his efforts with the very different people who made up the Clapham Sect. Synergy is discovering that *denominationalism* is not a dirty word but that different churches working together under Christ can produce startling results. Synergy is Carey working with Ward and Marshman and producing one of the greatest models of mission in history. Synergy is Luther discovering that his very despair prepared him for the discovery of the gospel and the principle that Good Friday experiences lead not to disaster but to resurrection. Synergy is Edwards preaching his metaphysical sermons and to everybody's surprise, including his own, lighting the fires of revival. Synergy is Wesley using the ragtag converts of Methodism as pastors and group leaders and thereby forming one of the most dynamic church movements of all time. Synergy is Bonhoeffer discovering that rare jewel of Christian community while being hunted and hounded by the Gestapo.

A classic decision-maker seeks synergistic results that go off the charts, not the calculated results worked out by accountants. Every decision we make should be made in light of the synergistic promise of Romans 8:28, that all things, even the personality differences and the financial squeezes, work out for good when we love God and are pursuing his purpose.

Great decision-makers don't grumble and complain their way through life. They know something that those on the road to mediocrity don't. They know that differences between people can be ingredients in the recipe of synergy. Classic decision-makers affirm the differences in people and accept the difficulties of each situation. They believe that the only way to get surprising results is to put in surprising ingredients.

Of Walden and the Word of God

The path of greatness is not just for success junkies. I've talked much about decision-making and mini-methods, but as I finish writing this book, filled with its remote ideas and ancient wisdom, I feel a more personal urgency to experience these ten ideas than merely to become a better pastor or leader. I want more than success in the boardroom or the classroom. I want to live an authentic life. It is an urgency Henry David Thoreau expressed in *Walden* when he said he wanted to reduce life to its essence so that when he came to the end of his life he would not wake up and "find out that I had not lived."

My sense of urgency, my desire to make decisions that matter, that enhance my life and the lives of others for the greater glory of God, comes partly from a fear that too much of my life is spent drifting through the gray fog of dullness and deadness. It comes from a fear that in my fortysomething years on this planet I may have really lived only half of that time. It is a fear described well by Tim Bascom:

> I'm not satisfied with the quality of my life. Yes, I'm comfort-able—better off than the vast majority of human beings. But I'm not satisfied. Whole days go by, sometimes weeks, and they feel lost. It maddens me. I've been given so many years, maybe seventy-five, eighty-five if I'm fortunate, but so much of that time seems to go by in a fog. When I am done, I fear I will look back and find I lived only twenty years altogether. That the rest was just putting in time, like a hostage being chained and blindfolded, waiting.[9]

And so I end this journey into the past with two more bits of ancient wisdom for those who want to feel alive and awake as they grope their way toward the path of greatness. Thoreau once said, "Only that day dawns to which we are awake." He spoke well. We need great ideas to awaken us from our mental and spiritual slumbers.

But the Bible captures in a much better way the desire of my heart for you the decision-maker and for myself the historian. In words spoken by the apostle Paul, we approach the fire that burns behind each of the ten great ideas and the star that points to the ultimate vision that should drive every decision we make:

I pray that you, being rooted and established in love, may have power, together with all the saints, to grasp how wide and long and high and deep is the love of Christ, and to know this love that surpasses knowledge—that you may be filled to the measure of all the fullness of God. (Eph 3:17-19)

For Discussion

1. Which of the above mini-methods would help improve your decision-making the most? Why?

2. Review the chart of the four classic marks. Which suggested activities are you currently doing to build the four marks in your church? What additional activities could be undertaken?

Notes

Introduction
[1]John Rodman, "Back on the Road to Life: The Pilgrimage of First Presbyterian, Quincy," *New England Journal of Ministry,* June 1981, p. 34.
[2]Ibid., p. 35.
[3]Richard Neustadt and Ernest May, *Thinking in Time: The Uses of History for Decision Makers* (New York: Free Press, 1986), p. xi.
[4]George Barna, *The Power of Vision* (Ventura, Calif.: Regal, 1992), p. 33.
[5]Ibid., p. 122.

Chapter 1: A Vision for Truth
[1]George Barna, *Virtual America* (Ventura, Calif.: Regal, 1994). Reported in *The Christian Century,* December 14, 1994, p. 1185.
[2]David Wells, *God in the Wasteland* (Grand Rapids, Mich.: Eerdmans, 1994), p. 150.
[3]Mark Noll, *The Scandal of the Evangelical Mind* (Grand Rapids, Mich.: Eerdmans, 1994), p. 252.
[4]Alister McGrath, *Luther's Theology of the Cross* (Oxford: Blackwell, 1985), p. 1.
[5]Martin Luther, "Heidelberg Disputation," in *Luther: Early Theological Works,* ed. James Atkinson (Philadelphia: Westminster Press, 1962), p. 290.
[6]Paul Althaus, *The Theology of Martin Luther* (Philadelphia: Fortress, 1966), p. 27.
[7]Ibid.
[8]Luther, "Heidelberg," p. 291.
[9]Althaus, *Theology of Martin Luther,* p. 34.
[10]Luther, "Heidelberg," p. 291.
[11]Althaus, *Theology of Martin Luther,* p. 32.
[12]Ibid.
[13]Ibid., p. 33.
[14]Luther, "Heidelberg," p. 291.
[15]Ibid.
[16]McGrath, *Luther's Theology of the Cross,* p. 159.
[17]Alister McGrath, *The Mystery of the Cross* (Grand Rapids, Mich.: Zondervan, 1988), p. 161.
[18]McGrath, *Luther's Theology of the Cross,* p. 158.

[19]Quoted in McGrath, *Luther's Theology of the Cross,* p. 169. See also the German edition of Luther's works, referred to as the *Weimar Ausgabe (WA),* 5:176, 32-33: "Crux sola est nostra theologia."

[20]Althaus, *Theology of Martin Luther,* p. 30.

[21]McGrath, *Luther's Theology of the Cross,* p. 181.

[22]Ibid.

[23]William Willimon, "Turning an Audience into the Church," *Leadership* 15, no. 1 (Winter 1994): 30.

[24]Ibid.

[25]Ibid., p. 33.

[26]Wells, *God in the Wasteland,* p. 185.

[27]George Barna, *Absolute Confusion* (Ventura, Calif.: Regal, 1993), p. 89.

[28]Wells, *God in the Wasteland,* p. 213.

[29]Some churches have used an earlier book of mine, *Doing Theology with Huck and Jim: Parables for Understanding Doctrine* (Downers Grove, Ill.: InterVarsity Press, 1993), to raise the level of theological consciousness in the congregation. This book uses some of the approaches of narrative theology to make theology more accessible.

[30]Kayode Soyinka, "Archbishop Tutu," *Africa Today,* September/October 1995, pp. 7-8.

Chapter 2: A Vision for Spirituality

[1]Kim France, "Generation Ex," *Elle,* March 1994.

[2]Douglas Coupland, *Life After God* (New York: Pocket Books/Simon & Schuster, 1995). *Generation X* was published in 1991 by St. Martin's (New York).

[3]"The Search for the Sacred: America's Quest for Spiritual Meaning," *Newsweek,* November 1994.

[4]Paul Vitz, *Psychology as Religion: The Cult of Self-Worship,* 2nd ed. (Grand Rapids, Mich.: Eerdmans, 1981), p. 103.

[5]Ibid., p. 122.

[6]John Calvin, *Calvin's Commentaries,* ed. Joseph Hartounian (Philadelphia: Westminster Press, 1958), p. 52.

[7]On the international impact of Calvin see W. Stanford Reid, ed., *John Calvin: His Influence in the Western World* (Grand Rapids, Mich.: Zondervan, 1982).

[8]John Calvin, *Institutues of the Christian Religion,* ed. J. McNeill, trans. F. Battles, 2 vols. (Philadelphia: Westminster Press, 1960), 3.1.1. References to the *Institutes* usually contain three numbers separated by periods. The first number refers to one of the four books into which Calvin divided his *Institutes;* the second number is the chapter within the specific book; the third number refers to the section within the chapter. In the text that follows, numbers in parentheses refer thus to the *Institutes.*

[9]Wilhelm Niesel, *The Theology of Calvin* (Grand Rapids, Mich.: Baker Book House, 1980), p. 128.

[10]*Institutes,* quoted in François Wendel, *Calvin: Origins and Development of His Religious Thought* (1950; reprint Durham, N.C.: Labyrinth, 1987).

[11]Alister McGrath, *Roots That Refresh: A Celebration of Reformation Spirituality* (London: Hodder & Stoughton, 1991), p. 124.

[12]Calvin's discussion of each of the six petitions is in 3.20.34-49.

[13]James Means, *Effective Pastors for a New Century* (Grand Rapids, Mich.: Baker

Book House, 1993), p. 17.
[14]Steven Covey, *The Seven Habits of Highly Effective People* (New York: Fireside, 1990).
[15]Patrick Morley gives excellent advice and guidelines for such accountablity groups in *The Man in the Mirror* (Nashville: Thomas Nelson, 1992), pp. 287-89.
[16]Os Guinness, *The Gravedigger File* (Downers Grove, Ill.: InterVarsity Press, 1983), p. 85.
[17]Ibid., pp. 81-82.
[18]Gordon MacDonald, *Rebuilding Your Broken World* (Nashville: Thomas Nelson, 1988). See especially the seven principles of spiritual warfare laid out in chapter 17.

Chapter 3: A Vision for Unity
[1]David Barrett, *African Initiatives in Religion* (Nairobi: Uzima, 1971), p. 148.
[2]R. Omanson, "The Church," in *Evangelical Dictionary of Theology*, ed. Walter Elwell (Grand Rapids, Mich.: Baker Book House, 1984), p. 231.
[3]Lesslie Newbigin, *Foolishness to the Greeks: The Gospel and Western Culture* (Grand Rapids, Mich.: Eerdmans, 1986), p. 146.
[4]Hans Küng, *The Church* (Garden City, N.Y.: Doubleday/Image, 1976), p. 357.
[5]Ibid.
[6]Winthrop Hudson, *American Protestantism* (Chicago: University of Chicago Press, 1961), p. 34.
[7]Michael Boland, "Biographical Introduction," in Jeremiah Burroughs, *The Rare Jewel of Christian Contentment* (1648; reprint Edinburgh: Banner of Truth Trust, 1964), p. 11. Much of the biographical information found in this chapter is gleaned from Boland and from the *Dictionary of National Biography*, vol. 3 (Oxford: Oxford University Press, 1917-).
[8]Quoted in Hudson, *American Protestantism*, p. 40.
[9]Paraphrased in Boland, "Biographical Introduction," p. 11.
[10]Ibid., p. 13.
[11]Hudson, *American Protestantism*, p. 41.
[12]Ibid.
[13]Ibid., pp. 41-42.
[14]Ibid., p. 42.
[15]Ibid., p. 44.
[16]Ibid., pp. 42-43.
[17]Ibid., p. 44.
[18]I should mention a warning that Peter Wagner has sounded about the dangers of "cooperitis." His analysis of the failure of Key '73 is a valuable reminder that unity is a means to a greater end. We want the world to see our oneness in order to draw them to Christ. According to Wagner, Key '73 lost this perspective and made unity the goal at the expense of evangelism. See his discussion in *Your Church Can Grow* (Ventura, Calif.: Regal, 1976), pp. 168-69.

Chapter 4: A Vision for Assurance
[1]The sources on Perkins's life are minimal. The excellent summary in the *Dictionary of National Biography* (London: Oxford University Press, 1917-), 15:892ff., is based on the most reliable accounts. The earliest account of Perkins's life is Thomas Fuller, *Abel Redivivus* (London: William Tegg, 1867), which originally

appeared in the 1640s. Samuel Clarke treated Perkins in 1675 in his *Marrow of Ecclesiastical History,* as did Benjamin Brook a century later.
[2]A pensioner was someone who paid his "commons," that is, common expenses of the college. A sizer was a student who could not afford the commons and was forced to work off his expenses during his college career. A scholar held a privileged position: commons were waived in light of the student's exceptional academic promise.
[3]Quoted in Ian Breward, *The Work of Willam Perkins* (Appleford, U.K.: Sutton Courtenay, 1970), p. 7. The story that Perkins was a drunkard who became converted by overhearing a women alluding to him as "drunken Perkins" and holding him up as a terror to a child was apparently created by Benjamin Brook. There is no evidence in the earlier sources of Perkins's life that this is genuine.
[4]The religious background against which Perkins and Puritanism appear can be quickly sketched. Mary Tudor (1516-1558), proclaimed queen in 1553, reinstituted Catholicism. She executed Protestant leaders like Thomas Cranmer, Nicholas Ridley, Hugh Latimer—some three hundred martyrs in all. Thousands went into exile in Strasbourg, Frankfurt and Geneva. There was little mourning in England when Mary (affectionately known to history as "Bloody Mary") died in 1558. Her death led to the ascension of the popular Elizabeth I (1533-1603). The daughter of Anne Boleyn (Protestant wife of Henry VIII), Elizabeth favored Protestantism. Indeed, her legitimacy required Protestantism, because her mother's marriage to the king was not recognized by the papacy. The exiles returned to England hoping to establish the models of church reform they had seen in Europe and had been taught in the Edwardian years, when Martin Bucer and Peter Martyr Vermigli lectured at Cambridge. Elizabeth's actions disappointed these zealous reformers. Her Acts of Supremacy and Uniformity in 1559 created the famous "middle way" of Anglicanism, seasoning Protestant doctrine and practice with Catholic accents. Her theology of the church was largely determined by the Forty-two Articles of 1553, revised in 1563 as the Thirty-nine Articles. Both Catholics and the "hotter sort of Protestants" opposed the Elizabethan settlement.
[5]*Dictionary of National Biography,* 15:893.
[6]H. Porter, *Reformation and Reaction in Tudor Cambridge* (Cambridge: University of Cambridge Press, 1958), p. 290.
[7]Ibid., p. 268.
[8]For a discussion of this fourth branch of Puritanism and its history see William Haller, *The Rise of Puritanism* (New York: Columbia University Press, 1938).
[9]The four steps of true conversion are elaborated on by Perkins in his *Whole Treatise of Cases of Conscience.* This work is to be found in Thomas Merrill, ed., *William Perkins (1558-1602): His Pioneer Works on Casuistry* (Nieuwkoop, Netherlands: B. DeGraaf, 1966), pp. 103-7.
[10]Ibid., pp. 39-40.
[11]Ibid., p. 61.
[12]Ibid., p. 56.
[13]Quoted in Mark Shaw, "The Marrow of Practical Divinity," Ph.D. dissertation, Wesminster Theological Seminary, 1981, p. 161.
[14]Ibid., p. 164.
[15]Ibid., p. 171.
[16]James Means, *Effective Pastors for a New Century* (Grand Rapids, Mich.: Baker Book House, 1993), p. 63.

[17]Mark Shaw, "Drama in the Meeting House: The Concept of Conversion in the Theology of William Perkins," *Westminster Theological Journal* 45 (1983): 71.

Chapter 5: A Vision for Worship

[1]J. I. Packer, preface to Soli Deo Gloria edition of the *Directory*, n.p. Unless otherwise noted, all references to the *Christian Directory (CD)* are taken from this edition. I wish to thank Dr. Timothy Beougher for reading this chapter and offering helpful suggestions.

[2]From his *Poetical Fragments*, quoted in Geoffrey Nuttall, *Richard Baxter* (London: Nelson, 1965), p. 44.

[3]Samuel Clarke, ed., *Christan Directory*, abridged ed.(London: n.p., n.d.), p. iv.

[4]F. J. Powicke, *The Reverend Richard Baxter Under the Cross (1662-1691)* (London: Jonathan Cape, 1927), p. 24.

[5]Nuttall, *Richard Baxter*, p. 108.

[6]*CD*, p. 90.

[7]Ibid., p. 158.

[8]Ibid.

[9]Ibid., p. 138.

[10]Ibid., p. 142.

[11]Ibid., p. 139.

[12]Each of these points is mentioned in ibid., p. 138.

[13]Ibid., p. 139.

[14]Ibid., p. 140.

[15]Ibid.

[16]Ibid., p. 139.

[17]These meditations are in ibid., pp. 139-42.

[18]Robert Webber, ed., *The Renewal of Sunday Worship*, Complete Library of Christian Worship 3 (Nashville: Star Song, 1993).

Chapter 6: A Vision for Renewal

[1]The story of the fire station and the community church appeared in Charles Colson's *The Body* (Dallas: Word, 1992), pp. 11-28.

[2]Os Guinness, *The Gravedigger File* (Downers Grove, Ill.: InterVarsity Press, 1983), p. 51.

[3]Ibid., p. 52.

[4]Ibid., p. 51.

[5]Ibid., p. 49.

[6]Quoted in Colson, *The Body*, p. 31.

[7]Colson, *The Body*, p. 184.

[8]J. I. Packer, *A Quest for Godliness* (Wheaton, Ill.: Crossway, 1990), p. 316.

[9]Quoted by Ian Murray, *Jonathan Edwards* (Edinburgh: Banner of Truth Trust, 1987), p. xvii.

[10]John Piper, *The Supremacy of God in Preaching* (Grand Rapids, Mich.: Baker Book House, 1990), pp. 65-66.

[11]Ola Winslow, *Jonathan Edwards* (1940; reprint New York: Octagon, 1979), p. 2.

[12]Jonathan Edwards, *Works* (1834; reprint Edinburgh: Banner of Truth Trust, 1974), 1:428.

[13]Ibid., 1:536.

[14]Ibid., 1:277.

[15]Ibid., 1:120.
[16]Ibid., 2:224.
[17]Quoted in Packer, *Quest for Godliness*, pp. 313-14.
[18]Quoted in ibid., p. 314.
[19]*Works*, 2:266.
[20]Ibid.
[21]Quoted in Packer, *Quest for Godliness*, p. 326.
[22]Packer, *Quest for Godliness*, p. 317.
[23]Ibid., p. 318.
[24]*Works*, 1:372.
[25]Compare *Distinguishing Marks of a True Work of the Spirit of God*, in *Works*, 2:266-69.
[26]Joseph Tracy, *The Great Awakening* (1842; reprint Edinburgh: Banner of Truth Trust, 1976), p. ix.
[27]Quoted in T. Faust and C. H. Johnson, eds., *Jonathan Edwards: Selections* (New York: Hill and Wang, 1962), p. 106.
[28]See *Narrative of Surprising Conversions*, in *Works*, 1:350-53. On holiness and conversion see Murray's discussion in *Jonathan Edwards*, p. 261.
[29]Packer, *Quest for Godliness*, p. 311. So central was the Spirit to the work that Packer seeks to summarize Edwards's concept of revival in a single sentence that gives particular prominence to the Holy Spirit: "Revival is an extraordinary work of God the Holy Spirit reinvigorating and propagating Christian piety in a community" (ibid., p. 318).
[30]This is the twelfth sign of a true work of the Spirit in Edwards's *Religious Affections*, 1:314.
[31]*Works*, 1:609.
[32]*Works*, 1:605.
[33]Richard Lovelace, *Dynamics of Spiritual Life* (Downers Grove, Ill.: InterVarsity Press, 1979), p. 41.
[34]Timothy Jones, "Great Awakenings," *Christianity Today*, November 8, 1993, p. 25.
[35]George Barna, *The Power of Vision* (Ventura, Calif.: Regal, 1992), p. 32.
[36]John Piper, *Desiring God* (Portland, Ore.: Multnomah Press, 1986), p. 78.
[37]*Discipleship Journal*, issue 66, 1991.
[38]Compare Packer's critique of the Finney method of evangelism in *Quest for Godliness*, pp. 292ff.
[39]See Colson, *The Body*, p. 194.
[40]See Mark Shaw, *Doing Theology with Huck and Jim* (Downers Grove, Ill.: InterVarsity Press, 1993), for one example of a positive presentation of biblical truth that attempts to glorify God by showing him to be the source of all satisfaction and salvation.
[41]See John Piper, *The Supremacy of God in Preaching* (Grand Rapids, Mich.: Eerdmans, 1990), pp. 81-105.
[42]Richard Lovelace, *Renewal as a Way of Life* (Downers Grove, Ill.: InterVarsity Press, 1985), p. 173.
[43]Piper, *Supremacy of God*, p. 11.
[44]Patrick Johnstone, *Operation World*, 5th ed. (Grand Rapids, Mich.: Zondervan, 1993).
[45]Piper, *Supremacy of God*, p. 11.

Chapter 7: A Vision for Growth
[1]Bill Hull, *The Disciple Making Pastor* (Old Tappan, N.J.: Revell, 1988), p. 19.
[2]Ibid.
[3]Elton Trueblood, *The Best of Elton Trueblood: An Anthology* (Nashville: Impact, 1979), p. 34. Quoted in Hull, *Disciple Making Pastor,* p. 19.
[4]A. Skevington Wood, *The Inextinguishable Blaze* (Grand Rapids, Mich.: Eerdmans, 1968), p. 15.
[5]Ibid., p. 15.
[6]Described briefly in A. Skevington Wood, *The Burning Heart: John Wesley, Evangelist* (Minneapolis: Bethany Fellowship, 1978), p. 38.
[7]Howard Snyder, *The Radical Wesley* (Downers Grove, Ill.: InterVarsity Press, 1980), p. 14.
[8]For a discussion of the view that Wesley's Methodism saved England from a violent revolution see Bernard Simmel, *The Methodist Revolution* (New York: Basic Books, 1973).
[9]John Wesley, *Journal,* ed. Nehemiah Curnock (London: Epworth, 1938), 3:71.
[10]Ibid., 5:26.
[11]*The Nature, Design and General Rules of the United Societies,* quoted in Wood, *Burning Heart,* p. 190.
[12]Wood, *Burning Heart,* p. 190.
[13]See the description in Snyder, *Radical Wesley,* pp. 54-58.
[14]Wesley, *Journal,* 3:285.
[15]Snyder, *Radical Wesley,* p. 60.
[16]Ibid., pp. 59-60.
[17]Ibid., p. 60.
[18]Ibid., p. 63.
[19]Ibid., p. 64.
[20]Quoted in Wood, *Burning Heart,* p. 198.
[21]C. Peter Wagner, *Your Church Can Grow* (Ventura, Calif.: Regal, 1976), pp. 111-26.
[22]Ibid., p. 161.
[23]*Letters,* 5:344; quoted in Wood, *Burning Heart,* p. 186.
[24]Dietrich Bonhoeffer, *The Cost of Discipleship,* 2nd ed. (New York: Macmillan, 1959), pp. 46-47.

Chapter 8: A Vision for the Lost
[1]Paul Borthwick, *How to Be a World-Class Christian* (Wheaton, Ill.: Victor, 1991), pp. 52-53.
[2]See the analysis by Robert Coote, "Bad News, Good News: North American Protestant Overseas Personnel Statistics in Twenty-five-Year Perspective," *International Bulletin of Mission Research* 19, no. 1 (January 1995): 6ff. Coote observes that some of the decline was a result of the way agencies reported short-term missionary statistics, but he concedes that there was a significant decline in actual numbers of career and short-term missionary personnel.
[3]This is the thesis of Ian Murray in "William Carey: Climbing the Rainbow," *Evangelical Review of Theology* 17, no. 3 (July 1993): 365.
[4]I am using Carey's own statistical estimates as published in his *Enquiry into the Obligations of Christians to Use Means for the Conversion of the Heathens* (1792), reprinted in Timothy George, *Faithful Witness: The Life and Mission of William Carey* (Birmingham, Ala.: New Hope, 1991).

[5]Murray, "William Carey," p. 357.

[6]Ibid., p. 358.

[7]Quoted in George, *Faithful Witness*, p. 57.

[8]Jonathan Edwards, *Works* (1834; reprint Edinburgh: Banner of Truth Trust, 1974), 2:306, note.

[9]John Ryland Jr., quoted in Murray, "William Carey," p. 361.

[10]David Bebbington, in *Eerdmans Handbook to the History of Christianity*, ed. Tim Dowley (Grand Rapids, Mich.: Eerdmans, 1977), p. 548.

[11]Given in George Smith, *The Life of William Carey* (Edinburgh: T & T Clark, 1885), p. 129.

[12]Bebbington in *Eerdmans Handbook*, p. 548.

[13]John Watts, "Baptists and the Transformation of Culture," *Evangelical Review of Theology* 17, no. 3 (July 1993): 331.

[14]Murray, "William Carey," p. 363.

[15]"Form of Agreement" (1805), reprinted in Smith, *Life of William Carey*, p. 442.

[16]Ibid.

[17]Ibid., p. 444.

[18]Ibid., p. 441.

[19]The booklet is divided into five sections: (1) whether the Great Commission is binding on the church today (yes, because we still baptize), the disobedience of those who have gone into missions and the promise of the presence of Christ, (2) a history of previous mission action, (3) a statistical survey of the present state of the world, (4) answering objections about the practicality of missions (distance, uncivilized cultures, danger, difficulties of getting food and meeting daily needs, language barrier), (5) practical steps to promote missions (pray, form agencies and give financially).

[20]Bebbington in *Eerdmans Handbook*, p. 550.

[21]Carey, *Enquiry*, in George, *Faithful Witness*, pp. E54-55.

[22]Bebbington in *Eerdmans Handbook*, p. 550.

[23]"Form of Agreement," p. 448.

[24]Ibid., pp. 448-49.

[25]Ibid., p. 449.

[26]Watts, "Baptists and the Transformation of Culture," p. 333.

[27]"Form of Agreement," p. 447.

[28]Ibid.

[29]Ibid., p. 442.

[30]Frederick Downs, "Reflections on the Enculturation/Social Justice Issue in Contemporary Mission," *Evangelical Review* of Theology 17, no. 3 (July 1993): 321.

[31]"Form of Agreement," p. 443.

[00]Bruce Nicholls, "The Theology of William Carey," *Evangelical Review of Theology* 17, no. 3 (July 1993): 378.

[33]Lamin Sanneh, *Translating the Message* (Maryknoll, N.Y.: Orbis, 1989), p. 102.

[34]"Form of Agreement," p. 450.

[35]Ibid.

[36]Ibid., p. 443.

[37]Quoted in Borthwick, *How to Be a World-Class Christian*, p. 15.

[38]Paul Borthwick, *A Mind for Missions* (Colorado Springs, Colo.: NavPress, 1987).

[39]John Piper, *Let the Nations Be Glad: The Supremacy of God in Missions* (Grand Rapids, Mich.: Baker Book House, 1993), pp. 115-66.

[40]*Cultivating a Missions-Active Church* (Wheaton, Ill.: ACMC [Association of Church Missions Committees], 1988), p. 32.

[41]Ibid., p. 14.

[42]Quoted in ibid., p. 17.

Chapter 9: A Vision for Justice

[1]Concerned Evangelicals, *Evangelical Witness in South Africa: A Critique of Evangelical Theology by Evangelicals Themselves* (Dobsonville, South Africa: Concerned Evangelicals, 1986).

[2]For a discussion of these events see David Walker, "Radical Evangelicalism: An Expression of Evangelical Social Concern Relevant to South Africa," *Journal of Theology for Southern Africa*, March 1990.

[3]Ernest Marshall Howse, *Saints in Politics: The "Clapham Sect" and the Growth of Freedom* (London: George Allen and Unwin, 1953), p. 28.

[4]Ibid., p. 29.

[5]Ibid., p. 7.

[6]See the review of this heritage in Richard Lovelace, *Dynamics of Spiritual Life* (Downers Grove, Ill.: InterVarsity Press, 1979), pp. 357-81.

[7]Ibid., p. 381.

[8]Quoted in John Pollock, *Wilberforce* (1977; reprint Tring, U.K.: Lion, 1986), p. 27.

[9]Ibid., p. 7.

[10]Ibid., p. 11, note.

[11]Ibid., p. 11.

[12]Howse, *Saints in Politics*, p. 25.

[13]Ibid., pp. 80-81.

[14]Ibid., p. 46.

[15]Ibid., p. 183.

[16]Ibid., p. 120.

[17]Ibid., p. 152.

[18]William Wilberforce, *A Practical View of the Prevailing Religious System of Professed Christians in the Higher and Middle Classes in This Country Contrasted with Real Christianity* (1797; reprint London: SCM Press, 1958), p. 113, note.

[19]Ibid., p. 7.

[20]Ibid., p. 119.

[21]Ibid., p. 115.

[22]Ibid., p. 117.

[23]Ibid., p. 147.

[24]The name was given apparently in 1844 by Sir James Stephen in the *Edinburgh Review*.

[25]Howse, *Saints in Politics*, p. 7.

[26]Pollock, *Wilberforce*, p. 308.

[27]Ibid.

[28]Ibid., p. 307.

[29]Ibid., p. 257.

[30]Ibid., p. 258.

[31]Howse, *Saints in Politics*, p. 4.

[32]Ibid., p. 5.

[33]Lovelace, *Dynamics*, p. 370. Lovelace identifies Ford Brown and Charles Foster as two scholars who have advanced this view.

[34]Ibid., p. 370.
[35]Wilberforce, *Practical View*, p. 103.
[36]Ibid., p. 104.
[37]Ibid., p. 118.
[38]Howse, *Saints in Politics*, p. 181.
[39]Pollock, *Wilberforce*, p. 259.
[40]Ibid., p. 129.
[41]Howse, *Saints in Politics*, pp. 31-32.
[42]Ibid., p. 33.
[43]Ibid., p. 7.
[44]Charles Colson, *The Body* (Waco, Tex.: Word, 1992), p. 367.
[45]Ibid., p. 366.
[46]Ibid., pp. 368-69.
[47]Ibid., pp. 371-72.
[48]Ibid., pp. 370-71.
[49]Albert Wolters, *Creation Regained* (Grand Rapids, Mich.: Eerdmans, 1985), pp. 76-77.
[50]Ibid., pp. 296-97.
[51]Lovelace, *Dynamics*, pp. 364-75.
[52]Timothy L. Smith, *Revivalism and Social Reform in Mid-Nineteenth-Century America* (New York: Abingdon, 1957).
[53]Lovelace, *Dynamics*, p. 399.

Chapter 10: A Vision for Fellowship
[1]Gene Edward Veith, *Postmodern Times: A Christian Guide to Contemporary Thought and Culture* (Wheaton, Ill.: Crossway, 1994), p. 19.
[2]Quoted in James Sire, *Why Should Anyone Believe Anything at All?* (Downers Grove, Ill.: InterVarsity Press, 1994), p. 58.
[3]Philip Elmer-DeWitt, "Cyberpunk!" *Time*, February 8, 1993, p. 62; quoted in Veith, *Postmodern Times*, p. 144.
[4]Veith, *Postmodern Times*, p. 165.
[5]Ibid., p. 79.
[6]Ibid., p. 15.
[7]The phrase is from Francis Schaeffer.
[8]Eberhard Bethge, *Dietrich Bonhoeffer* (New York: Harper & Row, 1977), p. 20.
[9]Ibid., p. 22.
[10]Ibid., pp. 52-53.
[11]Ibid., p. 60.
[12]Ibid., p. 194.
[13]Ibid., p. 202.
[14]Ibid., p. 297.
[15]Ibid., p. 385.
[16]Ibid., pp. 389-90.
[17]Ibid., pp. 772-73.
[18]Ibid., p. 830.
[19]Ibid., p. 831.
[20]Dietrich Bonhoeffer, *Life Together* (San Francisco: Harper & Row, 1954), p. 17.
[21]Ibid., p. 20.
[22]Ibid., p. 21.

[23]Ibid.

[24]Ibid., pp. 22-23.

[25]Ibid., p. 23.

[26]Ibid., p. 25.

[27]Ibid., p. 27.

[28]Ibid., p. 28.

[29]Ibid., pp. 31-33.

[30]Ibid., p. 32.

[31]Ibid.

[32]Ibid., p. 34.

[33]Ibid.

[34]Ibid., p. 35.

[35]Ibid., p. 37.

[36]Ibid., p. 77.

[37]Ibid.

[38]Ibid., pp. 77-78.

[39]Ibid., p. 115.

[40]Ibid., p. 114.

[41]Ibid., p. 122.

[42]Ibid., p. 39.

[43]Ibid.

[44]Richard Foster, *Celebration of Discipline,* rev. ed. (San Francisco: Harper & Row, 1988).

[45]Compare C. Peter Wagner, *Your Church Can Grow* (Ventura, Calif.: Regal, 1976), chap. 8.

[46]Ibid., chap. 7.

[47]Veith, *Postmodern Times,* p. 216.

[48]Ibid., p. 219.

[49]Ibid., p. 220.

[50]Erwin Lutzer, *Hitler's Cross* (Chicago: Moody Press, 1995), p. 207.

[51]The phone number for CURE is (714) 956-2873.

[52]George Lindbeck, "The Church's Mission to Postmodern Culture," in *Postmodern Theology: Christian Faith in a Pluralist World,* ed. Frederick B. Burnham (San Francisco: Harper & Row, 1989), p. 38.

[53]Ibid., p. 49.

[54]Ibid., p. 55.

[55]Lutzer, *Hitler's Cross,* pp. 195-96.

[56]Ibid.

[57]*Life Together,* p. 122.

Epilogue

[1]John Rodman, "Back on the Road to Life: The Pilgrimage of First Presbyterian, Quincy," *New England Journal of Ministry,* June 1981, p. 35.

[2]Richard Neustadt and Ernest May, *Thinking in Time: The Uses of History for Decision Makers* (New York: Free Press, 1986), pp. xv-xvi.

[3]Stephen Covey, *First Things First* (New York: Simon & Schuster, 1994), p. 103.

[4]For a good discussion of writing mission or vision statements, see ibid., pp. 307-21.

[5]This is John Piper's definition of Christian hedonistic faith in *Future Grace* (Portland, Ore.: Multnomah Press, 1995), p. 13.

[6]See the discussion of this method in Neustadt and May, *Thinking in Time*, pp. 105-6.

[7]Stephen Covey, *The Seven Habits of Highly Effective People* (New York: Fireside, 1989), pp. 262-63.

[8]Ibid., p. 262.

[9]Tim Bascom, *The Comfort Trap: Spiritual Dangers of the Convenience Culture* (Downers Grove, Ill.: InterVarsity Press, 1993), p. 51.